FOREIGN INVESTMENT IN CENTRAL AND EASTERN EUROPE

Also by Patrick Artisien

JOINT VENTURES IN YUGOSLAV INDUSTRY
YUGOSLAVIA TO 1993: BACK FROM THE BRINK?
YUGOSLAV MULTINATIONALS ABROAD (*with Carl H. McMillan and Matija Rojec*)
NORTH–SOUTH DIRECT INVESTMENT IN THE EUROPEAN COMMUNITIES (*with Peter J. Buckley*)
MULTINATIONALS AND EMPLOYMENT (*with Peter J. Buckley*)
DIE MULTINATIONALEN UNTERNEHMEN UND DER ARBEITSMARKT (*with Peter J. Buckley*)

Also by Matija Rojec

YUGOSLAV MULTINATIONALS ABROAD (*with Patrick Artisien and Carl H. McMillan*)
NEW FORMS OF EQUITY INVESTMENT BY YUGOSLAV FIRMS IN DEVELOPING COUNTRIES (*with Marjan Svetličič*)
INVESTMENT AMONG DEVELOPING COUNTRIES AND TRANSNATIONAL CORPORATIONS (*with Marjan Svetličič*)
TECHNOLOGICAL TRANSFORMTION OF THE THIRD WORLD: PROGRESS ACHIEVED AND PROBLEMS FACED: CASE STUDY OF YUGOSLAVIA (*with Marjan Svetličič*)

Also by Marjan Svetličič

GOLDEN NETS OF TRANSNATIONAL COMPANIES
JOINT VENTURES AMONG DEVELOPING COUNTRIES
EXPORT ORIENTED INDUSTRIAL COLLABORATION IN YUGOSLAVIA (*with Matija Rojec*)

Foreign Investment in Central and Eastern Europe

Edited by

Patrick Artisien
Lecturer in East European Economics
University of Cardiff

Matija Rojec
Senior Research Fellow
Centre for International Cooperation and Development
Ljubljana, Slovenia

and

Marjan Svetličič
Associate Professor of International Economics
University of Ljubljana, Slovenia

Foreword by Peter J. Buckley
Professor of Managerial Economics
University of Bradford Management Centre

St. Martin's Press

First published in Great Britain 1993 by
THE MACMILLAN PRESS LTD
Houndmills, Basingstoke, Hampshire RG21 2XS
and London
Companies and representatives
throughout the world

A catalogue record for this book is available
from the British Library.

ISBN 0–333–58228–4

Printed in Great Britain by
Ipswich Book Co Ltd
Ipswich, Suffolk

First published in the United States of America 1993 by
Scholarly and Reference Division,
ST. MARTIN'S PRESS, INC.,
175 Fifth Avenue,
New York, N.Y. 10010

ISBN 0–312–09112–5

Library of Congress Cataloging-in-Publication Data
Foreign investment in Central and Eastern Europe / edited by Patrick Artisien, Matija Rojec, and Marjan Svetličič : foreword by Peter J. Buckley.
p. cm.
Includes bibliographical references and index.
ISBN 0–312–09112–5
1. Investments, Foreign—Europe, Eastern. 2. Investments, Foreign—Former Soviet republics. 3. Joint ventures—Europe, Eastern. 4. Joint ventures—Former Soviet republics. I. Artisien, Patrick F. R., 1951– . II. Rojec, Matija. III. Svetličič, Marjan.
HG5430.7.A3F68 1993
332.6'73'0947—dc20 92–34123
CIP

Contents

List of Tables

List of Figures

Notes on the Editors

Patrick Artisien is Lecturer in East European Economics and International Business at the University of Cardiff. He is also Visiting Associate Professor at the European Institute of Public Administration in Maastricht, The Netherlands, and Visiting Research Fellow at the Centre for International Cooperation and Development in Ljubljana, Slovenia.

His previous publications include *Joint Ventures in Yugoslav Industry*, *Yugoslavia to 1993: Back from the Brink?*, *Yugoslav Multinationals Abroad* (with C. H. McMillan and M. Rojec), *North–South Direct Investment in the European Communities* (with P. J. Buckley), *Multinationals and Employment* (with P. J. Buckley), and *Die Multinationalen Unternehmen und der Arbeitsmarkt* (with P. J. Buckley).

Dr Artisien has acted as Consultant to the World Bank, The Organisation for Economic Cooperation and Development, *The Economist* and The International Labour Office. He is also a Partner in the Consultancy firm P. A. & M. R. Investments, specialising in economic, political and financial risk analysis in Central and Eastern Europe.

Matija Rojec is Senior Research Fellow at the Centre for International Cooperation and Development in Ljubljana, Slovenia. In 1989 he was appointed Head of the Centre's Foreign Direct Investment Department. Mr Rojec is permanent consultant to the Slovene Government in the area of foreign direct investment. He is currently engaged in drafting Slovenia's strategy on foreign direct investment. He has also acted as consultant to the OECD and the United Nations.

His recent publications in English include *Yugoslav Multinationals Abroad* (with P. Artisien and C. H. McMillan), *New Forms of Equity Investment by Yugoslav Firms in Developing Countries* (with M. Svetličič), *Investment Among Developing Countries and Transnational Corporations* (with M. Svetličič), *Technological Transformation of the Third World: Progress Achieved and Problems Faced: Case Study of Yugoslavia* (with M. Svetličič), and *Joint Ventures through Technical Cooperation among Developing Countries and their Economic Potential* (with M. Svetličič).

Marjan Svetličič is Associate Professor of International Economics in the Faculty of Social Sciences at the University of Ljubljana, Slovenia. He was formerly Director of the Centre for International Cooperation and Development in Ljubljana. Between 1988 and 1990 he was a member of the Executive Committee of the European Association of Development, Research and Training Institutes. He has also acted as consultant to several United Nations agencies. Dr Svetličič's publications include *Multinationals of the South, New Forms of Equity Investment by Yugoslav Firms in Developing Countries* (with M. Rojec), *Technological Transformation of the Third World: Progress Achieved and Problems Faced: Case Study of Yugoslavia* (with M. Rojec), *Joint Ventures through Technical Cooperation among Developing Countries and their Economic Potential* (with M. Rojec), and *Golden Nets of Transnational Companies*. He was formerly Editor of *Development and International Cooperation*.

Notes on the Other Contributors

Yuri Adjubei, Member of the Secretariat of the United Nations Economic Commission for Europe, Geneva.

Zbigniew Bochniarz, Visiting Professor, Hubert H. Humphrey Institute of Public Affairs, University of Minnesota, Minneapolis.

Peter J. Buckley, Professor of Managerial Economics, University of Bradford Management Centre.

William Crisp, Director of East European Operations, Business International, Vienna.

Cecelia Drazek, Policy Analyst, Abbott Laboratories, Abbott Park, Illinois.

John H. Dunning, ICI Research Professor in International Business, University of Reading.

Patrick Gutman, Assistant Professor of Economics, University of Paris I.

Wladyslaw Jermakowicz, Professor of Business, University of Southern Indiana, Evansville, Indiana.

Carl H. McMillan, Professor of Economics, Carleton University, Ottawa.

John Pinder, Visiting Professor, The College of Europe, Bruges.

David G. Young, Senior Manager, Price Waterhouse, Budapest.

Foreword

The excitement of research in international business is akin to that of an archer attempting to hit a moving target. In no area is this more true than current research into Central and Eastern Europe, where it is easy to slip into hyperbole in describing the changes that have so recently occurred. The dynamic nature of international business is fully captured in this volume.

Developments in Central and Eastern Europe pose three profound challenges. First, they present a challenge for business practitioners. New forms of doing business are required in the newly-emerging or rapidly reforming host countries of Central and Eastern Europe. For foreign investors, new operational modes are required and flexibility in all aspects of doing business is of the essence. This poses immense strains on control mechanisms and puts pressure on the rest of the enterprise. If the role of management is to adapt to change, then Central and Eastern Europe presents an ideal test. Second, change in Central and Eastern Europe poses a challenge to international business theory and models. This sets a large task for the (academic) analyst. Before existing theory can be fully confronted with evidence, a careful sifting and collation of empirical data has to occur. As most investments are recent and, as yet, unproven, many judgements are perforce provisional. Third, developments in Central and Eastern Europe present a crucial challenge to political leaders. Adaptation to new circumstances is always difficult but the degree of uncertainty in this case is very great. Attempts to reduce uncertainty through the establishment of firmly-based legal and political structures is one of the key tasks ahead in many host countries.

The collection of essays in this volume attempts to grapple with these issues. As the editors say, it is essential to be selective because of the vast diversity of both host-country conditions and foreign investors. Several points of great significance emerge: perhaps the most essential and most difficult lesson for all concerned is the importance of a long-termist approach. There are no easy solutions. It will be a long haul before the infrastructure, training and secure business practices which are essential for successful business development are in place. Short-term palliatives such as grants and other inducements to foreign investors are no substitute for these long-term pillars of success – but they may help to get some regions over a traumatic collapse of old certainties.

It is essential also to see the parallel with the development of academic explanation. The nature of evidence we require to judge the success of inward foreign investment is not always clear. It varies from micro-studies (cases) to economy-wide assessments of aggregate statistics. This book represents an essential first step to a full understanding of the three challenges of change.

Peter J. Buckley
Bradford

Part I
Contextual and Thematic Aspects

1 Foreign Direct Investment in Central and Eastern Europe: An Overview

Marjan Svetličič, Patrick Artisien and Matija Rojec

Central and Eastern Europe[1] have, since the turn of the decade, become a focal point for direct investment by Western multinationals, not least because of the unprecedented speed and intensity of the political and economic transformation in the area. Direct investment in Eastern Europe is becoming a factor in global resource flows: in the words of a UN observer, 'it may be useful to examine to what extent the countries of Eastern Europe will indeed attract multinationals, and what implications this may have for foreign direct investment (FDI) flows to other parts of the world'.[2]

As most former Eastern bloc countries, including Albania, have now undergone a change of government, it seems appropriate to examine whether a correlation exists between the magnitude of political change and the inflows of FDI in some of those countries. As the leading reformers, the Czech and Slovak Republics, Hungary, Poland and Slovenia freed most of their prices, lowered their trade barriers, embarked on ambitious privatisation programmes and flung open their doors to foreign businesses, the last were quick to explore the new possibilities which the area offered. The opportunities of selling to a market of some 400 million would-be consumers have never been greater, as once-rigid foreign trade systems are giving way to decision-making at local and factory levels.

Under Communist rule, the private sectors of the East European economies were severely restricted by the official ideology. In the words of America's leading scholar on East–West investment, Carl H. McMillan, 'attempts to accommodate foreign capital often took the form of treating foreign investment activities as a kind of enclave within the host economy. Now, as state enterprises are transformed into joint stock companies under new corporation laws and are privatised, 'foreign investment can be accommodated in ways which greatly enhance its potential impact on the host economy'.[3] Besides the traditionally 'ideologically sound' joint ventures, other organisational modes, such as majority holdings and wholly-owned subsidiaries, are now available to foreign investors.

But the complexities of the rapidly changing East European markets, the untested modes of privatisation and the still rudimentary legal frameworks remain daunting. Although FDI has increased over the past three years, with new deals being announced almost daily, Western firms have been slow to commit the large investment sums originally anticipated. Foreign investors are only too aware that the dismantling of the public sector in most of the former Communist countries has hardly begun; inflation is unacceptably high, industrial output is declining and the infrastructure often close to collapse. Hence, a balanced view needs to be taken between the seemingly unparalleled single largest opening of a new market, and the many pitfalls of an untested market where legal uncertainty, currency inconvertibility, supply problems and ownership restrictions linger on.

FDI legislation, a vital underpinning in the restructuring of the East European economic systems, was in fact introduced by most of these countries *before* the onset of democratisation. In this respect, we would argue that the political reforms were generated from the bottom up, by the economic needs of these societies, as a way out of their economic stagnation. Most former CMEA countries view FDI as a major restructuring instrument and as a vehicle for re-integration in the world economy. The skills and educational standards of their labour forces represent a positive starting point, as human capital is becoming a cornerstone of contemporary comparative advantages, and should act as a major incentive for multinationals to invest in the area.

The scope of this book is very wide, both in terms of countries covered and problems analysed. Selectivity, therefore, was deemed unavoidable: the countries under study include those which accumulated some experience of inward FDI, and others which were among the pioneers of foreign investment legislation. The host countries also differ in terms of size, economic structure, resource endowment, infrastructure, foreign trade orientation and integration in the world market. We believe that our representative sample provides a sound basis for at least some generalisations. Hungary's early move towards economic reforms made it one of the first East European countries to attract FDI. Poland's 'big bang' in January 1990 witnessed an upsurge of Joint Venture investments and placed it third in the league of FDI recipients, after the Commonwealth of Independent States (CIS) and Hungary. The CIS, with its vast market and natural factor endowment, selected itself. Finally, Slovenia, the economically most advanced country in Central Europe, has the longest experience of inward FDI, as a former constituent part of the Yugoslav federation, which first introduced FDI legislation in 1967.

This introductory note does not purport to present either a complete overview or a systematic analysis of FDI in former socialist countries. The main objective is to draw out some of the common characteristics and problems which these countries share, and which will influence economic strategies, both nationally and internationally, to and beyond the turn of the century.

In this series of essays on FDI in Central and Eastern Europe, we have included a chapter by Artisien and McMillan on East–West industrial cooperation. FDIs are only one facet of the general process of internationalisation of companies' activities; outward investments from Eastern Europe, as well as other forms of long-term inter-enterprise cooperation ought not to be neglected. Most countries' experiences have demonstrated that FDI is a final stage in long-term inter-enterprise cooperation: generally, outward investments follow *after* a company has been host to inward foreign investment. In this respect many of the former socialist countries provide an exception: their companies invested abroad *before* hosting FDI: the reason being that inward FDIs were prohibited for ideological reasons (see Artisien and McMillan in Chapter 3).

The similarities and differences which pertain to the countries under study in terms of their inward investment, also apply to their outward investments. The former Yugoslav federation is a special case, as a leader in the East European internationalisation league of firms, but occupying a somewhat mixed place in terms of management characteristics: the companies being less subject to state control than in other former CMEA economies, but more so than the private firms in capitalist countries (Artisien and McMillan). This aspect is particularly relevant as managerial and other differences among former socialist countries are frequently neglected.

Selected country studies form the basis and illustration of different models regarding the role of FDI in development strategies. Dunning (in Chapter 2) has suggested three models of development for the ex-socialist countries of Central and Eastern Europe in the field of FDI. These include:

1. The developing country model, characterised by the gradual attraction of inflows of foreign capital;
2. The reconstruction model, named after the experiences of the West German and Japanese economies in the immediate postwar years. The resource potential of the larger East European countries is comparable to that of the two most war-devastated countries, but the former are confronted with enormous institutional and attitudinal impediments;
3. The systemic model,[4] which combines both the developing country and reconstruction models, suggests that the willingness and ability of foreign investors rests mainly on the speed and extent to which the East European countries can alter their economic and legal systems, and on the ethos of their people towards entrepreneurship and wealth creating activities.

The three scenarios predict a different role for FDI; the reconstruction model, according to Dunning, points to the most significant involvement of foreign-owned firms. In his words, the former East Germany is already following the course of the reconstruction model, with Hungary and Czechoslovakia 'one or two steps behind'. Albania, Bulgaria and Romania fit more neatly into the developing country model. The systemic model depends on the nature of the systemic changes required and on the rate and efficiency with which they are introduced. This systemic change can be seen as a 'passport' for inward foreign direct investment, and in this context is relevant for all ex-socialist countries. All three models represent an attempt to rank factors pertinent to promoting FDI. FDI will clearly play a role in any model, but is likely to fluctuate according both to the form and stage of the host's economic development. What is specific, however, about this approach is that systemic changes will be a cornerstone in the East European countries' future strategies towards FDI.

Moreover, although these countries share a similar systemic background, their chances of attracting FDI will depend on a number of variables:

a) the path and intensity of the implementation of systemic changes;

b) location-specific advantages (resource endowment according to traditional theory);
c) infrastructural facilities;
d) human capital development (managerial, marketing and organisational skills); and
e) political and economic stability.

The starting point of each country *vis-à-vis* the aforementioned prerequisites differs. Some are more advanced in terms of infrastructure, but lag behind Western Europe by two or three generations (see Dunning). Others, like the CIS, are rich in resources. Generally, the comparative advantages of some of these countries do not outweigh the infrastructural drawbacks. FDI is more often than not the outcome of a mix of relevant factors, which have been developed to a satisfactory level. Failing that, they represent a barrier to FDI. Vast resources on their own cannot compensate for an underdeveloped infrastructure, which impedes the full exploitation of potential opportunities; this is pertinently highlighted by Adjubei in his coverage of the CIS (see Chapter 5).

Differences do exist in terms of the type of inherited economic structure, the intensity of international economic cooperation (particularly *vis-à-vis* the OECD countries), and the timing of the implementation of their transformation process. The former Yugoslav federation, which departed from central planning as far back as the 1950s and embarked on market-oriented reforms the following decade, is a special case, as Rojec, in Chapter 8, and Artisien and McMillan in Chapter 3, show.

By systemic changes we are not including solely those factors which would help create an adequate infrastructure for FDI, but those which would usher in a complete transformation of the economic system. Foreign investment laws creating special 'islands' for foreign capital, including free zones, are not sufficient. The whole essence of the system needs to become compatible with that of other market economies to be transparent and understandable to both foreign investors and local entrepreneurs. Any approach, in which policy makers continue to differentiate between domestic and foreign investors is doomed to failure. Only when foreign investors perceive that they are treated on a par with their local counterparts, will they be convinced of the long-lasting nature of systemic changes.

Instability and unpredictability are not restricted to the investment climate of the host countries: the attitudes of investing countries have added to uncertainty, reflecting their lack of knowledge of market and political conditions in Central and Eastern Europe. Crisp, in the Appendix, advises foreign investors to be prepared for long negotiations with host companies, and not to underestimate the time required to secure corporate approval.

Thus, the national treatment of FDI seems to be a precondition, as foreign investors look to stability. Thomas Sowell coined the phrase that former President Gorbachev's political genius for brilliant improvisations was precisely what should be avoided for the economy.[5] What investors need is an assurance that the goal-posts will not be moved during the lifetime of their commercial undertakings. Although preferential treatment may initially attract foreign investors, there is no certainty that these measures will be long-lasting. Foreign investors in Eastern Europe have been quick to acknowledge that incentives resulting in short term profits do not make up for infrastructural deficiencies in the host country in the medium term.

Preferential treatment and tax incentives are usually of a short-term nature, and have proved to be a useful instrument in allocating FDI to priority sectors in accordance with national development plans. However, as Bochniarz and Jermakowicz indicate in the case of Poland (Chapter 7), foreign investors have been more encouraged by the reduction of limits on the transfer of profits than by the general reforms of the past few years.

It does appear that the former CMEA countries overestimated the impact of FDI in the initial stages of the transition period to the market economy: foreign investment is seen as one of the most important instruments in economic restructuring, alongside privatisation. Thus, FDI legislation has been liberalised further in order to attract foreign capital. The dilemma, however, is that many of the Central and East European countries are competing with each other by offering a variety of FDI incentives without a full study of their potential effectiveness. This, in turn, generates instability in the FDI regimes, as less effective incentives are constantly downgraded or eliminated.

In the short term, the East European governments seem to have overstressed the legal environment which, although important, is not the foremost reason for attracting FDI: the investment climate ranks high in the motivation of first-time investors to Central Europe, where the outstanding remnants of ideological and systemic barriers have yet to be overcome.[6]

Most commentators would agree that, in the long term, the economies of Central and Eastern Europe offer a tremendous challenge and opportunity to foreign direct investors. Yet, at the beginning of 1990, the share of the countries comprising this area in total worldwide FDI flows was several times smaller than that of the less developed countries. Flows of FDI in the area are expected to go on increasing in absolute terms, but their relative weighting will lag behind that of the major hosts to FDI, namely the OECD countries.

To date, the East European countries, with a combined population of over 400 million, have attracted FDI stocks comparable with those of Ireland, Norway and Austria, each with a population of less than five million. Industrial market economies, with an average income per head equal to that of the most prosperous East European economies, have attracted fifty times more investment per head of population. The relative importance of foreign-owned enterprises in the economies of Eastern Europe remains extremely small. As Dunning shows in Chapter 2, in Poland in 1989 they accounted for only 1.9 per cent of all enterprises, 3.1 per cent of exports and 1.6 per cent of all employment. In the CIS at the end of 1990, according to Adjubei, FDI amounted to a mere 0.1 per cent of the book value of fixed assets and to 0.35 per cent of the value of total exports.

The potential for FDI clearly exists, but the preconditions of a full market economy have yet to be ushered in. In this transitionary period, FDI is best seen as a complementary (not a major) instrument in the restructuring process. FDI must be supported by other sources of finance: the efforts of the OECD countries in supplying economic assistance, including the establishment of the European Bank for Reconstruction and Development, are a useful start, but are too modest to establish a sound basis for the promotion of commercial flows of foreign capital.

The common denominator to economic recovery in Eastern Europe rests with the evolution of the political transformation, which in turn will be an influential factor on the FDI climate. The recent wars in the former Yugoslav federation confirm that no systemic changes can offset political unrest in the eyes of foreign investors. In Dunning's words, while foreign multinationals are uniquely able to supply many of the necessary ingredients for economic growth, a reshaping of attitudes to work and wealth creation, the redesigning of the legal and business frameworks, the costs of setting up a market system and the introduction of macro-economic policies, which stimulate domestic savings, are too substantial for individual companies to bear. Some progress on this front must be seen to be made prior to any substantial commitment of FDI.

Therein lies one of Eastern Europe's most daunting obstacles: the problem is not so much a lack of direct cooperation with Western companies, as an inappropriate economic structure which grew over a long period in conditions of semi-autarchic development. The newly independent republics of Slovenia and Croatia are a notable exception: their foreign-trade orientation towards the OECD countries has, for decades, been much higher than that elsewhere in Eastern Europe (see Rojec). Moreover, as Artisien and McMillan demonstrate, Yugoslav multinationals have been more active than their former CMEA counterparts in setting up a direct presence through subsidiaries and joint ventures on Western markets.

Thus, we would surmise that foreign investment can contribute to the structural transformation of the East European economies by raising productivity and efficiency in such a way as to create a basis for the future integration of their productive capacity in the international economy. As a small nucleus in the economies of Eastern Europe, FDI can generate spill-over effects far in excess of its own magnitude.

As Table 1.1 illustrates, since the turn of the decade the presence of foreign capital in Central and Eastern Europe has increased significantly. As of 1 October 1991, the overall number of foreign investment projects registered in the area was estimated to have grown to 31 060, as compared with 9121 a year earlier, and 2413 in October 1989. The total value of FDI in October 1991 grew to an estimated $10 120 million from half that amount, $5150 million, a year earlier.[7]

Notwithstanding these sharp increases, the absolute importance of FDI in the area remains modest: joint venture investments predominate in numbers, but less in the value of the capital involved. The figures represent commitments rather than actual transfers of funds; many of the FDI projects have yet to become operational or have already ceased operations. Adjubei estimated the underpayment of foreign capital contributions in the CIS at 26 per cent (this was based on a survey of thirty FDI projects). This suggests that, of the total foreign investment registered in the CIS ($5650 million) in October 1991, only $1470 million would have been transferred. A similar discrepancy does exist between the numbers of operational FDIs and of registered projects: one in three in the CIS, according to Adjubei. When these observations are repeated across Eastern Europe, as little as $3.1 billion could have been invested by the end of 1991 ($4.1

Table 1.1 Foreign Direct Investment in Central and Eastern Europe, 1989–91
(cumulative estimates of number and foreign capital in millions of dollars)

	15 October 1989		*1 October 1990*		*1 October 1991*	
	Number	*Foreign Capital*	*Number*	*Foreign Capital*	*Number*	*Foreign Capital*
CIS	1 000	1 846	2 051	3 208	4 500	5 650.0
Hungary	600	360	3 300	1 020	9 741	1 089.3
Poland	551	80	1 950	290	5 000	670.0
Czech and Slovak Republics	50	85	500	180	3 800	480.0
Bulgaria	25	–	70	–	800	300.0
Romania	5	–	570	66	6 061	231.4
Slovenia	182	136	680	386	1 158	699.5
Total	2 413	2 507	9 121	5 150	31 060	10 120.2

Source: ECE Data Bank.

billion if the former Yugoslav federation is included).

In spite of political and other uncertainties, foreign investors have been attracted to Central and Eastern Europe, where they have established pilot FDI projects, often in the form of small capital investments. The changing ownership structure in Eastern Europe has broadened the spectrum of potential Western investors, as state enterprises are no longer the sole option: among the growing alternatives are private firms, banks and joint enterprises.[8]

The impression gained from Western firms with previous experience of joint ventures in Eastern Europe is that they provide greater motivation and opportunity for contact between partners than licensing or cooperation agreements, and that the long-term benefits from such a strengthened relationship outweigh the multinationals' traditional insistence on control through wholly-owned subsidiaries. Patrick Gutman, in Chapter 4, emphasises that the East–West joint venture, as a strategic alliance, represents a half-way house between the 'pure market' and internalisation by multinational firms. Within this organisational mode, the East European countries benefit from technology and capitalist methods of management, whilst sharing the risks with the Western partners as well as the micro-economic costs involved in the modernisation process. As strategic alliances evolve and multinationals accept a shift from a majority – to a minority – direct investment model, their control over subsidiaries and joint ventures in Eastern Europe is increasingly exercised through technology and know-how, whether or not capital shareholding takes place.

The theme of joint ventures is also taken up in this book by Jermakowicz and Drazek, who compare the levels of *legal* liberalisation in the recipient countries, and find a high positive correlation between legal changes and the number of registered joint ventures. Arguably, the slowest pace of change has been in Hungary and Poland, which were among the pioneers of FDI legislation. The most radical legislative changes have taken place in the countries which were closest ideologically to a command economy, with Romania witnessing the most dramatic liberalisation, resulting in an impressive increase in joint venture registrations.

It should also be noted that:

- many FDI projects are small: their average value is estimated at about $500 000 and varies from $125 000 in Poland, to $1.5 million in the CIS. Resource-rich countries have tended to attract larger capital outlays;

- investments geared to import substitution and with a broad diversification of activities predominate; conversely, export-oriented projects are modest, and contradict the host countries' objective of strengthening their involvement in the international division of labour;
- the extended range of institutional possibilities for FDI, which now includes wholly-owned subsidiaries, has not been taken up by foreign investors, who continue to prefer the joint venture vehicle;
- East European nationals working or residing abroad, as well the Western subsidiaries of East European multinationals, are amongst the major investors in some countries, particularly Poland (see Chapter 7) and Slovenia (Chapter 8);
- FDI is frequently regarded by both foreign and domestic partners as a means of avoiding the foreign exchange and foreign trade restrictions by the host countries. In this respect it is merely a substitute for foreign trade transactions;
- there has been a strong inclination among foreign investors towards the service sector, particularly in the fields of consultancy and marketing, where the initial capital outlays are small;
- most foreign investors originate from Western Europe. In terms of numbers, the share of FDI projects involving European investors is the highest in Slovenia, the Czech and Slovak Republics, Hungary and Poland (between 80 and 90 per cent) and somewhat lower in the CIS (60 per cent) and Romania (57 per cent). In approximately 40 per cent of projects, 66 per cent in the case of Slovenia, the foreign parties are from the EC countries, and in about 25 per cent from EFTA. Western Europe also accounts for over 80 per cent of the total value of foreign capital in Poland, some 68 per cent in Romania, 63 per cent in Hungary, 60 per cent in the CIS and 55 per cent in the Czech and Slovak Republics. In terms of numbers, companies from the USA account for 7 per cent of all enterprises affiliated with foreign interests. In terms of capital, their involvement is highest in the CIS and Hungary (11 per cent), followed by Romania (9 per cent) and Poland (8 per cent). So far, Japanese firms have not shown a significant interest in investing in Eastern Europe;
- in terms of industrial breakdown, over half of foreign investment projects in the CIS are concentrated in the manufacturing sector. This is significantly lower in Hungary (40 per cent) and the Czech and Slovak Republics (32 per cent). Trade operations in the Czech and Slovak Republics and Hungary account for 20 per cent and 22 per cent respectively of FDI registrations.

Although the East European countries' needs for major inflows of FDI are high, the foreign investors' response seems unlikely to match them in the medium term. At the time of writing (May 1992) it is not obvious that the initial burst of enthusiasm of 1989–90 can or will be sustained. The experience of the former Yugoslav federation – the first socialist country to introduce FDI legislation in 1967 – shows that the initial euphoria, which prompted relatively large inflows of foreign investment, was followed by modest increases, which persisted until the sweeping legislative reforms of 1989. David Young (in Chapter 6) reinforces this argument in the case of Hungary, whose inward investment threshold expanded significantly during the period 1989–91. This increase, however, took place against the backdrop of negligible FDI prior to 1989, and similar exceptional rates of growth are not realistically expected in the coming years. Rojec (in the chapter on Slovenia) is equally cautious in his medium-term projections of direct investment flows to the countries of Central Europe, which he argues will remain subordinated to their Western counterparts. He lists the lack of financial capital, infrastructural deficiencies, the lack of strong market segments and of sophisticated buyers, as well as shortcomings in the fields of management and labour relations as major *natural* entry barriers to Western markets.

Whether FDI plays an increasingly important role in the restructuring of Eastern Europe will also hinge on global developments in the world economy, and more particularly on the extent and pace of integration of these countries *vis-à-vis* the Single European Market – a theme developed by Pinder in Chapter 10.

Finally, the future trends of FDI in Central and Eastern Europe will depend not only on investment opportunities and infrastructural conditions, but also on the world-wide availability of investment funds and their alternative destinations. The area under study has started to compete for FDI with developing countries and some industrial nations. McMillan points out that the rapid unification of Germany in 1990 served to concentrate West German investor attentions on Eastern Germany and away from Eastern Europe.[9] Dunning – in Chapter 2 – suggests that the former Socialist countries possess a major comparative advantage in human capital, which is both skilled and relatively cheap. Reuben Mark, Chairman and CEO of the Colgate-Palmolive Corporation – who was asked about his firm's motivation for investing in Eastern Europe, declared that 'a key factor was the high level of education of the population, well-developed technical skills and a great desire for Western products and lifestyles'.[10]

Notes

1. The terms 'Central' and 'Eastern' Europe are used interchangeably throughout this book by most contributors. They include the former European members of Comecon, namely Bulgaria, the Czech and Slovak Republics, Hungary, Poland, Romania and the Commonwealth of Independent States, plus Slovenia and the other republics of the former Yugoslav federation, Albania, and where appropriate, the former East Germany.
2. See P. Tolentino, 'Overall trends of foreign direct investment', *The CTC Reporter*, Spring 1990, United Nations, New York.
3. C. H. McMillan, 'Foreign Direct Investment Flows to the Soviet Union and Eastern Europe: Nature, Magnitude and International Implications', *Journal of Development Planning*, No. 20, 1991.
4. Systemic changes are necessary in the other two models, but here they play a central role.
5. See T. Sowell, What Capital Shortage?', *Forbes*, 19 August 1991.
6. See M. Svetličič, 'Promoting FDI in Vietnam: A Lesson from the Yugoslav Experience', *Asic-Pacific TNC Review*, No. 7, 1990. Although this article was written prior to the political transformation of Eastern Europe, the gist of the argument remains valid.
7. This represents a mere 2 per cent of total worldwide FDI flows in 1990. See *Transnationals*, Vol. 4, No. 1, March 1992.
8. See McMillan, op. cit.
9. McMillan, op. cit.
10. See *Columbia Journal of World Business*, Vol. XXVI, No. 1, Spring 1991, p. 19.

2 The Prospects for Foreign Direct Investment in Eastern Europe*

John H. Dunning

INTRODUCTION

Much has already been said, written and speculated about the subject of foreign direct investment (FDI) in Eastern Europe.[1] Almost daily, we read about new joint equity ventures being set up in the Soviet Union or Hungary; or of a strategic alliance being concluded between the Eastern and Western or Japanese firms; and, scarcely less frequently, about the efforts of one or other of the East European Governments to revamp its foreign investment rules and regulations, or to offer new tax concessions to make its country more attractive to foreign investors.

SOME FACTS AND FIGURES

Yet substantive and reliable data on the full extent of the participation by foreign firms in East European countries, are even the flows of investment into these countries, are hard to come by. Moreover, what data we do have are rarely comparable across countries or industrial sectors. This, in a way, should come as no surprise, as for so long, because of the absence of any proper financial or accounting procedures in Eastern Europe, most domestically produced economic statistics have been of dubious value.

Perhaps the best, and certainly the most publicised data we have, concern the number of joint ventures involving foreign (by which we mean non-East European) registered firms. As shown in Table 2.1, these reveal a rapid growth of the *intentions* of foreign firms to invest

* I am most grateful to Dr M. Svetličič for some most helpful comments made on an earlier draft of this chapter.

in Eastern Europe. At the beginning of 1988, 165 ventures involving foreign partners had been established. A year later, this figure had risen to 562; by March 1990 to 3575, and by July 1990, to 4979 and by December 1990 to over 10 000. More particularly, in the second half of 1990, there was a dramatic increase in new joint ventures registered in Central Europe.

However, as yet, only a small percentage – probably about 10 per cent – of these ventures, are currently operational. Most should be regarded as *potential* rather than *actual* investment commitments by multinational enterprises (MNEs). We do, however, know that, as of mid-1990, the highest proportion of joint venture start-ups had occurred in Poland and Hungary and in the service, rather than the manufacturing sectors.[2]

Table 2.1 also shows that the rate of growth of joint ventures is currently concentrated in three countries: the Soviet Union, Hungary and Poland. In the Soviet Union, where the growth potential of a large market is the main attraction, the estimated foreign capital invested in October 1990 was $3.2 billion; an amount about the same as the stock of inward investment in Sweden, Nigeria or Singapore. In Hungary, which is, perhaps, furthest along the road towards a market economy, it was $1.1 billion, about the same as the FDI stock in Pakistan. Uruguay or Cameroon; whereas, in Poland, where in spite of a larger population and long experience with joint venture capital,[3] the less stable political and social regime has limited foreign investment to around $340 million.

Who are the major foreign players in Eastern Europe? According to the United Nations Centre on Transnational Corporations (UNCTC),[4] of the 748 joint ventures reported as having been established in Czechoslovakia, Hungary and Poland by August 1989, 249, or 33.3 per cent, involved West German partners, 105, or 14.0 per cent, Austrian partners, and 73, or 9.8 per cent, US partners. Some later research by Patrick Gutman[5] shows that EC-based firms accounted for 42.1 per cent of the joint ventures in the USSR, and 30.9 per cent of those in Czechoslovakia in October 1990; 63.3 per cent of those in Poland, and 36.2 per cent of those in Hungary in January 1990. Austrian firms, however, were the leading investors (by number of joint ventures) in Hungary; while US and Finnish foreign investors were particularly active in the USSR. In the last year, there has also been a considerable upsurge of interest shown by Asian (and especially Japanese and Korean) investors in the larger East European countries. Some 65 or 8.5 per cent of the new joint

Table 2.1 Joint Ventures Registered in Eastern Europe 1988–90

	Population 1988 (million)	*1 January 1988*	*1 January 1989*	*1 January 1990*	*1 March 1990*	*1 July 1990*	*31 December 1990*
Soviet Union	286	23	191	1 261	1 480	1 734	2 800
Hungary	11	102	270	1 000	1 000	1 600	5 000 +
Poland	38	13	55	918	1 000	1 550	2 400
Czechoslovakia	16	7	16	60	60	60	n/a
Bulgaria	9	15	25	30	30	30	n/a
Romania	23	5	5	5	5	5	n/a
Total	383	165	562	3 274	3 575	4 979	over 10 000

Source: *European Commission*

ventures registered in the USSR in 1990 involved investment by firms from the Third World.

Which sectors tend to attract the most inward investment? An analysis of the sectoral distribution on the investment intentions by foreign firms reveals some noticeable differences. Within the manufacturing industry, which is currently attracting the most interest of Western capitalists in the Soviet Union and Poland, the former country seems to offer the best opportunities in most branches of mechanical and electronic engineering, whereas in Poland, the favoured sectors include food processing, textiles and wood products. In Hungary, business services, trade and transport undertakings currently account for 38 per cent of all approved applications by inward direct investment. In the Soviet Union, fast food chains and construction, and business services attract the largest share of operational investment. In Poland, the commercial trading sector, and in Czechoslovakia, the hotel and restaurant sector, stand out as the service sectors with the largest number of joint ventures. Although some Central and East European countries have extensive mining and other natural resources, there has been relatively little foreign investment in these sectors.

Of the more noteworthy individual investments (or investment intentions) by MNEs in Eastern Europe, mention might be made of a $3 billion capital stake by Volkswagen in the Skoda autoplant in Czechoslovakia; a $1.5 billion investment by the same company in a new production facility in Eastern Germany to produce the Golf and Polo range of cars; a $200 million investment by General Motors in a railway carriage and machine factory in Hungary; a $150 million participation by General Electric in Tungsram, Eastern Europe's leading light bulb manufacturer; Suzuki and Itoh's 40 per cent stake in a $10 billion venture to manufacture autos in Hungary; Gillette's joint venture in the Soviet Union to produce razor blades; ASEA Brown Boveri's acquisition of a majority stake in a leading Polish turbine and generating producer; and McDonald's multi million dollar stake in a chain of fast food restaurants in the Soviet Union and Hungary.[6]

As might be expected, the relative importance of foreign-owned enterprises in the economies of Eastern Europe is still extremely small. In Poland, it is estimated that in 1989, they accounted for only 1.9 per cent of all enterprises, 3.1 per cent of exports and 1.6 per cent of all employment. In other East European countries it was considerably less, although in some sectors, it is now starting to become significant. However, when one recalls that prior to 1987, the joint venture was not permissible at all in the Soviet Union, the opening-up of the economy to both international trade and investment has been quite remarkable.

THE PROSPECTS FOR MORE FOREIGN INVESTMENTS

So much for a thumb-nail sketch of the present state of foreign direct investment in Eastern Europe. What now of the prospects for the future? Most commentators agree that, taking a long-run perspective, the economies of Central and Eastern Europe offer a tremendous challenge and opportunity to foreign direct investors. Yet at the end of 1990, the countries comprising this area, which had a combined population of over 400 million, attracted about the same amount of investment as did Ireland and Norway, each of which had a population of less than five million. Even industrial market-oriented countries, with the same average income per head as the most prosperous of the East European economies, attracted forty times more investment per head of population. Assuming just a doubling of living standards and a near completion of the marketisation of the major East European economies by the year 2000, it would not be unreasonable to expect foreign and intra-East European investment to rise from its current $2–3 billion to around $100 billion – or about two-fifths of its current level in Western Europe. These, however, are just orders of magnitude of what *could* be achieved. The human and natural resources of Eastern Europe are impressive. What is lacking is the institutional structure, managerial and marketing expertise, effective (as opposed to potential) entrepreneurship, organisational capabilities and monetary incentives to efficiently utilise and upgrade these resources.

While foreign MNEs are uniquely able to supply many of the necessary ingredients for economic growth, a reshaping of attitudes to work and wealth creation, the redesigning of the business and legal framework, especially with respect to property rights and contractual relationships, the costs of setting up a market system, and the introduction of macro-economic policies, which encourage domestic savings, but accept the discipline of currency convertibility and an open trading system, are too substantial for individual companies – or in some cases for individual countries – to bear. These are the *real* costs of restructuring the economies of Eastern Europe; and, at least some progress on this front must be made, *and be seen to be made*, prior to any substantial commitment of direct investment funds by foreign MNEs.

ALTERNATIVE MODELS OF DEVELOPMENT

What then, is the most likely course or path of development in Eastern Europe? Let us consider three possible models or scenarios – accepting that the pattern and pace of restructuring is likely to vary, for example, between Hungary and Albania, or between Czechoslovakia and Bulgaria, or between Romania and Poland. The first is the *developing country* model. This hypothesis that, currently, the economies of the leading East European countries can be compared to those of some developing countries, and that just as these, notably Brazil, Korea, Thailand and Singapore, have moved along a particular development path or trajectory – from attracting little to attracting substantial inflows of foreign capital – so as they develop, East European countries will do the same.

While at first sight, this seems a plausible scenario, the assumptions on which it is based are not wholly appropriate. World Bank statistics suggest that, in the mid-1980s, the populations of most East European economies (Albania is the main exception) were considerably better educated, medically cared for, and housed, than even the most prosperous developing countries (Singapore and Hong Kong are exceptions). They also consumed more energy, and their R & D expenditure as a percentage of gross national product even approaches that of some Western economies.[7] On the other hand, industrial performances and commercial, transportation and communications infrastructures were generally no better than those of many middle-income developing countries, and considerably inferior to those of the fastest newly industrialised countries. And, the proportion of the gross national product absorbed by Central Government was two to three times that of the developing countries of the same income levels. Table 2.2 sets out some details of health and educational standards of a group of eight East European countries, including Yugoslavia.

The second model is to compare the present situation of the East European economies with that of West Germany and Japan after the

Table 2.2 Education and Health Facilities in East European Countries in the Mid or Late 1980s

	Education			*Health*			
	Primary	*Secondary (% of population in appropriate age group)*	*Tertiary*	*Population per Physician*	*Daily Calorie Supply*	*Infant Mortality (per 1000 of births)*	*Life Expectancy*
East European Countries:							
USSR	106	na	na	270	3399	25	67
Hungary	97	70	15	310	3569	16	70
Poland	101	80	18	490	3336	16	72
Romania	97	80	10	570	3373	24	70
Czechoslovakia	96	na	na	280	3448	13	67
Bulgaria	103	na	na	280	3642	14	72
GDR	106	na	na	440	3814	8	77
Albania	100	na	na	na	2713	24	72
Yugoslavia	95	80	19	550	3289	25	72
Developing Countries:							
Upper middle income Countries	101	54	20	1220	3117	42	68
Middle income Countries	101	67	17	2190	2846	52	66

Source: *World Bank: World Development Report 1990*

last World War. Let us call it the *reconstruction model*. This model has intuitive appeal in that it might be supposed that the resource potential of the larger East European countries is comparable to that of the two most war-devastated countries, but that to exploit these resources requires a fund of technological, organisational and management capabilities no less than that demanded by Japan and Germany in 1945. However, this model fails to take account of the enormous institutional impediments and the extent of the political and attitudinal change required by most East European nations *before* private enterprise (which, after all, was stifled for only a decade or so in both Japan and Germany) is prepared to undertake entrepreneurship and investment – including investment in R & D and manpower training – for economic restructuring and growth.

The third model is one which combines the more appropriate ingredients of the *developing country* and *reconstruction model* but also takes account of the macro- and micro-organisational changes necessary for economic progress. This might be called the *systemic model* – the word 'systemic' being chosen because it suggests that the willingness and ability of foreign (or, for that matter, domestic) investors rest mainly on the speed and extent to which East European economies can alter both their economic and legal systems, and the ethos of their people towards entrepreneurship and wealth-creating activities.

The three scenarios predict a different role for FDI. For example, depending on whether East European Governments adopt a German or Japanese strategy towards inward investment – and we think the former is much more likely – the *reconstruction* model points to the most speedy and widespread involvement of foreign-owned firms. The significance of foreign investment in the *developing country* model depends on the momentum and pattern of economic development, how this integrates into the world economy, and the kind of foreign participation it is likely to induce. Like the first scenario, the extent of foreign investment predicted by the *systemic* model depends on the nature of the systemic changes required and the rate and efficiency with which they are introduced; but the model does suggest a much slower initial participation of foreign firms due to the substantial establishment and learning costs they might have to incur in setting up production units and in marketing their products.

Because of the current differences in the economic development, political systems and institutional frameworks of the individual East European countries, it is likely that each country will follow a somewhat different path of integrating itself into the world economy. Hungary and Czechoslovakia are in fact already following the course of the reconstruction model.

By contrast, Albania, Romania and Bulgaria are more likely to fit into the developing country model. But much will depend on the speed and extent to which each country proceeds with its privatisation process; and how far it is able to stimulate both the entrepreneurial ethos of its people, and the upgrading of their expectations for better-produced and superior quality products.

In any event, the role of FDI is likely to fluctuate according both to the form and stage of economic development. This idea has been explored in the literature, using the concept of the investment development cycle (or path).[8] In a recently published paper, Teretumo Ozawa[9] suggests that, in her economic development, Japan passed through four stages of industrial restructuring. The first was in the 1950s and was marked by the production and export of labour-intensive and fairly low-skill products. As Japanese wage rates rose, and her human and technological capacity became more sophisticated, her comparative advantage shifted into scale-intensive, non-differentiated products: for example, heavy chemicals, steel, shipbuilding and so on. The third phase, which lasted from the mid-1960s to the early 1980s, was that in which Japan made considerable inroads into the international markets for mass production durable goods, for example motor vehicles and consumer electronics. The fourth stage, on which the Japanese economy is now entering, is that in which production and exports are highly innovatory and skill-intensive or, as Ozawa puts it, are Schumpeterian-type products. Depending on the policies of host Governments, inward FDI may play an important role in fashioning each of these development phases; but outward direct investment is not likely to materialise to any major extent until stages three and four are reached.

The likely future composition of economic activity and the role which foreign MNEs might play in industrial restructuring will depend very much on the particular competitive and innovatory advantages which individual East European countries can offer. Some limited guidance may be gained from an examination of the kind of US registered patents which the leading world enterprises attribute to their activities in Eastern Europe.

In an exercise conducted over the period 1969–86, John Cantwell identified the kind of industrial sectors in which Warsaw Pact countries recorded an above-average share of registered patents.[10] The chemical (excluding pharmaceutical) and mechanical engineering sectors both stood out, with both high research-intensive and labour-intensive sectors recording well below the average state of patents. Of the foreign firms which carried out the most technological activity in Eastern Europe, those of West European – and especially German MNEs – scored the highest, with those of US and Japanese origin well behind in second and third places.

THE ROLE OF MULTINATIONAL ENTERPRISES

What then of the role of MNEs in this restructuring process? In the mid-1980s, a collection of twelve country profiles concluded that MNE activity had had a significantly positive effect on trade, productivity and economic restructuring on most home and host countries.[11] It may, then, be reasonably expected that the opening of Eastern Europe to market forces will, by encouraging inward direct investment, markedly improve the economic lot of its citizens. If the experience of most countries in Western Europe and the more market-oriented developing countries is anything to go by, then foreign technology, management expertise and the access to foreign markets are likely to play a critical role in East European economic development.

However, it is our contention that such a role is likely to be different from that experienced by West European countries in the past, or developing countries today in at least three ways. First, the form of foreign participation is likely to be more pluralistic. It may well be that as in Western Europe the 100 per cent owned affiliate firms will eventually become the dominant form of participation by foreign firms. But we would also expect a multitude of collaborative agreements, subcontracting and networking arrangements, and crossing many different lines of economic activity, both along and between value chains, to be concluded. An example of such pluralism is shown in the motor vehicle industry where Volkswagen and Fiat are both substantially involved in various East European countries, but in several different ways.

Second, we would anticipate that at least the larger MNEs would respond to the challenges and opportunities of Eastern Europe in terms of its likely effect on their *global* marketing and production strategies. This is what is already largely happening in Western Europe and, to some extent, in the US and Canada as well. If current trends are anything to go by, Western and Japanese MNEs are unlikely to treat their East European affiliates as stand-alone ventures, but as part and parcel of a pan–European or even an international network of activities. This would suggest, that from the start, the functional and organisational strategies of European joint ventures, will, in so far as is permitted by the local partners, be locked into those currently pursued by the foreign firm. Western European firms, in particular, view Eastern Europe as offering an enlarged market for their products, thus better enabling them to spread increasing overhead costs of R & D and marketing, and by so doing, enabling them to compete more effectively with Japanese and US MNEs. In some sectors in which there is currently surplus production capacity in the Western world, both US and European firms are hoping that new markets, especially in the Soviet Union, Poland and East Germany will help absorb some of this capacity.

Third, there is every suggestion that, to some extent at least, the international community, and especially the European Community (EC) – has an enormous stake in the success of the political and economic restructuring of the erstwhile Communist bloc countries. By such means as direct grants, aid or loans; by the encouragement of private direct investment, for example by tax incentives and investment insurance schemes; by the provision of information about production and marketing conditions, laws and regulations in different West European countries; by action taken to improve economic transparency and promote a better understanding of Western investors of the business environment in Eastern Europe (for example, the PHARE programme); by assisting the education and training of East European technicians, scientists, accountants and the like; by the encouragement of industrial cooperation agreements between EC and East European firms; by technical advice on the appropriate macro-economic and structural adjustment policies for East European Governments to pursue, individual Western Governments, the European Commission, the EBRD[12] and various international agencies such as the World Bank, are likely to exert even more critical influence on the shape of an enlarged Europe in the 1990s than did (US) Marshall aid and similar schemes play in the design of Western Europe in the 1950s.[13] Certainly there is no shortage of ideas for the kind of multilateral aid programme which might be given to Central and East European countries. One particularly interesting suggestion – called the Strasbourg Plan for Central and Eastern Europe – was recently put forward by Michael Palmer, former Director General of the European Parliament.[14] Palmer contemplates that an economic package of around $16.7 billion a year is needed from the advanced industrial nations if economic restructuring in the seven Central and East European countries (including the former GDR) is to be completed in the next two decades or so. This equates with between 0.1 per cent and 0.5 per cent of the GDPs of the leading Triad countries in 1989.

However, as a *quid pro quo* for such financial aid, it is proposed that each of the recipient Governments should work out an overall plan for economic growth, and within the plan, a shopping list of priorities. The Governments should then launch a joint appeal to the international community. It is envisaged that priority should be given to radical improvement in transport and communication networks, a rapid reduction of environmental pollution, establishing an efficient market system, and encouraging currency stabilisation and balance of payments support. As with the earlier Marshall plan, the basic goal would be to establish the necessary conditions for private investment, including FDI, to be profitably undertaken.

We do not need to identify, in any detail, the ingredients of these necessary conditions. Suffice to assert that both the productive and institutional infrastructure of most Central and Eastern European countries is two or even three generations behind that of Western Europe. In a recently published assessment of the market building strategies in Hungary, Poland and Czechoslovakia, the OECD concluded that the only real progress that had been made was in the area of restoring property rights to private owners, removing some market imperfections (for example, consumer subsidies, and trade flow distortions), and increasing investment in education and labour skills.[15] But such are the prizes offered to firms by their resources and markets, and to Western democratic Governments by the prospects of a free and thriving market of 400 million inhabitants, that the incentive to overcome the huge barriers to restructuring is very great indeed. To this extent, I believe that a parallel can legitimately be drawn between the US interest in the economic and political recovery of West Germany and Japan, and that of the OECD nations in the future of Eastern Germany.

Again, at the risk of generalising, we would submit that the extent and pace at which East European economies will become fully integrated with the rest of Europe, will chiefly depend on three factors. The first is the ability of Governments to efficiently promote restructuring *and* to convince their own people that, in spite of additional economic hardships they will inevitably have to endure, there is light at the end of the tunnel, and the democratisation of markets will release a treasure of talents and entrepreneurship. The second determinant is the likely future course of the Soviet economy. The potential market of this economy is three times greater than the rest of Eastern Europe combined. If the Soviet Union flourishes, this is likely to create demand for products from the more advanced East European economies and hence encourage further foreign investment into them. The third determinant is the extent to which the necessary capital for long-stifled development can be found in a global economic situation in which the demands for such capital are so great. For apart from Eastern Europe, there are many claims on a supply of international savings. At the end of the day, capital constraints may well limit the pace of the economic regeneration of Eastern Europe.

We conclude this section with a review of two recent surveys of the opinions of business executives about the investment opportunities offered by different countries in Eastern Europe. The first is that conducted by *Financial Executive* and published in the September/October 1990 issue. Eastern Germany was perceived to offer the most attractive business environment to foreign investors, while Hungary was thought to afford the best indigenous assets for undertaking business. Some further details are set out in Table 2.3. Yugoslavia (which was included in the survey) and Czechoslovakia were ranked third or fourth – although, interestingly, Yugoslavia was believed to have the best history of entrepreneurship, yet the worst-but-one record of the speed of stability in economic reform. Currently, Romania and Bulgaria would not appear to be serious contenders for inward direct investment.

In another field study conducted by three US business school analysts in August 1990,[16] and based upon questionnaires completed by a sample of seventy-nine US business executives, it was found that of some eight possible modalities for exploiting East European markets, joint ventures with US minority equity interests was listed as the fifth most likely, following exporting from a West European subsidiary (ranked first), exporting from the US; licensing, bartering and countertrade. Joint ventures with a US majority interest was ranked seventh after management contracts; while the least likely form of entry was thought to be the wholly-owned subsidiary.

Concerning the perceived ability of East European countries to adapt to the changes required of them if they were to attract more

Table 2.3 Indicators of Attractiveness to Foreign Direct Investors

(a) Business Environment

	Standing with Western Banks	*Speed/stability of economic reform*	*Reliability of infrastructure*	*Extent of currency convertibility*	*Extent of profit repatriation*	*Extent of government bureaucracy*	*Average score*
East Germany	1	1	4	1	1	2	1.8
Hungary	4	2	2	2	2	1	2.2
Czechoslovakia	2	3	1	4	4	3	2.8
Yugoslavia	6	7	3	3	3	4	4.3
Poland	7	5	5	5	4	5	5.2
Bulgaria	3	4	7	6	7	7	5.8
Soviet Union	5	6	6	6	6	8	6.1
Romania	8	8	8	6	8	6	7.3

Source: *Financial Executive*, September/October 1990

(b) Business Asset attractiveness

	Existence of export-oriented business	*History of entrepreneurship*	*Average Score*
Hungary	1	2	1.5
East Germany	2	3	2.5
Yugoslavia	4	1	2.5
Czechoslovakia	3	3	3
Poland	5	5	5
Soviet Union	6	6	6
Bulgaria	7	7	7
Romania	8	8	8

Source: *Financial Executive*, September/October 1990.

investment, the respondents considered the progress made by Eastern Germany the most significant, followed by that of Poland, Czechoslovakia, and Hungary. Of the seven categories of change identified, the most progress had been made with political reform and the host-country attitude towards foreign direct investment; and the least progress in the upgrading of infrastructure. Finally, it was the opinion of the US executives that MNEs from Germany were likely to be the most likely future investors in Eastern Europe, with those from the USA and Japan following some way behind.

CONCLUSIONS

The resources and markets of Eastern Europe open up huge and exciting challenges to Western and Japanese firms, and to fledgling indigenous entrepreneurs. These opportunities are likely to be exploited in a variety of ways, notably through trade, joint ventures and strategic alliances between East European and foreign firms. Because they are the repository of much of the world's technological capability, managerial capabilities and organisational competences, MNEs are ideal vehicles for spearheading industrial restructuring through their ability to transfer technology and management skills; through their introduction of up-to-date industrial practices and quality control techniques; through their example and their spillover effects on local entrepreneurship, suppliers and competitors; and through their network of international linkages – with both large and small firms, they can provide much of the competences and initiatives for economic growth.

However, such investment will only occur if they advance the global strategies of companies. In a scenario of increasing shortages of capital but widening opportunities for growth, this places considerable burdens on the authorities of East European economies to offer the most favourable environment for value added activities – be these to produce goods and services for the domestic or international market. This is not (repeat not) simply a question of liberalisation of investment policies or of offering foreign investors generous fiscal incentives. Equally, if not more important, it is for Governments to create and sustain an economic and social environment in which both domestic and foreign firms can compete effectively, and to foster right attitudes by labour and management alike towards productivity improvements and competing in a global environment. While, as we have said, MNEs can supply some of these initiatives, particularly in so far as they link into the world economy, at the end of the day, it is the responsibility of Governments as custodians of the welfare of their citizens to set the commercial, institutional and attitudinal framework in which private enterprise can both flourish and provide the much-needed engine for economic development.

While the long-term future for FDI in Central and Eastern Europe is highly promising, the next decade or so is likely to be a particularly taxing time for both foreign investors and the Governments of host countries. The current recession, the collapse of intra-regional trade, brought about *inter alia* by the worsening economic situation in the Soviet Union, and the Middle East crisis, have each added to the already daunting restructuring problems facing most of Central and Eastern Europe. Indeed, economists predicted an even more severe recession for the region during 1992. In addition, uncertainties about legal instability, ownership restrictions, currency inconvertibility and supply constraints, and the absence of the required legal accounting and financial infrastructure are causing Western firms to reappraise the optimistic scenario on which they had earlier based their investment intentions. In the words of Carl McMillan,[17] 'The initial euphoria and the favourable business climate it engendered has now begun to wear off. The new mood is reinforced by greater awareness of the practical difficulties posed by investment in the area'.

These are sensible words. At the same time, it would be unfortunate if the pendulum of business attitudes and expectations should swing too much towards the pessimistic. One very recent encouraging sign is the commitment of the Heads of Governments of the seven leading industrial nations, to assist the Soviet Union in its efforts to move away from a command-dominated to a market-oriented economic system.[18] Should this commitment be translated into action, the medium-term future of FDI in Central and Eastern Europe is, indeed, a bright one.

Notes

1. For our purposes, we shall not consider Yugoslavia as part of Eastern Europe, although there are many similarities between that country and those dealt with in this chapter. In fact, of course, Yugoslavia has many institutional advantages over the rest of Eastern Europe, and, since the mid-1960s, has made considerable progress in the introduction of

market-oriented economic reforms, and the development of a cadre of managers and entrepreneurs.

2. About one-half of operative joint ventures involving foreign firms in the USSR are also in the service sector.
3. For example, in the decade before the political reforms, some 700 foreign enterprises were set up in Poland (June, 1990).
4. CTC Report No. 28, Autumn 1989.
5. Patrick Gutman, From *Joint Ventures to Foreign Direct Investment, New Perspectives in Eastern Europe and the Soviet Union*. Revised version of a paper presented at the international conference on 'Opportunities and Contracts for East–West Soviet Ventures', Moscow, 7–16 December 1990.
6. Further details of recent acquisitions and newly established joint ventures are given in Carl H. McMillan, *Foreign Direct Investment Flows to the Soviet Union and Eastern Europe: Nature, Magnitude and International Implications*, Carleton University, Ottawa, March 1991.
7. Although much of this expenditure was directed to defence and space-related activities.
8. See for example, Chapter 5 of J. H. Dunning, *Explaining International Production*, Unwin Hyman, 1988. The investment development cycle suggests that as countries develop their propensities to be invested in, or to engage in outward investment, they proceed through various phases with the inward/outward ratio being at its highest as countries approach full industrialisation.
9. T. Ozawa, 'Europe 1992 and Japanese Multinationals, Translating a subcontracting system in the expanded market'. In B. Bergenmeier, and J. L. Mucchielli (eds), *Multinationals and Europe 1992*, London: Routledge, 1991.
10. J. Cantwell, 'East–West business links and the economic development of Poland and Eastern Europe', University of Reading, Mimeo, 1990.
11. J. H. Dunning (ed.), *Multinational Enterprises, Economic Structure and International Competitiveness*, Chichester: John Wiley, 1985.
12. The European Bank for Reconstruction and Development, which has been set up with a capital of ECU 10bn to help finance market-oriented projects in Central and Eastern Europe.
13. For a review of these programmes, see The Commission of the European Communities, *Industrial Cooperation with Central and Eastern Europe: Ways to Strengthen Cooperation*, Brussels (Communication from the Commission to the Council and European Parliament), SEC (90) 1213, July 1990.
14. M. Palmer, *A Plan for Economic Growth in Central and Eastern Europe*, Mimeo, 1991.
15. As summarised in *International Economic Insights*, No. 2, March/April, 1991.
16. A. D. Mikhail, K. N. Nandola and S. B. Prasad, *Perceptions of US Executives on doing business in Eastern Europe and the USSR: testing the international exchange framework*, paper presented at the 16th Annual Conference of EIBA in Madrid, December 1990.

17. C. McMillan, 1991, op. cit.
18. As put forward in a six-point plan designed primarily to promote the trade of, and provide technical assistance to, the Soviet Union, agreed at the G7 Summit of Heads of Governments, held in London in July 1991. For details of this plan, see *The Financial Times*, 18 July 1991.

3 Some Contextual and Thematic Aspects of East–West Industrial Cooperation, with Special Reference to Yugoslav Multinationals

Patrick Artisien and Carl H. McMillan

INTRODUCTION

The integration of Eastern Europe into the world economy is a process that involves the expansion of direct investment as well as trade flows. The purpose of this chapter is to review the multinational activities of Yugoslav firms within the context of this long-term, postwar process, and to relate the Yugoslav experience to that of other East European countries. We shall also attempt to place Yugoslavia more broadly within the global movement by firms in the second half of the century to internationalise their production of goods and services through multinational entrepreneurship.

INTEGRATION INTO THE WORLD ECONOMY

Two sets of factors have tended in the postwar period to restrict the participation of the East European countries in the international economy. These countries had fallen into the Soviet sphere at the end of the war, as the result of wartime agreements and occupation by Soviet armed forces. With the emergence of the Cold War, geopolitical forces tended to isolate them from the mainstream of international economic intercourse, dominated by the industrially developed capitalist countries that formed the Western alliance.

Moreover, the East European countries were at this time busy patterning their societies after the Soviet model of socialism and all had launched their first five-year development plans. Non-market, 'administered' economies emerged in Eastern Europe, characterised by extensive state ownership of land and capital and comprehensive control by the ruling Communist Party apparatus. As a result, the East European economies became increasingly separated from the rest of the world by virtue of their socio-economic systems.

It is the gradual waning of both sets of forces, geopolitical and systemic, that has allowed the reintegration of the East European economies into the world economy. The Cold War began to diminish in intensity in the 1950s, with the death of Stalin and the termination of the Korean War. The trend gathered momentum with the *détente* policies of the 1960s and 1970s, and accelerated in the 1980s with the foreign policy course of cooperation set by the new leadership under Gorbachev.

A parallel trend in the area has been the search for alternatives to the Stalinist model of a socialist economy. Successive reform efforts have sought to decentralise resource allocation, to introduce market mechanisms and to move towards more mixed systems of ownership. This process too gained tremendous impetus from reforms instituted in the Soviet Union in the late 1980s, under the banners of Perestroika and Glasnost.

Yugoslavia has undergone the effects of both these processes, but the timing in the Yugoslav case has been markedly different from that of the other East European countries. The Tito–Stalin split in 1948 resulted in Yugoslavia's ejection from the Cominform and hence from the 'Soviet bloc'. The ensuing economic embargo imposed on Yugoslavia by the Soviet Union and its allies forced Yugoslavia very early to establish economic ties with the capitalist West. Moreover, Yugoslavia enjoyed Western favour in this period as a bloc 'defector', and was exempted from Western efforts to isolate the Soviet bloc economically.

Yugoslavia's adoption of a neutralist foreign policy position, however, and her alliance with Third World neutrals who also wished to avoid alignment with either opposing camp, kept her from closer political or economic association with West European neighbours. This distancing from the West was reinforced by the improvement in Yugoslav–Soviet relations after 1956 and Yugoslavia's 'observer status' (1964) in the bloc's economic association, the Council of Mutual

Economic Assistance (CMEA). It was only in 1970 that Yugoslavia entered into an analogous agreement of cooperation with the European Communities.[1]

Yugoslavia's expulsion from the Soviet bloc did not result in her rejection of socialism: instead she attempted to define her own, 'superior' form of socialist society. This meant the early abandonment of the Soviet 'command economy', and initiated the first East European attempt to reform the Soviet model. It did not, however, involve the adoption of a Western-style economic system, even of the highly mixed, West European variety. National economic planning was retained, if moderated; and, more importantly, political intervention in the economy remained much higher than in Western Europe. Moreover, except for agriculture, there was no move to reestablish private ownership. Instead, a unique form of 'social ownership' (workers' self-management) was instituted.

Thus, if the economic system that emerged in Yugoslavia in the 1950s and 1960s as the result of the reform process could be clearly distinguished from that of other East European socialist states, it also differed sharply from West European capitalist systems. These differences centred on the degree of state control over the Yugoslav economy (especially over prices, investment and foreign economic relations) and in the limited scope allowed for private economic initiative. In sum, there continued to be geopolitical and systemic impediments to Yugoslavia's participation in a world economy dominated by the advanced capitalist countries, although these impediments were somewhat different in nature from those that affected relations with the West or other East European socialist countries.

As a result of her foreign and domestic policy evolution over the postwar decades, Yugoslavia emerged as a country that consciously distanced itself from the processes of regional, political and economic integration in Western and Eastern Europe. At the same time, she sought, with mixed success, to develop a balanced pattern of economic relations with the CMEA countries, the European Communities and the developing countries of the Third World. It is with the latter two groups of economic partners that Yugoslavia has developed significant linkages at the level of the firm. The centralised character of state monopoly and control of foreign economic relations in other socialist countries restricted the scope for relations with them below traditional, state-to-state channels.

DEVELOPMENT OF INTERNATIONAL INTER-FIRM LINKAGES

Linkages at the level of the firm have been viewed by reformers in Eastern Europe as basic elements in the reintegration of the East European economies into the world economy. From this perspective, such linkages were essential to a strategy of economic reinsertion into a new, broader international division of labour. They would ultimately supplant the traditional system of centrally-determined trade and payments, that deliberately insulated the domestic planned economy from the external market, with a broad network of business ties that organically linked the two. The promotion of 'industrial cooperation' with foreign firms became a major objective of the East European socialist economies, beginning in the 1960s. The term in fact became one of the catchwords of improved relations in the new vocabulary of *détente*.

Industrial cooperation agreements took a wide range of organisational forms, from 'turnkey' contracts to the establishment of joint equity ventures.[2] Their essence was that the firms party to them would agree to pool certain of their capabilities in a common endeavour that would associate them for a relatively long, or even indefinite, period of time. Such agreements effectively established inter-firm partnerships, linking socialist state or cooperative enterprises with foreign, generally private, firms.

Legal limitations imposed on foreign direct investment in the socialist economies, designed to safeguard the principles of state ownership and control, tended to restrict inter-firm partnerships to non-equity, contractual forms. Without retaining any formal title to assets transferred to an Eastern location, the Western partner could nevertheless exercise some control, during the life of the agreement, over their use, over the allocation of income from them and over their disposal. In this way, industrial cooperation could perform some of the functions of more direct forms of investment and could substitute for them operationally in the face of legal and systemic constraints.[3] Thus the 'new forms of international investment' that have been identified as increasingly important in North–South relations were comparatively 'old' in the East–West context.[4]

Although there was much talk of complementarities and interdependencies between East and West, it is clear that the principal aim of industrial cooperation with the Western countries was to reduce the East's growing technological lag through the establishment of more effective channels for the transfer of Western technology to the socialist economies. This was at a time of rising Eastern dissatisfaction with the rate of indigenously generated technical progress and recognition of the need to institute a 'scientific-technical revolution' that would inject new dynamism into economies that were suffering from declining rates of growth in productivity. In East European relations with the Third World, where it was less developed, industrial cooperation was similarly seen as a channel for effective transfer of technology and know-how, but *from* the socialist countries, based on their industrial development experience, *to* the developing economies.

For Western firms, industrial cooperation offered the means of penetrating the bureaucratic buffer imposed by the Eastern state-trading institutions and of establishing direct links with production organisations in the socialist economies. Others in the West viewed it more generally, in the spirit of *détente*, as a means of transcending some of the traditional political and ideological, as well as the institutional, barriers to East–West contacts.[5]

By 1980, the seven European CMEA countries had concluded an estimated 2600 industrial cooperation agreements with Western firms.[6] For her part, Yugoslavia had concluded 713 such agreements.[7] Joint equity ventures in Eastern Europe comprised only 231 of this total (32 in Hungary, Poland and Romania and 199 in Yugoslavia).[8] Thus, at this time Yugoslavia was more active in establishing inter-firm links with the West than other East European economies.

Eastern and Western hopes that these agreements would attain the objectives set for industrial cooperation were unfulfilled, however. The failure to institute significant, complementary reforms of domestic economic institutions in Eastern Europe undermined the effectiveness of these external initiatives. Disillusion and mounting economic problems on both sides led to the stagnation of East–West industrial cooperation during much of the 1980s. Only at the end of the decade, with the political and economic changes in the Soviet Union and their repercussions in Eastern Europe, did the prospect of significant inter-firm links re-emerge.

GROWTH OF EAST EUROPEAN FOREIGN DIRECT INVESTMENT

Ideology was an important determinant of the nature of inter-firm ties. The principle of state (or social) ownership of the means of production formed the basis of official policy in Eastern Europe. For decades it virtually eliminated the possibility of foreign direct investment in the socialist economies, including direct investment by one socialist country in another. Once the possibility was formally allowed, traditional concepts of ownership continued to restrict the scope for foreign investment. It is only as the dominance of state and collective ownership in these economies came to be seriously questioned in the Soviet Union and Eastern Europe, at the end of the 1980s, that alternative forms of ownership, including foreign, began to develop significantly.

Over the course of the 1980s, a growing number of East European countries reacted to mounting internal and external disequilibria by relaxing restrictions on foreign investment. Their efforts to encourage foreign interest in joint equity ventures had met with little success, however, when the announcement in 1986 that the Soviet Union would invite foreign capital participation in this form began to attract the attention of Western investors. This interest spilled over to the East European countries, all of whom except the German Democratic Republic had, by this time, opened their economies to foreign participation in jointly-owned domestic enterprises. Spurred by the prospect of further liberalisation and reform, as well as by the continuing improvement in East–West relations, this interest translated into a spurt of investment activity. According to United Nations estimates, over 5000 agreements for the establishment of Joint Ventures in CMEA member countries had been registered by mid-1990. Most were located in the Soviet Union (1800), Hungary (1600) and Poland (1550).[9] In addition, some 3038 agreements had been registered in Yugoslavia by mid-1990. Although this growth reflected a considerable increase in interest, on both sides, the capitalisation of many of these ventures was very small. Often the partners on the Western side were not firms but individuals (typically expatriates of the Eastern host country).

Because of the rapid changes in Eastern approaches to ownership, the term 'Joint Venture' is increasingly inappropriate in describing the nature of these capital inflows to the East European countries. All of the countries now allow majority and even sole foreign ownership, and increasing numbers of new investments take this option. Moreover in Eastern Europe, privatisations are leading to foreign takeovers of existing state enterprises, in some cases up to 100 per cent. This trend is extending to the USSR as well, where new foreign investment and ownership legislation was introduced in 1990 (refer to Chapter 5 for details). There is also increasing scope in Eastern

Europe (and potentially in the Soviet Union as well) for the direct establishment of Western branches and subsidiaries).

The ideology of ownership restricted investments by socialist state enterprises in non-socialist economies to a far lesser extent. Soviet companies began to be established in Western Europe not long after the October Revolution. Some survived into the post-World War II period and to their ranks were slowly added a small number of East European (notably Polish) investments in the early postwar decades. The growth of foreign investments by Soviet and East European state enterprises only began to be significant, however, after 1965.[10] That the East European countries should, with regard to their own foreign direct investment activities, do unto others not as they would have others do unto them, tended to raise somewhat embarrassing issues of reciprocity. Pragmatic considerations nevertheless increasingly outweighed ideological and foreign policy inhibitions.[11] As a result, direct Eastern investments abroad became an important form of linkage at the enterprise level with economies, developed and developing, outside the socialist sphere.

Although a different ownership ('social' rather than 'state') dominated Yugoslav ideology and policy from the early 1950s, it had analogous effects. It made it difficult, in principle and in practice, to accept foreign direct investment in the Yugoslav economy. When the step was finally taken in 1967, in connection with a series of liberalising reforms of the economic system that were introduced in 1965, it imposed conditions on foreign investment that sought to protect the principles of social ownership.[12] On the other hand, like other East European regimes, the state has had fewer inhibitions about encouraging Yugoslav enterprises to invest abroad.[13] The dominance of social ownership has lately come into question in Yugoslavia, just as the state ownership has in Eastern Europe. In 1989, federal legislation was passed that allowed Yugoslav enterprises to adopt alternative organisational structures and encouraged competition among various forms of ownership in Yugoslavia.[14]

In Eastern Europe, including Yugoslavia, outward direct investment has been pursued for rather different purposes from those of inward 'investment', whether the latter took the form of industrial cooperation agreements or Joint Ventures. As noted earlier, the Eastern countries have allowed foreign (equity and non-equity) participation in their economies primarily to foster the modernisation of their industries, through acquisition of more advanced foreign technologies. Access to foreign technology has been very much a secondary aim of outward investments. The Eastern countries have invested abroad principally in support of their exports but sometimes in order to exploit their own technologies more directly. To this end, they have established in important Western markets their own trading and marketing firms, transport and shipping companies, banks, insurance firms and other financial service companies. In the Third World, where Eastern exports have often been linked to development projects, engineering and construction companies have played a major role.

Investment abroad in the establishment of an infrastructure essential to modern international commercial success has paralleled the growth of the East European countries' concern about their poor export performance, particularly in manufactured goods. The readiness to undertake foreign direct investments, despite ideological impediments and limited foreign currency funds to finance them, can be understood in this light.

The development of export-oriented, internationally competitive industries had been seriously neglected by traditional industrialisation strategies that focused instead on import substitution and accorded heavy protection to import-competing domestic industries. The need to shift to more export-oriented growth strategies and to adopt programmes of investment directed to this purpose has been a major theme of economic reform efforts in Eastern Europe. The development of export capabilities has been a growing consideration in industrial cooperation and Joint Venture policy as well. These external initiatives can thus be interpreted as a dimension of the East European reform process. As stressed earlier, the repeated failures of that process have undermined the effectiveness of these new external links.

Such considerations are reflected in the structure of foreign direct investments in the West undertaken by the East European countries and the Soviet Union. That structure is revealed by the accompanying tables. Table 3.1 shows that the countries most active as investors have been those that have introduced the most extensive economic reforms, namely Hungary, Poland and Yugoslavia. Together with the economic size of the investing country, this is one of the most important determinants of the inter-country differences in Table 3.1 in the level of investment activity (as indicated by the numbers of companies established abroad).

The predominance of investments in support of exports is clearly shown in Tables 3.1 and 3.2. Table 3.1 reveals that all of the Eastern

Table 3.1 Number and Geographical Distribution of Soviet and East European Companies in the West, end of 1989*

Country	*Bulgaria*	*Czechoslovakia*	*GDR*	*Hungary*	*Poland*	*Romania*	*USSR*	*Total*
Australia	1	1	0	2	4	0	4	12
Austria	6	2	3	33	12	1	6	63+
Belgium	2	3	7	2	7	0	12	33
Canada	2	5	1	1	3	2	6	20
Denmark	0	1	1	1	1	0	2	6
FRG	10	17	0	32	26	4	21	110
Finland	0	1	1	1	1	0	8	12
France	4	6	3	5	8	4	12	42
Greece	6	0	1	4	2	2	3	18
Italy	5	10	1	7	2	5	9	39
Japan	2	0	0	3	2	0	1	8
Luxembourg	0	0	0	1	1	0	1	3
Netherlands	1	4	6	3	5	0	4	23
New Zealand	0	0	0	0	1	0	0	1
Norway	2	1	0	1	1	0	3	8
Portugal	0	0	0	1	0	0	1	2
Spain	2	3	1	3	4	2	4	19
Sweden	2	4	2	2	6	0	4	20
Switzerland	2	2	2	7	5	2	6	26+
United Kingdom	5	11	6	16	16	4	13	71
United States	1	4	4	9	16	3	8	45
Total	53	75	39	134	123	29	128	581

* Directly and indirectly owned by Eastern parent organisations.
\+ There is multiple Eastern equity (Hu, Po, Ro) in one Austrian company and also (USSR, GDR) in one Swiss company.

Source: East–West Project, Carleton University, Ottawa, Canada

countries have targeted their Western investments primarily to countries that have been the major markets for their exports, with Germany far in front in this respect. Table 3.2 indicates that commercial activities (Group A) constitute two-thirds of all of the activities performed by Eastern companies in the West. Within this group, simple representation and trading account for nearly 80 per cent. Importing from the home country constitutes most of this; exporting to the home market is decidedly secondary.

These commercial companies in the West are an important component of the international distribution networks of the state monopolies that handle most of the foreign trade of the Eastern countries. Much of their trade with the West is conducted through these channels. The estimated annual value of turnover in 1986–88 by the commercial companies in the West of the seven European CMEA countries was about $25.1 billion, or 62 per cent of the total annual value of their exports to the OECD countries in those years. Comparable figures are not available for Yugoslavia, but the Yugoslav share is probably higher.

Yugoslavia differs from the other Eastern countries in the degree to which her foreign investments:

a) have been made by a relatively few, large trading companies. The sale of Yugoslav products and the marketing of tourist services made up 75 per cent of the various activities performed by Yugoslav companies in the West. Eighty-three Yugoslav companies, accounting for well over half of these commercial activities, are owned by eight, large Yugoslav trading companies: Exportdrvo, Generalexport, Gorenje, INA, Interexport, Iskra, Progres and Slovenijales.
b) perform relatively simple, import and travel agency functions and therefore have low average capitalisation. More than half of the Yugoslav commercial companies established in the West are little more than the foreign sales offices of Yugoslav trading companies that have incorporated them as separate juridical persons under host-country laws. Very rarely do they engage in such ancillary activities as product modification and servicing.

Other East European companies in the West are more diversified in both their activities and ownership structure. A larger share of the total (especially by value measures, such as capitalisation) are engaged in more complex marketing functions, in other trade-related

Table 3.2 Distribution by Activity of Soviet and East European Companies in the West, end of 1989*

Activity	*Bulgaria*	*Czechoslovakia*	*GDR*	*Hungary*	*Poland*	*Romania*	*USSR*	*Total*
GROUP A								
Representation	5	5	5	7	24	6	13	65
Trading	29	51	21	76	66	20	38	301
Trading/distribution	3	5	1	8	9	1	11	38
Trading/servicing	7	17	8	0	6	1	12	51
Trading/product mod.	1	0	0	0	1	0	11	13
Total	45	78	35	91	106	28	85	468
GROUP B								
Financial services	4	5	3	12	29	8	14	75
Transport services	7	3	4	6	19	1	34	74
Eng./const. services	4	1	2	7	4	0	2	20
Technical services	0	0	0	2	2	0	9	13
Business services	0	0	1	11	4	1	7	24
Consumer services	3	2	1	11	7	0	7	31
Total	18	11	11	49	65	10	73	237
GROUP C								
Fisheries	0	0	0	1	1	0	5	7
Resource extraction	1	0	0	1	0	0	0	2
Total	1	0	0	2	1	0	5	9
GROUP D								
Manufacturing	5	3	0	16	2	1	2	29
Total	5	3	0	16	2	1	2	29

* For companies which engage in multiple activities, each activity is counted separately.

Source: East–West Project, Carleton University, Ottawa, Canada.

functions such as financing, shipping and freight, or in forms of material production. Although there are differences among them in ownership structure, the seven CMEA countries on average have tended in their foreign investments to take on local partners much more frequently than the data show is the case for Yugoslavia. Only about 30 per cent of the nearly 600 companies in the West with capital participation by enterprises in the CMEA Seven were wholly owned, while the share of companies with sole Yugoslav equity was nearly 73 per cent.[15]

To sum up, Yugoslav investments in the West share many of the structural characteristics of those of other East European countries. Yugoslav investments overshadow other East European investments in the numbers of companies established. Most of the companies, however, are engaged in representative and agency functions for large Yugoslav trading and travel companies. Hence they tend to be small in capitalisation, although some handle a large trade turnover, and wholly owned. If less numerous, other East European and especially Soviet companies are more diversified in function and ownership, and tend to be larger.

Yugoslavia's economic involvement in the Third World, which she pursued as a basic tenet of her foreign policy diversification after the break with the Soviet Union, extended to the sphere of direct investments. The data reveal that, in this respect, Yugoslavia has been more active than most of the European CMEA countries. The only CMEA country with comparable LDC investments is Romania, which also pursued an active policy of Third World engagement as a counterweight to relations with the Soviet Union. Like Romania, Yugoslavia's Third World investments are concentrated (70 per cent) in Africa. Other East European countries have engaged in a more geographically diversified pattern of investments (Table 3.3). There is less difference between the CMEA countries and Yugoslavia in the distribution of investments in the Third World by activity, although Yugoslavia's share of non-commercial activities (production, transportation and construction) is somewhat higher than the CMEA average (Table 3.4). In ownership structure, Yugoslav investments in the Third World also resemble those of the CMEA countries in employing Joint Ventures with local firms as their most common form.

Table 3.3 Number and Geographical Distribution of Soviet and East European Companies in LDCs, end of 1989

Location	*Bulgaria*	*Czechoslovakia*	*GDR*	*Hungary*	*Poland*	*Romania*	*USSR*	*Total*
AFRICA	4	8	0	9	36	34	7	98
of which:								
Egypt	0	0	0	0	4	2	0	6
Libya	0	0	0	0	9	5	0	14
Morocco	0	0	0	0	0	3	1	4
Nigeria	2	4	0	6	8	3	1	24
ASIA	8	7	1	8	14	1	12	51
of which:								
India	5	5	1	7	2	1	3	24
Singapore	3	2	0	0	4	0	3	12
LATIN AMERICA	1	20	3	12	12	5	7	60
of which:								
Argentina	1	2	1	1	1	1	2	9
Brazil	0	3	0	3	4	0	1	11
Mexico	0	4	1	1	1	0	1	8
Peru	0	2	0	1	3	2	1	9
Venezuela	0	4	0	0	1	0	0	5
MIDDLE EAST	14	2	0	8	19	12	4	59
of which:								
Iran	1	1	0	1	3	1	2	9
Kuwait	2	0	0	2	0	0	0	4
Lebanon	6	1	0	1	2	5	1	16
Total	27	37	4	37	81	52	30	268

Source: East–West Project, Carleton University, Ottawa, Canada.

Table 3.4 Distribution by Activity of Soviet and East European Companies in LDCs, end of 1989*

Activity	*Bulgaria*	*Czechoslovakia*	*GDR*	*Hungary*	*Poland*	*Romania*	*USSR*	*Total*
GROUP A								
Representation	0	1	0	6	4	1	1	13
Trading	4	10	3	15	21	19	7	79
Trading/distribution	0	0	0	0	0	0	0	0
Trading/servicing	2	14	0	2	1	0	4	23
Trading/product mod.	0	3	0	1	0	0	1	5
Total	6	28	3	24	26	20	13	120
GROUP B								
Financial services	5	2	0	0	8	1	5	21
Transport services	8	0	1	1	18	1	8	37
Eng./const. services	1	4	0	4	10	2	0	21
Technical services	0	0	0	2	10	4	1	17
Business services	1	0	0	0	2	0	0	3
Consumer services	2	0	0	0	1	0	0	3
Total	17	6	1	7	49	8	14	102
GROUP C								
Fisheries	2	0	0	0	2	1	6	11
Resource extraction	1	1	0	1	1	26	0	30
Total	3	1	0	1	3	27	6	41
GROUP D								
Manufacturing	3	6	0	5	8	3	2	27
Total	3	6	0	5	8	3	2	27

* For companies which engage in multiple activities, each activity is counted separately.

Source: East–West Project, Carleton University, Ottawa, Canada.

THE SPECIAL CHARACTER OF THE SOCIALIST MULTINATIONAL ENTERPRISE

What special features (if any) characterise socialist multinational enterprises and how do they fit into the global multinational phenomenon? These are questions which have been addressed by McMillan in a recent book on the multinational activities of the European CMEA countries.[16] The relevant conclusions reached there are summarised below.

The Soviet Union and Eastern Europe have attained a position of some world significance as a source of foreign direct investment. In form and operation, the foreign investment activity of Soviet and East European enterprises bears notable similarities to the behaviour of the multinational enterprises of Third World countries. Both, in turn, share many of the characteristics of Western multinational enterprises. Available quantitative data suggest that the magnitude of investment activity by the CMEA countries is not greatly disproportionate to that of similarly engaged Third World countries, and CMEA investments are broadly comparable in functional range and geographical distribution to those of developing countries.

At the same time, Second and Third World multinationals have been restricted in their foreign direct investment activities by resource constraints that are less binding on OECD multinationals. Among these, the most important are capital constraints (especially in terms of funds available for foreign investment in convertible currencies) and managerial constraints (in terms of managers capable of operating effectively in a market environment).

Socialist state enterprises have established branches, subsidiaries and affiliates abroad for many of the same reasons that have motivated their capitalist counterparts. We have stressed the role of investments in support of trade. The need to adapt products to the requirements of foreign markets and to provide after-sale servicing, especially in the case of machinery and equipment, has pushed investments into new areas of a more technical than commercial nature. A certain progression has been observed from pure trading and marketing towards operations of a manufacturing character. Eastern enterprises have also invested directly abroad to exploit technical, financial and other advantages in order to generate higher foreign (especially convertible currency) revenues than could be gained by working through a foreign partner firm (under, say, a licensing arrangement). We find Eastern investments in banking, trade financing, transport, engineering services, tourism, hotels and restaurant services, that are not closely linked to Eastern commodity exports and provide independent sources of foreign currency earnings.

The CMEA countries may be viewed as 'state-investment' as well as 'state-trading' economies in the international arena. The multinational actors are state-owned enterprises subject at home to a considerable degree of central state direction and control. In foreign investment, as in foreign trade, socialist states have played a much more direct role than is the case elsewhere, even where multinationals are state-owned. In essence, this means that foreign investment, like foreign trade, may be used to pursue state objectives that transcend the interests of the individual state enterprise.

In practice, Eastern states may not exercise a high degree of strategic control over the multinational activities of state enterprises, allowing them to conduct their foreign operations on a comparatively decentralised basis. The degree of internal as well as external control over enterprise operations varies substantially among East European countries. Nevertheless, state control is residual and can be exercised, if circumstances require. A relevant example is the reported decision of the Soviet state in the summer of 1990 to 'encourage' Soviet banks located in the West to purchase Yugoslav debt. The intent was to reduce the accumulated Soviet trade deficit with Yugoslavia (which had reached some $2 billion) by having the amounts of debt purchased subtracted from the trade deficit figure, under an arrangement between the two governments.[17]

More generally, state ownership is reflected operationally in the subordination of foreign subsidiaries to the goals imposed on their parents by Eastern planners. Marketing companies may be required to maximise sales rather than profits to enable parent foreign trade organisations to fulfil export targets imposed by the foreign trade plan. For similar reasons, parents may sacrifice subsidiary profits by increasing their inventory and including the value in reports of export plan fulfilment. Western multinationals can and do subordinate subsidiary profits to global profit, or other, strategic goals. To an extent unparalleled elsewhere, however, considerations of macroeconomic policy have been directly incorporated into socialist multinational operations.[18]

Yugoslavia shares with the other East European countries the special characteristics of the socialist multinational enterprise. It is less in their form and operation abroad than in their organisation and subordination at home that socialist multinational enterprises are distinct from multinational enterprises based in other socio-economic systems. Yugoslav multinationals are rooted in an economic system where private enterprise is the exception and where market allocation has been restricted by party administrative intervention. Although Yugoslav enterprises are less subject to state control than enterprises in more centralised social systems, they are certainly more so than private enterprises in a capitalist system. The managers of large Yugoslav companies abroad are generally experienced in operating a successful firm in a market economy, but they often reveal the perspective of senior bureaucrats, taking the view of the state with regard to the goals of the firm in many matters.

For example, a number of managers of Yugoslav commercial companies in Western countries stressed in interviews the need to extend operations beyond trade to technical and production activities. In this way, they felt that they could become a conduit for the transfer of advanced technology to Yugoslav producers. Only in this way would Yugoslavia remain competitive in the host-country market. Obviously this is a perspective that transcends the profit goals of the individual company to incorporate important macroeconomic goals of the Yugoslav state.

The reader may wonder to what extent this 'socialist' analysis of the East European multinational enterprise will continue to apply. Indeed, most East European countries are now ruled by non-Marxist parties, and have explicitly rejected the socialist label.

We must recognise that the East European societies and economies are in flux and that the transformation underway will ultimately affect the character of their multinational activities. In particular, as the private sectors of these economies grow in size and strength, they will extend their activities abroad to multinational operations. This, combined with the marketisation of the Eastern economies, will serve ultimately to eliminate the special, 'socialist' character of the East European multinational enterprise. The process will vary in tempo and nature among the Eastern countries, with the transformation of the German Democratic Republic, as the result of German reunification, representing an extreme case. Otherwise we can realistically expect that East European economies will remain far more 'mixed' in character than West European economies. It would therefore seem premature to abandon differentiation based on systemic features. It will no doubt be some time before the vestiges of the former societies have been eliminated to such an extent that our characterisation of East European multinational enterprises no longer applies.

We conclude by relating trends in the flows of investment that we have analysed in this chapter. The opening up of the Eastern economies to foreign direct investment led, especially after 1986, to a rapid growth in inflows. As we have seen, the number of instances (foreign-owned companies, including banks, established) exceeded eight thousand by mid-1990. By the same measure, and including Yugoslavia, outflows numbered about 1100 (827 in the West and 268 in the South). However, many of the inflows remained investments 'on paper' – little more than registrations – while the outflows (especially those directed to the OECD economies) were well-documented instances of currently operational companies.[19] In terms of size, investments into and out of the region tended on average to be small. They were largest for the USSR, where the average total capitalisation of Soviet companies abroad was $5.6 million, and that of joint enterprises registered in the USSR was $4.8 million. There is considerable variation about the average in both cases. Moreover, the figures are subject to exchange rate fluctuations and the value for inflows is generally exaggerated by the overvaluation of the rouble and other Eastern currencies at official exchange rates.

If inward investments continue to grow at this present pace and become increasingly operational, they will clearly exceed outflows. In some ways, this is as it should be. The old status of the region as a net investor *vis-à-vis* the West was anomalous and due to administrative restrictions on inflows. This result depends, however, upon whether Eastern Europe continues to be regarded as an interesting target for investment. Meanwhile, outflows from the area are anything but stagnant, and the political conditions for them are increasingly favourable. In the three-and-a-half year period from 1987 to mid-1990, the seven European CMEA countries established nearly a hundred new companies in the West alone (all fully operational). The most active investing countries have been Hungary and the Soviet Union, with Germany and Austria as the favoured locations. In the period from January 1989 to mid-1990, Yugoslav enterprises established 190 new companies abroad. According to the German Economic Ministry, Yugoslav direct investment in Germany totalled DM323 million at the end of 1988, well above the value of German investment in Yugoslavia (DM185 million).

To sum up, as the century enters the final decade, direct investment is a dynamic area of East–West economic relations. Flows in both directions are playing a major role in the integration of the Eastern economies into the world economy. These developments should be recognised as the growing internationalisation of production and services in the East–West context and the extension of multinational operations to East–West relations in both directions.

Notes

1. For details of and background to the EC's Trade and Cooperation Agreements with Yugoslavia, see, *inter alia*, P. Artisien and S. Holt, 'Yugoslavia and the EEC in the 1970s', *Journal of Common Market Studies*, Vol. XVIII, No. 4, June 1980; and P. Artisien, 'Belgrade's closer links with Brussels', *The World Today*, Vol. 37, No. 1, January 1981.
2. The various forms are listed and described in C. H. McMillan, *Industrial Cooperation, East European Economies Post-Helsinki*, Joint Economic Committee, US Congress, US Government Printing Office, Washington, DC, 1977, p. 1182, Table 1. See also United Nations Economic Commission for Europe, *East–West Industrial Cooperation*, New York, 1979.
3. See McMillan, op. cit. (1977), p. 1192.
4. See C. Oman, *New Forms of International Investment in Developing Countries*, Paris: OECD, Paris, 1984.
5. See, for example, H. V. Perlmutter, Emerging East–West Venture: The Transideological Enterprise, *Columbia Journal of World Business*, IV, 5, September–October, 1969.
6. Data on East–West industrial cooperation agreements vary depending upon the definition used to classify agreements. These data are based on the definition adopted by the United Nations. See C. H. McMillan, 'Trends in East–West Industrial Cooperation', *Journal of International Business Studies*, Fall, 1981.
7. Federal Secretariat for Foreign Economic Relations, Belgrade.
8. See United Nations Economic Commission for Europe, *East–West Joint Ventures*, New York, 1988; and P. Artisien, *Joint Ventures in Yugoslav Industry*, Gower, Aldershot, 1985.
9. United Nations Economic Commission for Europe, *East–West Joint Venture News*, No. 5, July 1990.
10. See C. H. McMillan, *Multinationals from the Second World*, Macmillan, London 1987.
11. The influence of ideological considerations on East European approaches to foreign direct investment is discussed in McMillan, op. cit., 1987, especially in Chapter 4.
12. See C. H. McMillan and D. P. St Charles, *Joint Ventures in Eastern Europe, A Three Country Comparison*, C. D. Howe Research Institute, Montreal, 1974; and P. Artisien, op. cit., 1985.
13. See P. Artisien, C. H. McMillan and M. Rojec, *Yugoslav Multinationals Abroad*, Macmillan, London, 1992.
14. The new measures allowed foreign firms to set up wholly-owned subsidiaries, mixed enterprises such as Joint Stock and Limited Liability

companies, banks and insurance organisations. For further details, see *Business Eastern Europe*, Vol. XVIII, No. 11, 13 March 1989; and Vol. XVIII, No. 12, 20 March 1989.

15. On the ownership structure of CMEA companies in the West, see Table 8 (p. 22) of *The East–West Business Directory*, 1990–91, Carleton University/Duncan Publishing, 1990.
16. McMillan, op. cit., 1987, Chapter 8.
17. Reported in *Business Eastern Europe*, Vol. XIX, No. 326, August 1990, p. 259.
18. For more discussion of these points, see McMillan, op. cit., 1987, pp. 71–2.
19. Those in the West are listed in *The East–West Business Directory*, 1990–91, op. cit.

4 Joint Ventures in Eastern Europe and the Dynamics of Reciprocal Flows in East–West Direct Investments: Some New Perspectives[1]

Patrick Gutman

INTRODUCTION

At the beginning of 1989 most Socialist countries[2] allowed joint venture partnerships with Western capital. Only East Germany and Albania did not permit them. Was the concept of 'exportation de capitaux',[3] organically linked to that of imperialism, now acceptable to Eastern Europe? Or had the concept of Foreign Direct Investment lost its ideological content to become a mere 'exportation de capital'?[4]

Recent events call for a re-examination of the understanding of joint ventures in Eastern Europe. First, the easing of the legislation governing Foreign Direct Investment and the near-generalisation of this practice introduce a new context for Western capital. Second, a particular role is conferred to the joint venture formula in the twin-track process of modernisation and implementation of the reforms. These two points make the exercise indispensable, even if at present it is difficult to appreciate the exact scope of the phenomenon. It is premature to judge the current experience with regard to the internal dynamics of the planned economies. We shall therefore conduct a general reflection rather than a precise evaluation of the recent practice.

Many past analyses of joint ventures in the Soviet Union and Eastern Europe have been characterised by a descriptive, practical, institutional and/or juridical approach. Joint ventures were almost always considered as a separate subject, although in fact, they are simply one of many organisational modes applied in the strategy of acquiring and assimilating foreign technology. To treat joint ventures as a separate subject often results in not discussing the actual choice of organisational modes. Furthermore, most past studies and articles on joint ventures located in Eastern Europe – with a few exceptions – lack a theoretical or analytical framework. In general there is no linkage between Western Direct Investment in Eastern Europe and Socialist Direct Investment in the West. Indeed, until today, the *dynamics* of reciprocal flows in East–West direct investments has not been studied.

From a theoretical point of view, it is important to emphasise the recent acceleration of Western investment in Eastern Europe as well as the development of East European investment in the OECD countries. These two phenomena reflect the acceptance of a shift from international trade to internationalisation of production in the East–West context. They also fit into the current formation of the 'System of the World Economy' (as put forward by Charles-Albert Michalet). In this broader framework, we will attempt to demonstrate that the recent acceleration in the rhythm of joint venture creation in Eastern Europe (in the wake of liberalising measures in foreign direct investment legislation) introduces a new perspective on the dynamics of reciprocal flows of direct East–West investments.

First, we examine the concept of joint ventures as applied in the Soviet and East European contexts. Here, it is advisable to consider the specificity of joint ventures in East–West relations in terms of an alliance strategy.

Second, we survey the character – typical or not – of joint ventures set up in Eastern Europe, and compare them with the foreign direct investment model generally followed by Western capital. The context is that of New Forms of Investment versus Direct Investment.

Finally, we review the impact of the new wave of Direct Investment in Eastern Europe on the dynamics of reciprocal flows in East–West investments, by referring to Vernon's theory of the product life cycle and the hierarchy of productive systems.

THE JOINT VENTURE FORMULA IN EASTERN EUROPE AS A STRATEGIC ALLIANCE

Joint ventures are without doubt an important form of East–West Industrial Cooperation, as they institutionalise relations between partners. Beyond the classical approach – in terms of the typology of different organisational modes – taken by many authors and institutions, we should emphasise that the joint venture fits into the concept of the 'Contractual Economy',[5] and represents a half-way house between the 'pure market' and 'internalisation' by multinational firms. In this context, East–West joint ventures conform entirely to International Inter-Firm Agreements.[6]

We view the emergence of an increasing number of East–West joint ventures, particularly since 1987, as stemming from the spreading of international Inter-Firm Agreements, particularly those in the main OECD countries since the end of the 1970s.[7] These strategic alliances were all the more developed in the OECD countries, which were going through a period of intense technological change entailing high investment costs. In such circumstances a partnership provided a particularly convenient answer to risk management.

There is a time lag between the significant development of East–West co-enterprises which we observe at present, and the implementation of International Inter-Firm Agreements in the West: this development can be seen as the search for a strategic alliance. It appears that a partnership with the West, through the creation of a joint venture, constitutes one of the means chosen by many East European countries to push forward their modernisation programmes.

Within this organisational mode, the East European countries benefit from technology and capitalist methods of management, whilst sharing the risks with the Western partner as well as the micro-economic costs involved in the modernisation process. The distribution of risk, inherent in the notion of joint ventures, is a key factor in explaining the choice of organisational mode. The pursuit of alliances is a recurrent theme in most papers covering this subject, even though a Gosplan economist has reversed the perspective by entitling one of his papers 'A partner *for* the West',[8] in order to encourage more Western firms to set up joint ventures in the former Soviet Union.

Although the development of joint ventures with Western capital in the ex-Socialist countries conformed to the strategic alliances observed in the 1980s, it is necessary to point out that these ventures brought together firms that belonged to different socio-economic systems.[9] Their specificity lies in the fact that East European partners preferred partnerships with their Western 'adversaries' to those with their COMECON allies: the number of East–East joint ventures to date remains very small. Their development encountered several obstacles, including strong centripetal tendencies from the ex-Soviet Union, which often insisted on 'Soviet-centred' joint ventures, as well as the traditional problem of rouble convertibility.

This shift from allies to opponents is not neutral: it recalls, in a modern and adapted form, the de Witte system.[10] In supporting Gorbachev's modernisation programme, the West tried to prevent the reversibility of perestroika and glasnost, to ensure that the ex-Soviet Union remained tied to the World economy and its political institutions. Western assistance via joint ventures was not in itself a new phenomenon in the USSR: it is in keeping with a historical tradition. This view is supported by at least two precedents: the foreign investment and borrowings in the period 1870–1914 under the Czarist regime, and the concessions policy launched by Lenin and Krasin at the beginning of the NEP. Yet these two experiences are not strictly comparable. In the first case, a massive export of capital financed Russia's economic development, whilst securing for the foreign investor a key position in most industrial and banking sectors.[11] On the other hand, the concessionary policy of the NEP did not have the same dimension or impact:[12] it was deliberately limited within the framework of a tactical strategy, and barely comparable to the 'exportation de capitaux' in the Leninist sense. It is better understood as an 'exportation de capital', in the Michalet tradition, namely the export of productive capital, which allows the relocation of the source of value added.[13]

Next, we turn our attention to equity joint ventures and their relevance to the 'exportation de capital'. Few authors, if any, have addressed the question of equity joint ventures in these terms. Carl McMillan, however, has emphasised that capital acquisition (capital accumulation in Marxist terms) was not, in itself, the prime objective of joint ventures, as the Communist regimes preferred to access long-term credits and loans on the international money markets (most notably Eurodollars).[14]

According to the United Nations Centre for Transnational Corporations, between 1975 and 1987, the accumulated capital of equity joint ventures did not exceed 0.25 per cent of the total amount of capital borrowed through the international credit mechanism.[15] It is clear, therefore, that over the last twenty years, the so called 'International Credit Economy' has played an essential role in East–West economic relations, even if at times it had to slow down because of the East European countries' external constraints. In practice,

Western capital did not seem to have a genuine alternative between a policy of direct investment in Eastern Europe, and the International Credit Economy. Unlike the Third World, where foreign direct investment and the International Credit Economy went hand in hand,[16] in Eastern Europe, until recently, the Communist regimes checked the expansion of foreign direct investment.

From a chronological viewpoint, it was noticeable that the policies of debt stabilisation recorded a level of success between 1982 and 1984. When the effects of those policies started to wear off, the liberalisation of foreign direct investment took off. The economic revival that took place after the abrupt break in the policies of structural adjustment, coupled with the imperative of modernisation of manufacturing equipment,[17] led to a renewal of the debt crisis after 1985. In this context, the increasing use of equity joint ventures can be regarded as a means of reducing the external constraint, while continuing to benefit from the Western technology necessary for modernisation. Joint ventures add a degree of freedom *vis-à-vis* the modernisation *v.* indebtedness dilemma, thus avoiding a clear-cut choice.

In fact, the thesis that the International Credit Economy is giving way to foreign direct investment also applies outside Eastern Europe: this was recently endorsed by the Trilateral Commission, whose authors, Giscard d'Estaing and Kissinger, *inter alia*, opposed the massive injection of credit into the ex-Soviet Union, and instead advocated the promotion of equity joint ventures for the production of goods. They added that these firms could benefit from the same guarantees as the sales of capital goods.[18] This scheme recalls both the Pisarist project of 'Transideological society', and the will to reduce the supply of public credits guaranteed by Western states. In this line of reasoning, it is important to emphasise that the growth of joint ventures in Eastern Europe is more than merely a new wave of Western Direct Investment: it is a new context.

Indeed, the objective is to facilitate the transition from an international credit economy – in which the West bears the risks – to an 'exportation de capital' in the sense defined above. Multinationals would no longer solely be vehicles for technology transfer, but would be in a position to bring about a genuine relocation of production. The latter would contrast strongly with the disguised relocation of production, which is currently generated through the export of turnkey plants and buy-back agreements.[19] The transfer of value would not necessarily go through resulting products by means of compensation, but could be operated by re-exporting the products of the joint venture. The stake for Western capital is therefore important: the East European countries would cease to be an atypical link developed by the internationalisation of capital, but would become more fully integrated into the 'World Economic System'.

In this respect, the opening up of Central and Eastern Europe to foreign capital can be examined against the alternative backdrops of traditional direct investment and the New Forms of Investment. This would establish whether joint ventures in Eastern Europe conform to the pattern of foreign direct investment generally followed by Western capital.

THE INVERSION OF THE TRADITIONAL MODEL: A SHIFT TO MAJORITY-OWNED FOREIGN DIRECT INVESTMENT

Studies which concentrate on the development of multinational enterprises suggest that, up until the mid-1960s, these firms – particularly in the USA – preferred to exercise a high degree of control over their foreign subsidiaries, which explains the high proportion of wholly- and majority-owned affiliates.[20]

This 'traditional' model of direct investment, which relied on maximising the subsidiary's 'subservience' to the parent company, was made possible by whole or majority ownership of the equity. Then, when confronted with the growing demands of host nations – mainly from the Third World – multinationals gradually opted for a direct investment model, which left more room for local partnerships. By regaining the majority stake in the statutory capital, the host countries manifested a will to assert their sovereignty. In accepting this shift from a majority- to a minority-direct investment model, multinationals aimed for risk minimisation. This strategic evolution does not, however, imply a loss of control over the subsidiaries: instead of being exercised exclusively through capital ownership, the new strategy relies more on control through technology and know-how, whether or not capital shareholding takes place. It is precisely this dissociation between capital ownership and technology transfer which constitutes the specific element of what Charles Oman has coined 'The New Forms of Investment'.[21]

In the framework of the debate between the New Forms of Investment and Traditional Direct Investment, equity joint ventures are paramount; that is, they form part of the investment process. As Oman reminds us, the minority equity joint venture is typically a New Form of Investment: 'A joint venture normally implies that at least two firms or economic groups share the assets, risks and benefits of a firm or investment project. The economic group comprises private, public or state firms. The capital distribution is regulated according to either the shares of the partners or other contributions, including technology, management and access to world markets. According to this definition, a joint venture is classified as a New Form of Investment if the host country partner holds at least 50 per cent of the capital. We exclude from our definition those joint ventures where the foreign partner holds a majority of the equity'.[22]

It is evident, from this definition, that the joint ventures established in Eastern Europe in the early 1970s represented New Forms of Investment, long before the emergence of the concept. This also applied to most other organisational modes of East–West Industrial Cooperation, confirming Oman's typology.

From 1971 to 1988, joint ventures in Eastern Europe, with their minority foreign participation and the frequent capitalisation of equipment and technology,[23] were perfect illustrations of New Forms of Investment. At the same time they represented an inversion of the traditional direct investment model of Western capital, which in its early stages generally takes the form of wholly- or majority-owned investment, before shifting to minority-owned or contractual ventures.

In reality the phenomenon is doubly atypical from the West's viewpoint. Not only did the implementation of the first wave of joint ventures in Eastern Europe (1971–88) correspond to an inversion of the direct model traditionally followed by Western capital,[24] but since 1989, we have observed a reversal of that perspective. In other words, there has been a significant shift from the New Forms of Investment to the traditional direct investment model. Western firms in the Soviet Union have, since April 1989, been allowed to become majority shareholders, whilst in Hungary they may enjoy total control of joint ventures (following a law passed in December 1988). Only Bulgaria has not set any ceiling on foreign direct investment since 1980 (see Table 4.1).

Just under 85 per cent of the total number of joint ventures in COMECON at the end of 1988 were located in the Soviet Union and in Hungary. The evolution of regulations in these two countries has already prompted other nations to modify the provisions which previously restricted foreign participation: Poland and Czechoslovakia are two cases in point.

The two laws adopted by the Polish Diet on 23 December 1988 (which became operative on 1 January 1989) had important implications for foreign direct investment in that country. Whilst introducing more liberal fiscal provisions, the law governing equity joint ventures simplified the investment regime by adopting a united framework for the foreign operator, covering state, private and cooperative enterprises in the production, business and service sectors. Western partners can from now on become majority partners and hold up to 100 per cent of the statutory capital.[25]

Czechoslovakia, for her part, has tolerated inward direct investment since August 1985 under certain prescribed conditions, without resorting at the time to any specific law.[26] Some ten joint ventures were set up in this way between 1986 and January 1989, when a law passed in 1988 became applicable. This allows the foreign partner to have majority control, and applies retrospectively to joint ventures established before 1989.[27] Thus, 1988 was a turning point: it saw four members of COMECON – the USSR, Hungary, Poland and Czechoslovakia – prepare to switch over from a minority to a majority foreign direct investment regime.

These recent changes have introduced a new context in which to encourage more Western firms to set up business in Eastern Europe. The liberalisation of foreign direct investment, combined with recent political changes, has been a turning point in the post-war history of countries which demonstrated an open reticence to Western capital. The imperatives of modernisation without excessive indebtedness, and of export promotion of manufactured goods on world markets, helped those countries to overcome the ideological barriers responsible for this historically dated approach to foreign investment, and ushered in a more pragmatic attitude. The latter fits into the managerial revolution currently sweeping through Eastern Europe.[28] Foreign direct investment is now perceived more as the export of technical means of production and know-how, than as the 'exportation de capitaux'. The normalisation and expansion of foreign direct investment – most notably the acceptance of majority-owned joint ventures – exemplifies the desire to offer an alternative to the classical forms of technology transfer in East–West Industrial Cooperation. In this context, the recourse to majority-owned foreign direct investment as an alternative organisational model has a double objective: the search for a learning process coupled with a higher degree of internalisation (see Figure 4.1).

The creation of joint ventures is intended to allow the East European countries to benefit from technology and capitalist know-how in

Table 4.1 Summary of Joint Venture Regulations in the CMEA Countries prior to 1988

	Romania	*Hungary*	*Bulgaria*	*Poland*	*Czechoslovakia*	*Soviet Union*
Year when rules first issued	1971	1972	1980	1986	1986	1987
Approving authority	State Council	Ministry of Finance	Council of Ministers	Ministry of Foreign Economic Relations	The Federal Ministry having jurisdiction	The USSR ministry or agency or Council of Ministers of the Union Republic, having jurisdiction
Maximum foreign participation	49%	49%; exceptions possible	No upper limit	49%; exceptions possible	49%	49%
Purchasing from						
(a) domestic markets	in convertible currencies	as local enterprises	as local enterprises	as local enterprises	as local enterprises	as agreed in the contract with Soviet enterprises
(b) foreign markets	free	must obtain foreign trade permit	must obtain foreign trade permit	must obtain foreign trade permit	must obtain foreign trade permit	free
Marketing to						
(a) domestic markets	in convertible currencies enterprises	only through wholesale market	directly to the domestic market	directly to the domestic market	directly to the domestic with Soviet enterprises	as agreed in the contract
(b) foreign markets	freely in convertible currencies	must obtain foreign trade permit	must obtain foreign trade permit	must obtain foreign trade permit	must obtain foreign trade permit	free
Currency transfers abroad	only out of JVs own currency earnings	only out of JVs own currency earnings	only out of JVs own currency earnings	Limited by: (1) 15–20% of currency earning to be sold to Polish banks (2) Right to foreign currencies proportionate to share in statutory capital	to be defined in the foreign currency permits	only out of JVs own currency earnings

Income tax rate Incentives: lower tax rate	30% Case by case: – first profitable year: tax free – following 2 years: 15.30%	40% (1) Case by case (2) Production and hotels: first 5 years - 20%; from 6th year - 30% (3) activities of outstanding importance: first 5 years tax free; from 6th year - 20%	20% Case by case: first 3 years: reduction to be negotiated yearly	50% (1) first 2 years tax free (2) export: each 1% of production exported = 0.40% reduction in tax rate	50%	30% (1) case by case (2) first 2 years from declaring profit, tax free
Withholding tax	10% if transferred abroad		10% if transferred abroad		25%	20% if transferred abroad (unless provided otherwise in a tax treaty)
Posts to be occupied by host-country nationals			(1) Chairman of Management Board (2) Chairman of Board of Directors	Manager or Chairman of Management Board	Presiding members of management bodies	(1) Chairman of the Board (2) General Manager
Rules on salaries of employees (a) domestic employees	(a) Rules of state enterprises	To be specified in employment contract for both domestic and foreign employees	(a) Bulgarian law	To be specified in joint venture contract or by decision of joint venture organs for both domestic and foreign employees	Czechoslovak rules for both domestic and foreign employees; Ministry of Labour may grant right to deviate	(a) Soviet law
(b) foreign employees	(b) To be specified by the Board of Directors		(b) To be specified in employment contract			(b) To be specified in contract

Source: UN–ECE, 1988, Table 2, p. 72.

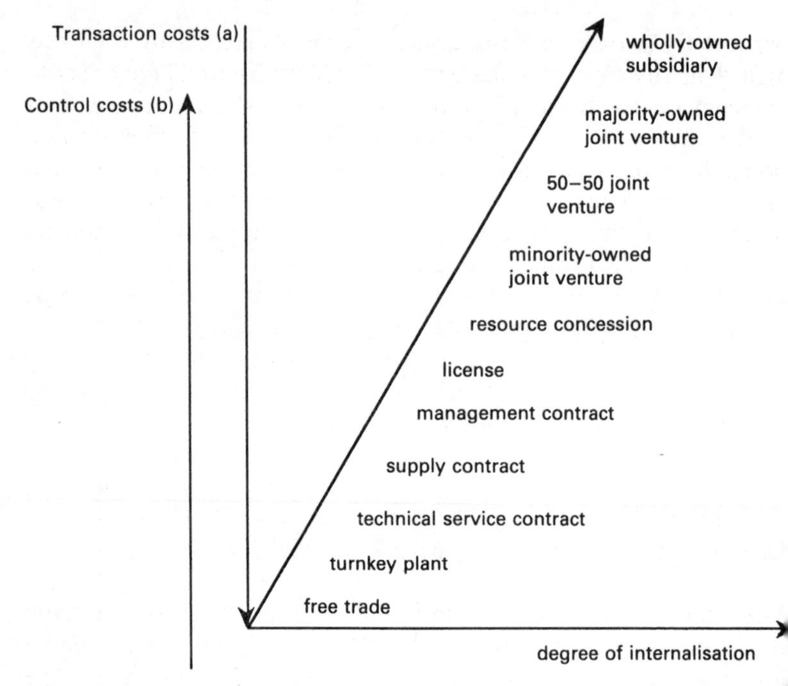

Figure 4.1 Form of Foreign Participation and Growth of Transaction and Control Costs According to the Growing Degree of Internalisation

Source: J. L. Mucchielli, *Les firmes multinationales: mutations et nouvelle perspectives*, (Paris: Economica, 1985), p. 209.

an appropriated form by favouring active assimilation (learning b doing), as opposed to passive assimilation, which often characterise the import of Western technology and equipment.[29] It is the very ga between technology transfer and industrial workmanship whic prompted the authorities of the planned economies to look for associ ates rather than distributors in order to increase the efficiency of th investments.

The need for a higher degree of internalisation, which led to th formation of joint ventures with Western capital, reflects a shift fron an inter-firm to an intra-firm logic. It remains unclear whether th increase in costs – transaction and control costs – resulting from th shift to majority-owned joint ventures will be compensated by th stability associated with greater control.

The implementation of transactions governed by internalised pro cedures may prove to be less expensive than market exchanges,[3 particularly in Eastern Europe where negotiation costs are relatively high.[31] In any case, it is the price which Western firms must pay to overcome entry barriers. Moreover, it helps them increase their market share in the face of the import substitution and export promotion policies of the planned economies. In practice, in a large number of cases, the choice is not strictly between the export of capital goods to and foreign direct investment in Eastern Europe, but rather between accepting a joint venture or staying out of the market. Since 1987 the Soviets have promoted joint ventures as a 'privileged' mode in their negotiations with Western industrialists. Co-enterprises have been used as an alternative to the import of industrial complexes, by combining the advantages of 'learning by doing' with marketing guarantees, without bearing the full risks.

THE DYNAMICS OF RECIPROCAL FLOWS IN EAST–WEST DIRECT INVESTMENT: SOME NEW PERSPECTIVES

Most studies of joint ventures in Eastern Europe do not take account of the macro-economic evaluation of the stocks and flows of direct investment generated by the creation of equity joint ventures. The major reason is the total absence of official investment statistics.

In 1989 none of the East European countries had a Balance of Payments sufficiently detailed to provide estimates of the value of capital imports. Even if they had, as McMillan points out,[32] the problem would not be totally resolved because of the difficulties of correctly quantifying direct investment. The contributions to the statutory capital of co-enterprises take one of many forms, and are likely to be excluded from registration statistics, if they appear not to be strictly relevant to the 'capital import/direct investment' label. The United Nations Economic Commission for Europe's data bank is the most comprehensive source for *numbers* of joint ventures set up in Eastern Europe. This is, however, not the case for aggregated data of stocks and flows of Western direct investment, for which neither the reports of the United Nations Centre for Transnational Corporations, nor the OECD, IMF or World Bank financial statistics, are of assistance. Clearly this is a gap to be filled, particularly as the emergence of an increasing number of equity joint ventures in the East European countries is changing radically the dynamics which has prevailed until now.

Legislative restrictions on inward investments into Eastern

Europe, together with a lack of genuine enthusiasm on the part of Western firms, led to the surprising position that, until the late 1980s, the East European countries were net exporters of capital to the OECD countries. This trend was linked to the systemic differences between planned and market economies, and to the mutual distrust which prevailed until recently.

These observations are tested below against established foreign direct investment theories, in particular Vernon's product life cycle model. The facts underlined above take on a new dimension, as they constitute a paradox of Vernon's theory. This theory does not allow us to take into account the 'upward mobility' of direct investment from countries downstream of the manufacturing process to those situated further upstream. Nor does it consider the development of reciprocal flows in foreign direct investment between countries at similar levels of development. We may then wonder whether the emergence of an increasing number of equity joint ventures involving Western firms in Eastern Europe will not reverse the dynamics of East–West reciprocal flows of investment.

First, we present the data, which prompted us to raise the existence of the paradox, namely the emergence of direct investment from Eastern Europe. Second, we attempt to demonstrate that a return to the 'norm' in the dynamics of reciprocal flows of East–West direct investment already exists in respect of the hierarchy of productive systems, not withstanding the 'upward mobility' of investment from East to West.

1972–88: The paradox of East–West direct investments, with regard to Vernon's theory and the hierarchy of productive systems

The 1970s and 1980s were momentous decades for the East European countries, as they gradually rejoined the International Division of Labour. This change in attitude was translated at two levels, through the development of international trade and in the emergence of a process of internationalisation of production in the West and South. McMillan has suggested that this phenomenon of multinationalisation, which originated in the COMECON countries, expressed a qualitative evolution in the external relations of planned economies.[33] It symbolises an intent to break away from the more rigid concepts which prevailed earlier, particularly with regard to the perception of foreign direct investment. From a theoretical viewpoint, the multinationalisation of socialist firms reflected the adoption of the concept of 'The International Division of Labour' in its broadest interpretation (the export of productive capital), in the wake of the rejection of Stalin's thesis of 'Two World Markets'.

In spite of the small magnitude of direct investment flows from COMECON to the West and South (0.3 per cent of the world stock of foreign direct investment in 1979[34] and 0.1 per cent in 1983,[35] it is worth noting that, between 1972 and 1988, the East European countries' direct investments in the West exceeded the inward investments from that area. *The East–West Business Directory*[36] estimated the level of capitalisation by COMECON countries in the OECD at $610 million in 1985 (see Table 4.2), nearly five times that of the OECD countries in Eastern Europe (estimated by Maciej Lebkowski and Jean Monkiewicz at $120–130 million for 1984).[37]

Perestroika does not seem to have altered the preference for direct investment abroad. Recent editions of the *East–West Business Directory* show that, between 1986 and 1988, the USSR increased its level of capitalisation in the OECD by more than 50 per cent, and the value of its financial assets by over 25 per cent – both at current prices (see Tables 4.2 and 4.3).

This recent trend reflects a will to make the multinational process more dynamic. Ivan Ivanov, the Vice President of the State Commission for Foreign Economic Relations, declared to the International Chamber of Commerce in Paris in December 1988: 'The USSR must be treated not only as a business partner, but also as a foreign investor'.[38] Poland and Hungary, too, have increased their presence in the OECD countries: between 1986 and 1988, Poland increased her level of capitalisation by 192 per cent, whilst that of Hungary went up by 20 per cent (with her financial assets in the West going up by more than 65 per cent).

The direct investment stake by COMECON in the West takes on its full significance if we appreciate that commercial joint ventures, on average, acted as a vehicle for more than one-third of socialist exports to the OECD countries in 1985–86.[39] In Poland and Hungary it reached 50 per cent, in Bulgaria 94 per cent, whilst in the USSR it was closer to the average (36.6 per cent). Profitability, however, was not above average, as illustrated in the case studies of recipient countries.[40] It seems, however, that the main objective was the search for market outlets rather than the quest for significant profit margins, which would account for the *commercial* nature of the joint

Table 4.2 Capital Invested by CMEA Countries in OECD Countries (millions of current dollars), 1981–88

Country	*End of 1981*	*Beginning of 1985*	*End of 1986*	*1988*
Bulgaria	17.2	12.9	27.0	29.5
Czechoslovakia	18.5	12.7	30.1	38.3
GDR	4.9	9.3	14.3	9.3
Hungary	37.6	32.3	40.0	48.5
Poland	50.6	60.7	23.0	67.1
Romania	99.5	40.9	40.7	41.4
USSR	320.2	440.2	378.1	583.2
Total CMEA (7)	548.5	609.0	553.2	817.3
Percentage invested in banks	61.1	70.6	66.0	71.6

Source: *The East-West Business Directory*.

Table 4.3 Financial Assets held by CMEA Countries in OECD Countries (millions of current dollars), 1980–88*

Country	*End of 1980*	*Beginning of 1984*	*1985*	*1988*
Bulgaria	2.7	–	–	165.2
Czechoslovakia	207.8	–	–	–
GDR	–	–	–	–
Hungary	524.2	20.9	675.4	1 133.6
Poland	629.0	836.6	823.5	866.6
Romania	1550.2	1 142.5	1 143.3	1 184.2
USSR	7480.2	9 990.2	8 420.5	10 662.8
Total CMEA (7)	10 394.1	11 991.2	11 062.7	14 012.4

* excluding the Western branches of East European banks.
Source: *The East-West Business Directory*.

ventures. In other words, the volume of turnover prevails over profitability, for it constitutes a vital source of convertible currency. It seems, therefore, that COMECON investments in the West are part of a structural phenomenon and unlikely to be modified. Consequently, only a real increase in Western investment in Eastern Europe could alter the dynamics of the period 1972–88.

The post-1988 years: The new wave of Western direct investment in Eastern Europe, or a return to the dynamics of East–West reciprocal flows consistent with the hierarchy of productive systems

In its 1988 report, the United Nations Centre for Transnational Corporations emphasises that equity joint ventures recorded a strong upturn in the 1980s. For the whole of COMECON, their total number increased from 43 at the end of the 1970s, to 867 at the end of 1987, a twenty-fold increase (see Table 4.4). A more detailed analysis, however, reveals that this dynamism owes much to the 'Polonia' firms, which consist entirely of Polish capital, as the foreign stake is held by Polish nationals residing abroad.

Even if, for Balance of Payments reasons, the capital imports of 'Polonia' firms are recorded as a direct investment, they appear to be a function of the transfer policy of Polish expatriates to the domestic community, rather than a genuine internationalisation of foreign productive capital. Furthermore, if we rely on investment flows, and not on the number of joint ventures, the implementation of the 'Polonia' firms no longer represents a major import of capital, as is illustrated below. With the exception of the 'Polonia' firms, Table 4.4 underlines the marginal character of joint ventures in Eastern Europe up to the mid-1980s: in 1984 they numbered less than fifty. Moreover, a yearly average increase of some six joint ventures between 1980 and 1984 for the whole of COMECON hardly reflects dynamic growth. It comes as no surprise, therefore, that Lebkowski and Monkiewicz valued at between $120 and $130 million the total Western capitalisation in equity joint ventures in Eastern Europe at the end of 1984.

Table 4.5, which shows the yearly flows of new joint ventures in COMECON, underlines their slow development. Hungary, one of the pioneers of inward investment in Eastern Europe, recorded a mere twenty-five joint ventures between 1972 and 1983,[41] amounting to $50 million in foreign capital.[42] By the end of 1986, the *total* capital invested in joint ventures in Eastern Europe (including the local share) was close to $500 million.[43] If we hypothesise further that the domestic capital share amounted to half the total statutory capital, we put the level of Western capitalisation in COMECON at the end of 1986 at about $250 million. This figure, however, appears to have been inflated: the 1988 Report by the United Nations Centre for Transnational Corporations (based on the national statistics of the East European countries) estimated the level of Western capitalisation in COMECON at only $200 million (including the contributions

Table 4.4 Distribution of Joint Ventures in the CMEA Countries (number of cases)

Country	*End of 1970s*	*1984*[a]	*End of 1987*[b]	*End of 1988*[c]	*Beginning of 1989*[d]
Bulgaria	–	8	15	21	25
Czechoslovakia	–	–	2	11	11
Hungary	4	32	110	150	270g
Poland 'Polonia'	30	633	703[e]	767[e]	na
Poland 'Joint Ventures'	–		13	26	55
Romania	9[h]	7[h]	5[h]	5[h]	5[h]
USSR	–	–	19	162	190[f]
Total CMEA (6) (excluding "Polonia")	13	47	164	375	556
Total CMEA (6) (including 'Polonia')	43	680	867	1142	na

Sources:
[a] UNCTC (1988), Table XVIII.1, p. 301.
[b] UN–ECE (1988), Table 3, p. 107.
[c] UN–ECE (1989a), Table 7, p. 62.
[d] UN–ECE (1989a), p. 9, A.
[e] J. Kwiatkowski & M. Sowa (1989), p. 8.
[f] of which approximately thirty joint ventures have a foreign share originating in the CMEA or Less Developed Countries.
[g] the gap between 270 (beginning of 1989) and 150 (end of 1988) is explained in the text.
[h] this includes one firm (ROLISHIP) with a Libyan foreign share, which explains why the total of 375 at the end of 1988 (excluding the Polonia firms) differed from the UN–ECE source (ECE/Trade/162/Rev. 1, Table 7, p. 62) from which ROLISHIP is excluded. The new total is then 374.

of Polish expatriates to the 'Polonia' firms). This suggests, in turn, that the vast majority of equity joint ventures in Eastern Europe was characterised by a very low level of capitalisation.

According to Lebkowski and Monkiewicz, the average foreign share in the statutory capital of joint ventures amounted to:[44]

- $600 000 in Romania at the end of 1977, due to the relatively large size of the projects[45] and the restricted number of joint ventures;
- $600 000 in Hungary in the mid-1980s; and
- $46 600 in Poland at the end of 1984.[46]

Table 4.5 shows further that, between 1972 and 1986, a mere eighty-two joint ventures were set up, representing 21.7 per cent of the total joint venture stock at the end of 1988 (excluding the 'Polonia' firms). 1987 marked a turning point, when stocks doubled over the previous year. The most decisive year, arguably, was 1988 when 169 equity joint ventures were established, worth half of the total stock. This acceleration was accounted for, mainly, by the upsurge in the number of Soviet joint ventures, which followed a hesitating start in 1987. These represented 58 per cent of the increase in 1988. In Hungary, the number of joint venture registrations accelerated after 1986–7, whilst in Poland, the legislative changes introduced in April 1986 started to bear fruit in the late 1980s. The provisional data for 1989 showed that the two most active recipient countries – Hungary and the USSR – hosted in excess of 250 equity joint ventures each.

According to the *Hungarian Trade Journal*, 220 joint ventures were registered by the end of September 1988, of which three quarters were reported to be operational; sixty-seven ventures were set up in 1987 and another eighty during the first ten months of 1988. These figures tally with the estimate of 270 in early 1989, put forward in Table 4.4. Persanyi[47] estimated at $250 million the total injection of direct Western investment in the Hungarian economy in 1988, a clear improvement on 1983 when foreign capitalisation was estimated by the same author at $50 million.[48] The growing number of joint ventures, and the increase in the average size of the initial statutory capital invested, account for this trend. Ivan Toldy–Ösz estimated that the latter was close to $1 million, and would have gone up to $2.1 million in 1988,[49] had the three large banking joint ventures established before 1987[50] been excluded from the capital stock of the 220 co-enterprises. According to the same source, the total capitalisation (domestic and foreign) of the 220 Hungarian joint ventures was

Table 4.5 Annual Flow of New Joint Ventures in CMEA countries (1972–88)

Year	*Bulgaria*	*Czechoslovakia*	*Hungary*	*Poland*		*Romania*	*USSR*	*Annual Flow (excluding 'Polonia' firms)*	*Global stock (excluding 'Polonia' firms)*	*Cumulative frequency of stock (excluding 'Polonia' firms) as a percentage*
				Polonia firms[a]	*Joint ventures*					
1972						1		1	1	0.26
1973			1			3		4	5	1.32
1974			2			1		3	8	2.11
1975			1			1		2	10	2.64
1976				1		2		2	12	3.17
1977				3		1		1	13	3.43
1978				12				0	13	3.43
1979			1	30				1	14	3.70
1980			4	76				4	18	4.76
1981	2			154				2	20	5.29
1982	1		5	252				6	26	6.87
1983			11	491				11	37	9.78
1984	4		10	633				14	51	13.49

1985	1		14	712[b]				15	66	17.46
1986			16					16	82	21.69
1987	7	2	46	703	13[c]		19[c]	87	169	44.70
1988	5	9	38	767	35[c]		122[c]	209	378	100.00
Total	20	11	149	767	48[c]	9[d]	141[c]		378	

Sources:

1 UN–ECE (1988), Table 3, p. 107 for Romania.
2 UN–ECE (1989a), Tables 1 to 6, pp. 10–62 for other CMEA Countries excluding 'Polonia' firms.
3 M. Lebkowski & J. Monkiewicz, (1986) Table VII, p. 120 for 'Polonia' firms up to 1985.
4 J. Kwiatkowski & M. Sowa (1989), p. 8 for 'Polonia' firms in 1987 and 1988.

Notes:

[a] Statistics in terms of stock.
[b] As of mid-1985.
[c] Joint ventures involving a CMEA or LDC foreign share are excluded.
[d] Four of the nine joint ventures in Romania which stopped their activity mostly before 1978, included Romavia, Romelite and Elarom. See F. Louvard (1985), p. 62.

around $420 million at the end of September 1988.[51] In parallel with the legislation liberalising inward foreign investment, a nascent privatisation movement aims at attracting foreign capital. This perspective presages a linkage between foreign direct investment and privatisation.

In Poland, the implementation of the 'Polonia' firms constitutes a fairly unique experience. In its initial provisions, the law of May 1976 limited their activity to small-scale production between domestic partners, and their life span was restricted to ten years. The specificity of the Polish model lies in its orientation towards small firms with low capitalisation. According to Monkiewicz and Lebkowski, the total foreign capital at the end of 1984 was estimated at $30.3 million, representing an average foreign share of $46 600.[52] In a more recent article, Krystyna Szymkiewicz reports that, between 1976 and 1986, some 700 'Polonia' firms attracted about $100 million,[53] with a modest average capitalisation per firm of $140 000. This suggests that the 'Polonia firms have so far been marginal to the Polish economy, with 0.4 per cent of the economy's total sales, and 0.1 per cent of small-scale production.[54] Although the scope of their activities was widened in 1982, their relative weighting remained unchanged during the following years.[55] The registration procedure for these firms has since been tightened, for at least two reasons: they exacerbated wage differentials among Polish workers, whilst allowing the emergence of a class of *nouveaux riches* and speculators, two practices perceived as too 'sensitive' to permit their unchecked expansion. This would explain the Polish government's decision to widen the scope for direct investment to foreign capital by liberalising on four successive occasions (in 1979, 1982, 1986 and 1988) the investment legislation. This begs the question of whether the government sought to promote equity joint ventures with Western capital as an antidote to the 'anarchic' development of the 'Polonia' firms. The law of April 1986 was a major turning point, in that it offered conditions which were more favourable to Western capital than to the 'Polonia' firms, although the latter were not excluded from its scope. According to Elisabeth Nadjer, foreign exchange provisions confirmed this discrimination.[56] In 1987–8, forty-eight joint ventures with a total capital investment of $31.4 million were established (that is, an average capitalisation close to $650 000 and an average foreign share of $230 000).[57] Clearly, these figures are merely indicative: six co-enterprises have a statutory capital exceeding $1 million each, of which one is in excess of $7 million, thus raising the average level of capitalisation. It is apparent that joint ventures, as a conduit for foreign capital, have been more successful than 'Polonia' firms: their average capitalisation ($650 000) and foreign equity ($230 000) are some fivefold those of 'Polonia' co-enterprises. The new wave of liberalisation ushered in by the December 1988 law is likely to be an inducement for yet more foreign investment. Under this legislation, the foreign partner is entitled to hold up to 100 per cent of the statutory capital, provided a minimum of Zl25 million has been invested. After a three-year tax exemption (up to six years in priority sectors), joint ventures' profits are taxed at 40 per cent, a 10 per cent reduction on the 1986 legislation. Each per cent of output exported results in a 0.4 per cent lowering of taxation, above the minimum tax rate of 10 per cent. Reinvested profits are exempt from taxation, and the foreign partner can repatriate up to 80 per cent of profits.[58]

Since April 1989, direct Western investment in Poland has fitted in with the new political and economic situation. The legalisation of Solidarity, the foreign trade reforms and collapse of communism have been major stimuli for foreign investors. The very day Solidarity was legalised, President Bush announced an economic aid package for Poland, which consisted of about $1 billion and was aimed at promoting the reforms.[59] Two of the package's eight points were specifically linked to American direct investment in Poland: 1) Assistance from OPIC (The Federal Organisation for the Guarantee of Private Investment Abroad) for US firms investing in Poland; 2) The promotion of debt-equity swaps to allow US firms to acquire shares in Polish enterprises. This principle is not new: as early as January 1989, the then Polish Prime Minister on a visit to Bonn, had sought to secure a declaration of intent for the conversion of German debt into direct investment. Clearly, Poland intends, through foreign direct investment, to reduce, or at least service, her external debt. In early 1989, Andrzej Wojcik, the then Secretary of State for Foreign Economic Relations, declared: 'Poland cannot afford to spend more than $8 billion a year on imports, when those imports come from Western countries and are payable in convertible currencies. The import of foreign capital in this manner facilitates the repayment of the foreign debt (close to $40 billion). Investing in Poland should also constitute a financial investment in the long run'.[60]

Because of the speed at which joint ventures have emerged in the USSR, the assessment of their capitalisation and average foreign share has been fraught with difficulties. Variations reflect the small size of the sample and large flows of new co-enterprises added to the existing stock. For these reasons, we have divided the twenty months

Table 4.6 Evolution of the Capitalisation and Foreign Share of Joint Ventures in the USSR (May 1987–December 1988)*
(number of joint ventures and millions of roubles)

Period	*Joint ventures*		*Capitalisation (A)*		*Foreign share (B)*		*Ratio B/A*
	number	*%*	*value*	*%*	*value*	*%*	*%*
May–Sept. 87	8	4.70	65.3	8.23	23.2	7.71	35.52
Oct. 87–Feb. 88	21	12.35	134.1	16.90	47	15.62	35.04
March–July 88	43	25.29	227.4	28.66	89.1	29.62	39.18
August–Dec. 88	98	57.64	366.5	46.19	141.5	47.04	38.60
Total	170	100.00	793.3	100.00	300.8	100.00	37.91

* Out of 170 joint ventures, 142 have a Western partner, and twenty-eight include capital from COMECON and the less developed countries.

between May 1987 and December 1988 into four five-month periods, and used monthly statistics from the United Nations Economic Commission for Europe[61] to illustrate trends in levels of capitalisation and foreign equity.

Table 4.6 suggests that the growth of joint ventures has been a gradual phenomenon, reflecting the initial caution of Western firms: a mere twenty-three ventures were set up in 1987, of which nineteen had Western equity. From May 1988, the monthly registration of joint ventures began to exceed ten, with a marked acceleration in November and December 1988 (twenty and twenty-seven registrations respectively). By the end of 1988, the total capitalisation of the 170 joint ventures amounted to R793.3 million ($1282 million),[62] of which the foreign share totalled R300.8 million ($486.1 million). In spite of the large increase in joint venture numbers, Table 4.7 shows a considerable drop, over time, in both the average capitalisation per joint venture (from R8.2 million in period I to R3.7 million in period IV), and the average foreign share.

The drop in capitalisation levels is partly explained by the large number of small joint ventures in the service sector which only require a small start-up capital. These figures were a disappointment to the Soviet authorities, which complained about the lack of Western investment in high capitalisation joint ventures. It is probable that a study of comparable statistics prompted the Soviet authorities to modify the investment legislation: a decree passed on 2 December 1988 allowed foreign partners to become majority owners of the

Table 4.7 Capitalisation and Average Foreign Share per Joint Venture in the USSR (May 1987–December 1988) (millions of roubles)

	Period	*Average Capitalisation*	*Average foreign share*
I:	May 87–Sept. 87	8.162	2.900
II:	Oct. 87–Feb. 88	6.385	2.238
III:	March 88–July 88	5.288	2.072
IV:	Aug. 88–Dec. 88	3.739	1.443
TOTAL		4.666 (or $7.54 million)	1.769 (or $2.85 million)

Source: Calculated from Table 4.6

equity, as an incentive to increase the level of the start-up capital.

The 170 joint ventures discussed above were established in the period leading up to December 1988, and included twenty-six with capital from COMECON and the LDCs. If the latter two are excluded from our calculations, the average capitalisation of the remaining 142 ventures amounts to R4.478 million ($7.236 million), with an average Western share of R1.633 million ($2.639 million). Thus, the *total* capitalisation of the 142 Soviet–Western co-enterprises is close to $1027.5 million, and the *total* Western equity approaches $374.7 million.

No estimates were made for Bulgaria and Czechoslovakia, where the value of the statutory capital for most joint ventures was unknown. The exceptions were three Czechoslovak joint ventures, where Western capitalisation averaged $10 million.

When the estimates are added up on a country by country basis – see Table 4.8 – it does appear that Western direct investment in Eastern Europe recorded rapid progress since 1984, when Lebkowski and Monkiewicz valued it at between $120 and $130 million.

Although these figures must be treated as estimates, we noted that Western capitalisation between 1984 and 1988 increased six-fold, from $120–130 million to $716 million (at current values). This suggests further that the levels of Western capitalisation at the end of 1988 exceeded the *total* capitalisation (domestic and foreign) of joint ventures in Eastern Europe at the end of 1986, estimated at $500 million by the United Nations Centre for Transnational Corporations.

If we compare the estimates for the beginning of 1989 with the

Table 4.8 Western Capitalisation in Joint Ventures in Eastern Europe since 1972 (millions of dollars)

Western capitalisation in joint ventures in:	*Estimates end of 1988*	*Estimates beginning of 1989*
Hungary	250	325
USSR	374.4	950
Poland ('Polonia' firms)*	30.4	30.4
Poland (Joint Ventures)	11	11
Romania*	40	40
Czechoslovakia	10	10
Bulgaria	na	na
Total COMECON	715.8	1 366.4

* For Romania and Poland's 'Polonia' firms, we have used sources from M. Lebkowski and J. Monkiewicz, 1986, pp. 627 and 634.

dynamics of reciprocal flows in East–West direct investments, we conclude that Western capitalisation in Eastern Europe ($1366 million) has been vastly superior to that of COMECON in the OECD countries ($817 million), according to *The East–West Business Directory*. In 1988 Western investment in Eastern Europe witnessed a revival, whilst 1989 marked the beginning of the inversion in the dynamics of reciprocal flows in East–West direct investments. The liberalisation of the investment legislation in COMECON clearly had an impact.

Thus, we have observed an expansion of foreign direct investment in Eastern Europe, in parallel with a normalisation in the dynamics of reciprocal flows of East–West investments. Foreign direct investment in Eastern Europe has become one of several organisational modes. The perception by the Socialist authorities of inward direct investment evolved from an 'apprehension' in terms of the 'exportation de capitaux' (in the Leninist sense) to an 'apprehension' in terms of the 'exportation de capital' (as a technical means of production, as understood by Michalet). Indeed, the liberalisation of the legislation has enabled Western investors to choose between minority- and majority-owned joint ventures. In terms of ownership, this should facilitate the integration of the East European countries into the internationalisation of production. From this perspective, Western direct investment in Eastern Europe should rapidly become a multiple of East European investments in the West, particularly if joint ventures in the ex-USSR continue to grow both in terms of numbers and capital.

Normalisation should return to reciprocal flows of East–West investment as the East European countries become once again net importers of capital (that is of direct investment). This conforms more readily to the hierarchy of productive systems. If indeed there is a return to 'the norm' because of the inversion in the dynamics of reciprocal flows of East–West direct investment, this does not allow us to conclude, on the premise of Vernon's theory, that the paradox has disappeared. The upstream movement of direct investment from East European to OECD countries – that is from less developed to more developed countries – persists, illustrating why normalisation is not a sufficient condition for the disappearance of the paradox.

Notes

1. Translated from Patrick Gutman, 'Sociétés mixtes à l'Est et dynamique des flux réciproques d'investissements directs Est-Ouest: nouvelles perspectives' in W. Andreff (ed.) (1990), *Réforme et échanges extérieurs dans les pays de l'Est*. By permission of L'Harmattan Publishers.
2. Eastern Europe throughout this chapter refers to the seven CMEA members, namely the USSR, and the six East European countries. Yugoslavia is excluded from the scope of this analysis.
3. Charles-Albert Michalet distinguishes between the 'exportation de *capital*' in the singular, and the 'exportation de *capitaux*' in the plural. The latter refers to *finance* capital in accordance with Lenin's interpretation in *Imperialism: The Highest Stage of Capitalism*, whilst in the former, the emphasis is on the role of technical means of production in relocating the production process abroad.
4. In this case, the emphasis is on *productive* capital in accordance with Michalet's interpretation in *Le Capitalisme mondial*.
5. For a detailed presentation of the concept of 'contractual economy', see Michalet (1988).
6. See C. H. McMillan (1978).
7. See K. Ohmae (1985) for a general presentation of strategic alliances between the most industrialised poles of the World Economy (USA, Europe and Japan; that is, the Triad). For its European manifestations, see the CEREM–LAREA (1986) study, and the United Nations Economic Commission for Europe (UN – ECE 1988), Appendices II, III and IV.
8. O. Morgatchev (1988).
9. See the study by the United Nations Centre for Transnational Corporations, UNCTC (1988a).

10. Count de Witte was the Finance Minister under Czar Alexander III. During this period, the loans granted to Russia by her allies were equivalent to the price of maintaining treaties signed between them. See A. Besançon (1976), pp. 76–7.
11. For details of the extent of foreign capital penetration in Russian industry at the turn of the century, see A. Rowley (1982), pp. 185–6 and 235; and R. Girault and M. Ferro (1989), p. 62.
12. Alec Nove gives the following figures: 0.6 per cent of industrial production for the sixty-eight concessions which existed in 1928. See A. Nove (1969), p. 89.
13. C. A. Michalet (1976), pp. 80–91.
14. C. H. McMillan (1986), p. 261.
15. See UNCTC (1988b), p. 308.
16. See W. Andreff (1987), pp. 57–60.
17. *Economies et Sociétés*, XXII, No. 2, 1988, G, No. 43.
18. *Le Monde*, 12 April 1989, p. 35.
19. See P. Gutman (1988b) for the functioning of the mechanism and its principles.
20. UNCTC (1978), Table III.25, p. 229.
21. See C. Oman (1984).
22. Ibid.
23. For details, see J. P. Saltiel (1987), p. 294.
24. The choice of this period is based on the fact that the USSR allowed inward direct investment in 1987.
25. See *MOCI*, No. 854, 6 February 1989, p. 8.
26. See J. Blaha (1988), p. 38.
27. *Business Eastern Europe*, 2 January 1989, p. 3.
28. This interpretation in terms of a managerial revolution is close to that of Marie Lavigne. See M. Lavigne (1989), p. 2.
29. The problems of assimilation and diffusion of Western technology have been explored elsewhere. See M. Bornstein (1985) and P. Hanson (1981).
30. This is one of the determinants in the process of internalisation. See P. Joffre and G. Koenig (1985), p. 157.
31. As P. Hanson and M. Hill have shown in a study of chemical plants set up in the USSR by British engineering companies. See P. Hanson and M. R. Hill (1979), p. 594.
32. See C. H. McMillan (1986), pp. 264–5.
33. See C. H. McMillan (1987). For an analysis of that book, see P. Gutman (1988a).
34. See W. Andreff (1987), p. 38.
35. See UNCTC (1988b), Table 1.2., p. 24.
36. *The East–West Business Directory* is published by the Institute for Soviet and East European Studies at Carleton University, Ottawa. It lists contact points with OECD countries for the conduct of business with Eastern Europe, the Soviet Union and Yugoslavia.
37. See M. Lebkowski and J. Monkiewicz (1986), p. 637.
38. See Carl McMillan's preface in Pierre Grou's book: P. Grou (1989), pp. 5–6.

39. *The East–West Business Directory*, 1989, Table 6, p. 16.
40. See G. Hamilton (1986); and P. Artisien, C. H. McMillan and M. Rojec, *Yugoslav Multinationals Abroad*, Macmillan, London, 1992.
41. Istvan Toldy-Ösz, the editor of *Register* 109, estimated at 21 the number of joint ventures created between 1972 and 1983. See *The Hungarian Trade Journal*, February 1989, Vol. 39, No. 2, p. 6.
42. See F. Persanyi (1989), p. 29, and P. Marer (1986), p. 152.
43. See UNCTC (1988b), p. 302.
44. See M. Lebkowski and J. Monkiewicz (1986).
45. Particularly OLTCIT, a joint venture created with Citroën with an initial statutory capital of F500 million. See P. Gutman (1980), pp. 67–9. See also *Les Echos*, 28 October 1988, p. 9.
46. In order to attract more foreign capital, provisions have been introduced which set a minimum level of investment. This was set at $50 000 in April 1986, with a view to enlarging the capital contributions to the 'Polonia' firms.
47. F. Persanyi (1989), p. 29.
48. Ibid.
49. See I. Toldy-Ösz (1989), p. 6.
50. Namely the Central European International Bank Ltd, an off-shore bank created in 1979; the Citibank Budapest Ltd, established in 1985; and the Unicbank Ltd founded in 1986. These three banks had a starting capital of about $20 million. See the *Hungarian Chamber of Commerce* (1988), pp. 14, 49, 84.
51. See I. Toldy-Ösz (1989), p. 6.
52. See M. Lebkowski and J. Monkiewicz (1986), p. 634.
53. See *Le Monde Affaires*, 31 October 1987, p. 11.
54. See M. Lebkowski and J. Monkiewicz (1986), p. 632.
55. Based on our own calculations from the Polish General Statistics Directory, 1988.
56. See E. Nadjer (1986), p. 113, quoting K. Plesinski (1986), p. 2.
57. See UN–ECE (1989a), Table 4.4, pp. 33–8.
58. See UN–ECE (1989a), p. 5.
59. See *Le Monde*, 19 April 1989, p. 4.
60. See *MOCI*, No. 854, 6 February 1989, p. 8.
61. See UN–ECE (1989b), Table 1, p. 5.
62. On the basis of $1.61605 per rouble. This is an average of the 1987 (1.582275) and 1988 exchange rates (1.6501), based on a monthly average for 1988.

Part II
Empirical Country Studies

5 Foreign Investment in the Commonwealth of Independent States: Growth, Operations and Problems

Yuri Adjubei*

INTRODUCTION

This chapter addresses itself to the first wave of foreign capital inflows in the economy of the former constituent republics of the Soviet Union.

The scale and structural characteristics of FDI in the former Soviet Union (including the countries of origin of foreign partners, and the size and industrial/regional breakdown of the investments) have been closely monitored elsewhere.[1] This survey focuses instead on the motives, scope and problems encountered by foreign investors, against the backdrop of rapidly deteriorating economic conditions and political unrest in the Commonwealth of Independent States (CIS).

It should be noted that foreign capital inflows in the USSR were initially restricted to joint ventures between foreign and local companies, whilst the participation of foreign capital in the privatisation of state companies, contrary to the experience of other East European countries, is still at the embryonic stage.[2]

The disintegration of the Soviet Union and the setting up of a new Commonwealth of Independent States at the end of 1991 are likely to have dramatic implications for the investment climate in the successor-states of the USSR, and the strategies of foreign investors.

* The author works for the Secretariat of the United Nations Economic Commission for Europe. The views expressed in this chapter are his own, and do not necessarily reflect those of the Secretariat.

At the time of writing (February 1992), only a first contour of the new, and still highly unstable, system of relationships within, and among these states, has taken shape. It is likely, however, that the major stumbling blocks to foreign investment operations which were present in the former Soviet Union will persist, if in a somewhat modified form, in the new Commonwealth. Therefore, the accumulated joint venture experience of coping with difficulties remains valid in the medium term.

EVOLUTION OF THE LEGAL FRAMEWORK

The history of foreign investment in the Soviet Union goes back to 1987, when the first Government decree legalising joint ventures was passed.[3] Since then, various new regulations have addressed different aspects of foreign investment, on a comparable basis to those of other East European countries.

Major landmarks in the evolution of the foreign investment regime allowed Soviet production co-operatives to participate in joint ventures in which foreign partners may hold a majority share (December 1988).[4] Under a new 'Law on Enterprises', introduced on 1 January 1991, foreign persons are entitled to set up joint ventures. Presidential Decrees, published on 26 October 1990, authorised Soviet persons to enter into foreign investment agreements, permitted wholly-owned foreign subsidiaries on Soviet territory, and guaranteed the right of foreign investors to repatriate profits. Furthermore, foreign investors were granted explicit rights to set up joint stock and limited liability companies, trade foreign currency for roubles at commercial exchange rates, and participate in banking activities.[5] The Legislation on the privatisation of enterprises, adopted both at the Union level and by some former Soviet republics, has laid the foundations for foreign business interests to take part in this process.

In sum, the sequence of legislative changes governing foreign investment activities in the USSR was broadly of a liberalising nature, notwithstanding some administrative setbacks, which hindered the operations of some foreign firms.[6] More significantly, some progress was achieved between 1987 and 1991 in creating a legal framework for FDI in the Soviet Union and, at that time, its constituent Republics.

The Foreign Investment Legislation passed in July 1991 incorporated all the previous regulations on foreign investment, and endorsed explicit guarantees for the property rights of foreign investors. The right of foreign companies to repatriate capital, as well as profits 'legally' earned in the Soviet Union was also confirmed.[7]

By the end of 1991, at least nine former Soviet republics[8] had adopted their own foreign investment regulations. The Law on Foreign Investment in the Russian Federation is highlighted below.

Under the Russian Law passed on 1 September 1991, foreign investors enjoy the same rights as their domestic counterparts, and only in exceptional circumstances relating to the public interest, can foreign investment be nationalised, requisitioned or confiscated. In this eventuality, 'prompt, adequate and effective' compensation (including the loss of profits) is guaranteed. The Law also guarantees the foreign investors' right to purchase foreign currency at market rates for transfers abroad.[9] The law does not restrict the areas of activities of foreign investors; only those enterprises engaged in banking, insurance and financial services must obtain licenses from the Central Bank and the Ministry of Finance respectively. Companies in which the foreign share exceeds 30 per cent are allowed to export their own products and to retain the convertible currency proceeds from exports. A 'national' regime of taxation for foreign investors grants them preferential treatment when operating in 'free economic zones'. The Law also laid the foundations for the participation of foreign companies in the acquisition and privatisation of Russian enterprises. Foreign investors are also authorised to take out concessions for the extraction of mineral resources, and are protected from subsequent contractual revisions.[10]

While codifying the basic conditions of foreign entrepreneurship in a single document, the Russian Foreign Investment Law still excludes foreign investors from land ownership, and imposes some restrictions on the acquisitions of local enterprises.[11] This suggests that the concept of 'national treatment' of foreign investors is not being implemented consistently. More significantly, in the post-socialist era, foreign investment regulations constitute only one facet of the overall foreign investment climate. The application of laws at national and local levels, and more broadly, the operational environment of private entrepreneurship, will determine how successfully foreign capital integrates in the domestic economy.

THE MAGNITUDE OF FOREIGN INVESTMENT

According to data from the Soviet State Committee on Statistics, some 4200 foreign investment projects were registered on the territory of the former USSR as of 1 July 1991, with a total statutory capital of R10 billion.[12] This compares favourably with 2905 joint venture registrations at the beginning of 1991, 1274 in early 1990, 191 at the start of 1989 and a mere 23 contracts in early 1988. In spite of this impressive growth in the number of inward foreign investments, the successor states of the Soviet Union have increasingly lagged behind the other countries of Central and Eastern Europe: their combined share in the total number of foreign investment registrations in the whole area is estimated to have declined from just under 40 per cent at the beginning of 1989, to 22 per cent at the start of 1991, and 17 per cent in mid-1991.[13]

On 1 January 1991, the aggregate foreign contribution in the statutory capital of registered joint ventures had reached $3151.7 million.[14] This estimate, however, is most likely to inflate the value of foreign capital: first, although their exact number is unknown, many joint ventures have not, for various reasons, transferred the registered amounts of capital.[15] Second, the official exchange rate, which until November 1990 was used to convert rouble values into dollars, can hardly be considered a realistic measure of the real purchasing power of the two currencies in investment transactions. Recently, because of the accelerated depreciation of the rouble *vis-à-vis* convertible currencies, the commercial exchange rate, applicable in foreign investment and trade transactions since November 1990, has also lost any relevance to the market clearing rate.[16] Consequently, any valuations resulting from the use of the commercial rate should be considered as the *upper* limit of foreign investment in the ex-Soviet Union to date. This being said, according to this measure, the accumulated foreign capital in January 1991 (R2009.7 million) was estimated to be worth $1209.0 million. As a point of comparison, in early 1991 foreign investment in Hungary amounted to about $1.2 billion. More accurate and up-to-date estimates of foreign capital in the former Soviet Republics have been hampered by the lack of reliable primary information on joint venture registrations on the one hand, and the rapid depreciation of the rouble, on the other.[17]

If problems of statistical comparability are disregarded, and the cumulative inflows of foreign capital are contrasted with the book value of productive fixed assets[18] of the former Soviet Union, the former amounted to a mere 0.1 per cent of the latter at the end of the third quarter of 1990. The ratio of foreign investment to *non-state* productive fixed assets (that is, those belonging to co-operatives and private citizens) was estimated at 0.93 per cent for the same period.[19]

The total number of *operational* FDI projects in the former Soviet Union grew from 307 at the beginning of 1989 to 1027 on 1 January 1991, whilst their weighting in the total number of FDI registrations increased from 24 to 36 per cent. By the end of the third quarter of 1991, in the twelve republics, which were formed on the ex-Soviet territory (excluding the Baltic states), 1570 joint ventures were operational. Of these, 1278 had already started production.[20]

The total number of joint venture employees increased from about 18 000 in the Autumn of 1989 to 103 700 on 1 January 1991, and to 163 800 nine months later. This last figure, which excludes the Baltic States, makes up for approximately 0.1 per cent of the total labour force in the respective former Soviet Republics.[21]

In 1989, at current prices, the output of enterprises with foreign capital was worth R877 million; this rose to R4335 million in 1990 (a five-fold increase). These figures are equivalent to 0.09 per cent and 0.43 per cent, respectively, of GNP.[22] When compared with the same period in 1990, by the end of the third quarter of 1991, the output of joint ventures had almost quadrupled to R8834.4 million, or 0.56 per cent of GNP.[23] This suggests that, in 1991, the output of enterprises with foreign participation continued to grow in real terms, while the overall level of economic activity plummeted.

In terms of industrial breakdown, in 1990 about 53 per cent of joint ventures' output was accounted for by mining and manufacturing. About 14 per cent of goods and services was produced by enterprises classified under 'Research and Development', 4 per cent by firms in trade and catering, and 3 per cent in construction. 'Other industries', including personal and business services, banking and insurance, accounted for more than 23 per cent of output.

From these data, and with due regard to the statistical problems involved,[24] it can be seen that the share of mining and manufacturing in the total output of goods and services of joint ventures is only marginally lower than the weighting of the industrial sector in the gross social product of the former Soviet Union.[25] This casts doubt on the complaints of some observers, who blame foreign investors for concentrating their activities in the service and foreign trade sectors.[26]

At the current early stage of foreign penetration, when the starting-up of operations requires considerable imports of machinery and equipment, it comes as no surprise that, in aggregate terms, joint ventures have recorded a negative foreign trade balance. This amounted to R293.5 million in 1989, and increased to R712.0 million (or 7 per cent of the overall foreign trade deficit) in 1990.[27] During the first three quarters of 1991, foreign investment-related exports grew much faster than imports: at current prices, the former increased over six-fold, while the latter rose by 18 per cent. As a result, the deficit in joint venture foreign trade dropped to R61 million, as compared with the overall positive ex-Soviet foreign trade balance of R7.2 billion.[28]

At the macro level, the impact of FDI on the economy of the former Soviet republics has so far been marginal. However, the influence of foreign investment operations on individual industries and product lines – although less tangible – may well turn out to be significant. Although joint ventures contribute a mere 1.0 to 1.2 per cent of the overall output of food and consumer goods, in conditions of ubiquitous scarcities in the consumer market, FDI can contribute to the local supply of certain goods, particularly in larger cities.[29]

Of particular relevance are the 'demonstration' and 'presence' effects of enterprises associated with foreign partners, which disseminate styles of decision-making, management and marketing so far unknown to most domestic enterprises.

MOTIVATION

When planning a foreign venture, regardless of location, prospective investors generally seek to exploit existing or potential advantages in the host economy, whilst maximising their own competitive superiority in technology, know-how and marketing. In the case of the former Soviet Union, these company-specific advantages are combined with:

- a relatively inexpensive and qualified labour force, including a high percentage of well-trained specialists (for example, applied researchers in natural sciences, engineers and programmers);
- abundant natural resources and energy, favouring the location of material- and energy-intensive industries (such as the production of bulky chemicals);
- in some cases, a significant pool of locally developed technology

and human capital which can only be commercialised through foreign capitalisation.

The aforementioned company-specific and locational factors make the markets of the former Soviet republics a sound prospect for expansion in the medium term. Of particular attraction to the foreign investors are the high levels of domestic demand for some raw materials and manufactured products (*inter alia*, personal computers, telecommunications and copying equipment, chemicals, drugs, high-quality paper and consumer durables), as well as a wide range of business and personal services which are either unavailable on the local market or imported.

The testing of these hypotheses clearly requires more information on foreign investment than is currently available. However, an attempt to break down foreign investment projects according to the aforementioned comparative advantages of Western investors[30] suggests that by the end of 1990, in the ex-Soviet Union, just under 60 per cent of foreign capital was committed to undertakings, which combined Western technology and expertise with relatively inexpensive local labour. Another 14 per cent was invested in enterprises, which relied additionally on commercialising local technology with the assistance of foreign partners. In the medium term, these projects are predominantly oriented towards the domestic market. By contrast, immediate export prospects exist for joint ventures which process and commercialise domestic natural resources – which have attracted 24 per cent of foreign capital. Given the increasing interest of both foreign investors and host Governments in this type of ventures, their share is likely to grow in the future.

OBSTACLES AND SOLUTIONS AHEAD

Many of the obstacles confronting foreign investors in the former Soviet Union are common to the other East European economies facing the transition from central planning to a market economy. Understandably, the scope and repercussions of these problems vary from country to country and between individual firms. However, in the case of the Soviet Union and post-Soviet Independent States, these problems have been compounded by the rather slow pace of transition, as well as by inconsistent and contradictory governmental decisions. The experience of Western investors to date reveals a variety of operational difficulties: among these are the imprecise character and unpredictable changes in regulations pertaining to foreign investment; bureaucratic obstacles and delays in government registrations; a lack of suitable accommodation for company offices and foreign employees, and of local managers trained to conduct business in a market environment; difficulties in reconciling local and Western systems of accounting; and problems relating to labour motivation and industrial relations practices.

The scope of this chapter restricts our discussion to problems which can be singled out as major stumbling blocks, and are likely to influence the investment climate in the medium and long terms. These obstacles include:

- an underdeveloped business infrastructure, poor local and international communications and transport, and inadequate information and data facilities;
- unavailability and/or inadequate quality of local supplies of raw materials and components for production;
- difficulties in raising finance and obtaining financial guarantees from local banks;
- the non-convertibility of domestic currencies combined with obstacles to the free flow of funds, including the repatriation of profits abroad.

For decades, the *business infrastructure* in Eastern Europe has suffered from under-investment. On the territory of the former Soviet Union the telephone network has nine lines per hundred inhabitants (one line per hundred in Siberia). This contrasts with between thirty and forty in Western Europe (sixty-six in Sweden).[31] A mere 1500 international telephone lines on the territory of the ex-Soviet Union serve a population of 290 million.[32]

The UK-based Telecommunications Research Centre has estimated that modernising the telecommunications network in Eastern Europe would cost some $350 billion over the next fifteen years.[33] A ten-year telecommunications development programme, elaborated at the beginning of the 1990s by the Ministry of Communications of the former USSR, called for a total investment of R70 billion (over $40 billion at commercial exchange rates).[34] The transportation network is in equal need of modernisation: Soviet railways have recorded yearly freight losses estimated at $10.5 billion. The total amount of investment needed to substantially upgrade the railway network in the former Soviet Union is estimated to be in excess of $158 billion.[35] These estimates suggest that enormous investment opportunities exist in the field of infrastructure. Foreign capital has been active in this sector, and is likely to make a growing contribution in shaping the future business environment. For example, the Belgian subsidiary of Alcatel CIT, the French telecommunications conglomerate, has set up a joint venture – Lenbell Telephone – from which the Ministry of Communications has contracted to purchase digital telephone lines worth $2.8 billion over the next twenty years: as part of this deal, the State is committed to purchase 250 000 telephone lines within the next two years. Lenbell is also planning to introduce digital exchanges for private switchboards. A second joint venture to produce micro-chips, which are a key element in the switches used by the Alcatel system, has also been agreed.[36] In December 1991, the Telezarya joint venture, which involves Italian partners, commissioned its first automatic switchboard, 'Linea UT', in Vyborg, near the Finnish border. Commercial production is scheduled for mid-1992, when some 100 000 new subscribers will be connected.[37] The production and marketing of digital exchanges is expected to reach 1.5 million lines a year, and the sales 2.3 billion ECUs in the next two decades.[38]

Similar ventures have also been set up in the other former Soviet republics. In Kiev, a joint venture with Siemens, in which the group has planned to invest $95 million, started producing digital communication switches in 1991. Its initial capacity – of 1 million digital lines a year – is expected to rise to three million lines by the end of the century.[39] In addition, a recently-established consortium of American, Japanese, West European and South Korean firms plans to lay a fibre-optic cable across Siberia which would link the countries of the Asian Far East with Europe via the Russian Pacific region. The transcontinental fibre-optic cable will provide 8000 digital telephone channels, and this number may eventually be quadrupled. The construction which started in 1991, is scheduled for completion in 1994–5.[40]

The former Soviet republics also suffer from a severe shortage of photocopying equipment, which was only recently released from excessive bureaucratic regulations. There are only forty photocopiers per million inhabitants in the ex-USSR, compared with 300 per million in Latin America. Clearly, foreign investment has a role to play in filling this gap: for example, the British subsidiary of Rank Xerox has created three joint ventures in various republics, including an assembly plant in Kazakhstan which plans to produce 1000 copiers a year by 1993. At the end of 1991, the company's joint ventures already had a revenue of $30 million. *The Financial Times* forecasts a four-fold increase in sales of photocopiers on the territory of the former Soviet Union by 1995.[41]

The availability and quality of local inputs are a frequent problem to the foreign investor worldwide. In Eastern Europe and the ex-Soviet republics, it is exacerbated by the legacy of a centralized system of material supplies and the monopoly of state-owned enterprises, which often operate obsolete production facilities. Linked to this problem is the absence of incentives for subcontractors to supply parts according to internationally recognised quality standards. The quality of supplies has been a major preoccupation for foreign investors in the engineering industry, which is encouraged by Governments to subcontract the manufacturing of components and parts to local firms, rather than import.[42] A survey of joint ventures in the Soviet electrotechnical industry, conducted in the Autumn of 1989, highlighted the subcontracting problems of manufacturers, whose products had a relatively high value added (including enamelled cables and specialised drilling lathes in the electronics industry, electrical consumer goods and street lighting equipment.[43]

Foreign investors have sought to overcome the obstacle of poor quality in local supplies both through internalisation and the market. With the former, they have invested in the joint ventures' supply lines and built up vertically-integrated production networks. This appears to be the preferred solution of one of the pioneers of joint entrepreneurship in the former Soviet Union, Lenwest, of which the German shoemaker Salamander is a partner. Lenwest started operations in April 1988 with a yearly output of one million pairs of shoes, which it plans to increase to 10.6 million pairs a year in 1993, when the plants are fully modernised. In the initial stages of production, Lenwest experienced difficulties in acquiring local raw materials of standards acceptable to the Western parent. This quality problem was overcome through th planning of another joint venture involving the participation of German partners and a leather processing factory in Kursk. Simultaneously, Lenwest embarked on a co-operation agreement with a Leningrad-based Soviet-Italian joint venture, Skortek, which produces shoe insoles and heels from polymeric materials.[44] A similar solution to the problem of supply was adopted by McDonald's joint venture in Moscow which internalised the whole chain of inputs, from potato growing to the catering of food services.[45] Another American food processing company, Archer Daniels Midland Co., which is involved in a beer-brewing joint venture located to the north-west of Moscow, concluded that it would have to invest in all stages of the brewing process from malting operations to the modernisation of bottling.[46]

The creation of an integrated chain of affiliated enterprises with its own sourcing and marketing outlets has advantages and drawbacks for the investor and the host economy. The investor has uninterrupted access to inputs of acceptable quality, but loses a degree of flexibility when new and more efficient suppliers emerge. Eventually, the main beneficiary of such a scheme is the consumer (or buyer of intermediate inputs) of high quality products. At the same time, the local economy may forgo some potentially important spill-over effects in terms of new technology, quality control and innovative management.

The alternative market solutions to supply-side failures lie with the emergence of alternative suppliers, such as co-operatives and private enterprises, which do not belong to the outdated system of centralised resource allocation. These subcontractors are in their infancy in the successor-states of the Soviet Union, and, although the market perspective of economic reforms has become transparent in most independent states, they often have to overcome stringent resistance from the local authorities, which are jealous of their success.[47] However, these new competitors are rapidly outperforming the state agencies because of their greater reliability, customer-tailored service and promptness of input delivery.[48]

The financing of foreign investment operations remains one of the most acute problems, given the small size of the average investment and the growing operational risks under the mounting economic and political instability in the former Soviet republics. The distribution between external and domestic sources of finance is illustrated below. In 1989 and in the first half of 1990, joint ventures in the Soviet Union were the recipients from domestic and external sources of some sixty convertible currency loans valued at R1 billion. Of these, R180 million were extended by the Vneshekonombank (Bank for Foreign Economic Relations, or BFER), which also guaranteed an equivalent amount.[49] The above figures compare unfavourably with the number of joint ventures operational at the end of June 1990 (703), the total number of foreign investment registrations (1754), and their capitalisation by foreign partners to date ($2.9 billion at current official exchange rates). When seeking external finance (primarily in convertible currencies), domestic enterprises associated with Western firms face the related problems of loan availability and guarantees.

With regard to *domestic* sources of financing, borrowing difficulties stem essentially from the legacy of the centralised credit system and are further exacerbated by the present scarcity of foreign exchange.

Before the Law on Banking Activity was passed – which extended convertible currency and rouble loan financing to commercial banks – this was the exclusive right of the Vneshekonombank. The latter was usually reluctant to exercise financial obligations *vis-à-vis* joint ventures, and was very selective in supplying credits and guaranteeing loans to foreign investors. Although there was no official ban on credit-oriented projects, most of these were reported not to have been endorsed.[50] Large industrial projects, however, which incorporated state structures capable of guaranteeing credit repayment, qualified more easily for direct loans from the BFER.[51]

When foreign investors did not enjoy preferential treatment from the Vneshekonombank, they could secure financial resources by enlisting a local bank among their founders. This was the case, for example, of the UK–Soviet joint venture Intershelf, in which Promstroybank (Bank for Industrial Construction) had a 10 per cent share of the statutory capital. This, however, did not necessarily guarantee convertible currency loans, as these transactions were tightly controlled by the BFER, and any joint venture wishing to borrow convertible currency required authorisation from the Bank.[52]

Problems also arise when foreign investors try to draw on the lending capacity of *Western* institutions: here, the question of appropriate guarantees from the local partner comes to the forefront.[53] Understandably, Western financiers hesitate to make loans to newly established and mostly small mixed companies with no solid guarantees. Conversely, this type of financing is generally more accessible to larger enterprises, which intend to export a high proportion of their output or have guaranteed returns in foreign exchange from the domestic market. A typical example is that of the French construction company, Bouygues, which set up the joint venture Aerokhiva with the Soviet airline Aeroflot for the building of a hotel in Khiva, Uzbekhistan. Most of the project's finance – $66.8 million – is to be raised through the French banks, and is guaranteed by the French export credit agency, Coface, and La Banque Française de Crédits à l'Exportation.[54] Another instance is that of the London-based Moscow Narodny Bank, which, together with the Finnish bank Postipankki, has arranged for the funding of the Finnish–(ex)Soviet joint venture Chudovo R. W. S., which produces high-quality veneered plywood sheeting. The credit, guaranteed by the Ministry of the Timber Industry, will be repaid through the hard currency earnings of exports to Western Europe.[55]

The recently adopted Russian Law on Foreign Investment legalised the use of joint venture property as a collateral for fund-raising. It is expected that this will alleviate the problem of financial guarantees in the Russian Federation, at least for those companies with foreign capital, which have already accumulated property.

Other Western sources of finance have included investment funds specifically targeted at investment financing in Eastern Europe and the former Soviet Union: their number has been growing over the past two years, and, by the end of 1991, the total amount of capital committed to the region via these funds was estimated to be $1 billion.[56] At the beginning of 1991, the Stepp Financial Group and the Canadian consulting firm Gowling, Straty and Handerson, set up an investment company jointly with the Union of Lessees and Entrepreneurs on the Soviet side. The new company, with the statutory capital of $100 million (Canadian), is intended to finance foreign trade and investment projects in the CIS in machine-building, agriculture and forestry, instrument engineering, telecommunications, and oil extraction and processing.[57] In late 1990, another larger fund was jointly set up by the American investment management company, Batterymarch, and the State Commission for Military-Industrial Production. The founders intend to raise between $400 million and $1000 million, to be invested in new high-technology companies with a foreign input: these are emerging in the defence sector of the ex-Soviet Union as a result of the ongoing conversion effort. By the end of 1991, six commercially-viable projects were identified, including the production of health-care and computer equipment, and commercial aircraft.[58] Fund-raising activities, albeit on a smaller scale, have also been undertaken by some Japanese companies.[59]

On the domestic side, it is expected that the creation of a modern banking system in the sovereign republics will facilitate the financing of projects with foreign participation. The establishment of a whole range of commercial banks with partial foreign ownership would contribute to the de-monopolisation of banking and the diversification of sources of finance.[60] The recently founded International Bank of Moscow, with a statutory capital of R100 million (subsequently revalued at R275 million, of which 80 per cent consists of convertible currencies), raised with the participation of German, Finnish, Italian and French partners, illustrates this new generation of financial institutions.[61] In September 1991, the International Bank of Moscow initiated the first syndicated loan (worth $20 million) to a joint venture (Logovaz).[62]

Finally, additional sources of finance available to foreign investors are being created through the revival of stock exchanges and investment companies: 1990 saw the opening of the Moscow International Stock Exchange – with a statutory capital of R10 million – and of the Central Stock Exchange (R59 million).[63] The largest investment company in Russia to date – the Russian Investment Joint-Stock Society, or Renako – has a statutory capital of R1.2 billion. The company plans to participate in the forthcoming privatisation and to set up other companies, with the task of implementing individual investment projects.[64]

Arguably, the absence of an adequate mechanism for the transfer abroad of profits, stemming from the non-convertibility of the rouble, ranks as a major impediment to Western firms.[65] The stance of the Government *vis-à-vis* profit repatriation has been liberalised gradually over the past few years. Both the Soviet and Russian Laws on Foreign Investment, as well as comparable laws in the Baltic States, the Ukraine and Belarus, guarantee the right of foreign investors to transfer their profits abroad, and endorse mechanisms for the legal purchase of foreign exchange. The same right is generally guaranteed by Bilateral Investment Protection Treaties. However, the legal basis for profit repatriation does not exclude exchange risks in conditions of foreign exchange shortages.

The strategies of foreign firms *vis-à-vis* convertible currency earnings differ according to their marketing policies and the size of the investment. A survey of forty-six joint ventures conducted in the Soviet Union between October 1987 and September 1989 showed that twenty-eight enterprises (61 per cent of the sample) planned to generate convertible currency earnings by developing export markets, sixteen (35 per cent) and six enterprises (13 per cent) respectively relied on the Western partner for output distribution and counter-trade arrangements; another seventeen companies (37 per cent) intended to sell to the domestic market in convertible currency.[66]

In 1990, as many as 309 joint ventures, or 37 per cent of those producing goods or services at the end of that year, marketed their products abroad.[67] During 1990 and the first three quarters of 1991, the exports of foreign investors amounted to 0.47 per cent and 1.6 per cent respectively of their total value (excluding the Baltic states in

1991), and expanded in real terms, while the foreign trade of the former Soviet Republics plummeted.[68] In many cases, exporting by these enterprises was the result of 'convertible currency self-sufficiency' requirements, which may compel joint ventures to engage prematurely in buy-back arrangements.

Rare examples of successful export performance aside,[69] most operational joint ventures sell their output on the domestic market. So far, sales for convertible currency have remained a reliable source of foreign exchange for a number of joint ventures in industries with high levels of demand, including computer hardware and software, legal and business consultancy, transport, insurance, hotel and catering services, and entertainment. In Russia, the Presidential Decree of 15 November 1991 forbade the marketing of goods and services for convertible currency on Russian territory as of mid-1992.[70] If this decision is implemented in full, it will create operational problems for companies which have secured a marketing niche.

When the purchase of convertible currency was prohibited, enterprises with a foreign capital input which billed their output in roubles, could cover their foreign exchange costs and transfer profits abroad in one of two ways. For large joint ventures high on the host government's list of priorities, the Western partner's right to transfer back profits may have been granted on an *ad hoc* basis. This applied, in particular, to consortium-type foreign investments. Under an internal clearing system, members of consortia with large convertible currency earnings agreed to sell part of them for roubles to other members, with the objective of balancing the money requirements of all partners.

This idea was popular some two or three years ago, when a co-operation agreement was signed by the American Trade Consortium and the Soviet Foreign Economic Consortium on 30 March 1989. This involved several large US corporations (Archer–Daniels–Midland, Chevron, Eastman Kodak, Johnson and Johnson, RJR Nabisco and Mercator Corporation), and paved the way for US investment of up to $10 billion in twenty-five joint ventures over the next two decades.[71] Profit repatriation was guaranteed by the host Government, which secured access by the American Consortium to readily exportable raw materials and fuels: for that purpose, the Chevron corporation undertook to refine petroleum from the Korolev oil field in Western Kazakhstan.

In spite of expectations, the consortium-type of foreign investment did not yield any tangible results in the disintegrating Soviet Union.[72] This reflected a shift in decision-making away from the centre to the republics, coupled with the growing scarcity of foreign exchange.

THE IMPACT OF THE DETERIORATING ECONOMIC AND POLITICAL SITUATION

The last two years have borne witness to a worsening economic situation in the former Soviet Republics. According to official sources, in 1990 GNP fell by 2.3 per cent, and Industrial Gross Output by 1.2 per cent. Inflation was estimated to have risen by 5 per cent during the same period, and the equivalent of R1 billion worth of output was lost as a result of strikes and labour stoppages caused by social and political conflicts.[73]

In 1991 the economic slump worsened: GNP fell by an additional 17 per cent and Industrial output by 7.8 per cent. In the first three quarters of 1991 the value of goods which failed to reach the consumer rose to R31.6 billion. About 1000 enterprises had to interrupt production because of shortages in material inputs: as much as R4.5 billion worth of goods were lost as a result. In the same year, wholesale prices in industry increased by two and a half times on a year by year basis, and the official consumer price index almost doubled.[74]

There are indications that prospective investors have been dissuaded by the economic malaise and inconsistencies in economic policy. After peaking in the fourth quarter of 1989, when the monthly foreign investment registrations numbered between 105 and 108, the comparable figures for the first quarter of 1990 fell to seventy-eight, to sixty in the third quarter and to less than fifty in the fourth. At the same time, companies which engaged in joint ventures tended to select short-term profit-making projects, which entailed small capital commitments. The average capitalisation of joint ventures registered in the Soviet Union decreased from R6.9 million in 1987 to R2.0 million in 1990. The average foreign contribution to the statutory capital of these enterprises (at current official exchange rates) dropped from \$3.9 million in 1987 to \$1.2 million in 1990.[75] Of the foreign investments registered in 1990, less than 4 per cent had foreign capitalisation in excess of \$5 million. In over 78 per cent of joint ventures, the foreign share in the statutory capital was equal or below \$1 million.[76] Although the aggregate data are not available, press reports suggest that in 1991, despite an increase in the number of investments, their average capitalisation remained low.[77]

The disruption of economic ties among enterprises has been compounded by political unrest in some of the republics. In the period preceding 1990, the shares of Estonia and Lithuania in the capitalisation of joint ventures (2.8 per cent and 1.7 per cent) were larger than their contributions to the National Income (0.6 per cent and 1.4 per cent, respectively, in 1988). During 1990, however, these shares fell to 0.2 per cent and 0.1 per cent. On a smaller scale, this was also the case for Moldova.[78]

The growing political instability at regional level has also affected operational joint ventures. A joint venture plant involving Péchiney and the French banking pool led by the Crédit Lyonnais in Kanaker, Armenia, started producing aluminium foil in January 1990. When supplies were interrupted by the economic blockade later that month, operations could only be resumed thanks to a 2000 km air bridge between Kuibychev and Erevan.[79]

The growing scarcity of goods on the domestic market has also undermined the potential for counter-trade. The export licensing procedures introduced in March 1989 greatly hindered some joint ventures, which had formerly covered their convertible currency expenses and repatriated profits via this channel.

Accelerating rates of inflation, not least through the administrative escalation of prices, have overhauled the cost structures of feasibility studies and, in some cases, endangered the existence of enterprises. An example is that of the price of beef charged by the Soviet partner in McDonald's joint venture which increased from R2.4 per kg in February 1990 to R14 in November 1990. Over the same period, the office rent increased ten-fold.[80]

Recent months have borne witness to the improving investment conditions in Russia and some of the other independent states (in particular Kazakhstan, the Ukraine and the Baltic republics). This relates primarily to the political and legal components of the investment climate, namely, the transition to democracy, the adoption of foreign investment legislation and of guarantees for foreign investors. In the economic sphere conflicting government decisions have contributed to a volatile situation.

In Russia, changes in taxation and foreign economic relations have significantly increased business uncertainty. This is illustrated in the field of tax legislation. In 1991, for joint ventures where foreign participation did not exceed 30 per cent, the basic level of tax on profit was set at 45 per cent in the first quarter, and at 35 per cent in subsequent quarters. If the foreign share exceeded 30 per cent of the equity, a 30 per cent tax was levied on profits in the first quarter, and 25 per cent subsequently. In December 1991, the Russian parliament passed a new law on the taxation of profit (effective as of 1 January 1992) which established a 32 per cent flat tax rate for both foreign and domestic companies. Thus, the implementation of the 'national treatment' principle raised taxation levels for companies with a foreign stake in excess of 30 per cent. This was compounded by higher banking, brokerage and trade intermediation charges. At the same time, a new value added tax of 28 per cent was introduced as a counter-inflationary measure, and applied not only to material production but also to services.[81]

A month later, however, the Russian Government cut the rate of VAT to 15 per cent,[82] apparently, as a result of concerted lobbying by entrepreneurs.

In spite of these conflicting signals and high volatility of regulations, foreign investors have revived an interest in the former Soviet Republics. In November 1991, Madrina A. G. of Germany committed $300 million (30 per cent of the capital) to the largest joint venture to date on the territory of the former Soviet Union. The new enterprise, named after its Soviet partner Elektrosila, will be producing generating and power equipment, as well as consumer goods.[83] Fiat of Italy recently signed an agreement of intent to acquire a stake (estimated at 30 per cent) in the largest Russian car-manufacturing company, VAZ, which is earmarked for privatisation.[84] After two years of negotiations, the French oil company, Elf Aquitaine, signed a contract for oil prospecting and extraction in the Saratov-Volgograd region, which entails an investment of several hundred million dollars in exploration, and several billion at the production stage. The details of the contract so far have not been disclosed, but it is likely to be a production-sharing agreement for a period of twenty years. A similar contract with Elf Aquitaine is being negotiated in Kazakhstan.[85]

FUTURE PROSPECTS

On the one hand, the likelihood is that the single market of the former Soviet Union will be split up among its republican segments, separated both by customs barriers and different currencies. Political instability and border disputes between some of the independent states cannot be excluded, and are likely to raise the risk threshold for foreign investors. For these reasons, the governments of the developed market economies may be less willing to guarantee and finance investments in the politically unstable republics.

On the other hand, the dismantling of the Soviet Union has made some republics more responsive to the potential advantages of foreign investment, and encouraged them to adopt a more liberal stance towards attractive projects with foreign participation.

Recently, Russia and Kazakhstan, both well endowed in natural resources, have become more favourably disposed towards foreign investors wishing to develop their oil, gas and timber reserves. Press reports confirm this trend in some other former Soviet republics. The pressing need for convertible currency, which can be earned through the export of natural resources, opens better prospects for multinationals, which have some experience of large-scale concessions, joint venture and production-sharing agreements in the primary sector.

In terms of economic efficiency, the prospects for foreign investment in the Commonwealth of Independent States depend largely on the direction and spread of market reforms: the stabilisation of local currencies and the uninterrupted supply of high quality inputs are high on the list of priorities.

In the short to medium term, several large foreign investment projects, enjoying the patronage of political leadership, may be implemented. These are most likely to be in the exploitation of natural resources, and in manufacturing, alongside the privatisation and defence sector conversion programmes. The inflow of capital from small and medium-sized enterprises is likely to be more closely linked to the economic recovery and the restored political stability of the CIS.

In the long term, assuming a decisive breakthrough in market-oriented reforms, it is probable that the 'comparative' advantages of the economies of the former Soviet republics will play a more appropriate role in foreign investment decisions.

Notes

1. See, for example, the recent statistical survey of foreign investment in the Soviet Union, in ECE *East–West Joint Venture News*, No. 7, February 1991.
2. For example, on 1 October 1991 out of the total of 19 201 industrial enterprises in the Russian Federation, only ninety-four (0.4 per cent) were joint-stock companies producing 0.9 per cent of industrial output

(*Ekonomika i Zhizn'*, No. 49, December 1991). The first acquisition of a Russian company by a foreign firm took place in July 1991, when the Dutch Royal Begemann Group acquired 100 per cent of the stock of Tsemach – a cement machinery producer – for $7 million (*Business Eastern Europe*, 26 August 1991).

3. *East–West Joint Ventures: Economic, Business, Financial and Legal Aspects*, United Nations, New York, 1988, p. 183.
4. ECE *East–West Joint Venture News*, No. 1, 1989.
5. ECE *East–West Joint Venture News*, No. 6, 1990; *Izvestiya*, 15 March 1991.
6. A presidential decree, adopted in January 1991, which authorised the security forces to search through the premises of joint ventures and examine their books, can be cited in this respect. This 'anti-market' decree was repealed in October 1991 (*Izvestiya*, 22 October 1991).
7. See *Vneshnyaya Torgovlya*, 1991, No. 8.
8. Armenia, Belarus, Estonia, Latvia, Lithuania, Kyrgyzstan (Government Decree), the Russian Federation, the Ukraine (Law on foreign investment guarantees) and Uzbekistan.
9. The application of a more beneficial rate of exchange was made conditional on the import-substitution effects of individual investment projects.
10. Supplement to *Ekonomika i Zhizn'*, No. 34, August 1991.
11. Foreign investors were forbidden to purchase roubles for this purpose at market exchange rates and, instead, were obliged to use the much less beneficial special rate of the Central Bank, which did not exceed R8–10 per dollar, as compared with R110 per dollar at the 'official market rate'. (*Izvestiya*, 23 January 1992). Therefore, a certain double standard was applied: for most investment expenditure, foreign companies were obliged to transfer their capital, valued in foreign currency, into roubles at arbitrary exchange rates set by the Central bank, while reverse transfers had to be effected at current market rates which undervalued the rouble.
12. *Statisticheskii Press-Byulleten'*, No. 24, 1991, p. 29.
13. If not otherwise stated, the data originate from the ECE database on joint ventures.
14. This cumulative figure relates to foreign shares in the statutory capital of 2050 joint ventures registered as of 1 January 1991, for which the registration records were filled in.
15. Thus, a sample survey of thirty registered joint ventures in the Soviet Union has revealed an average under-payment of contributions amounting to 26 per cent (*Ekonomika i Zhizn'*, No. 4, January 1990, p. 21). The *Commersant* weekly notes that 80 per cent of dormant joint ventures registered in 1990 could not start operations because the foreign partners had failed to contribute their share of the statutory capital (*Commersant* (English edition) 31 December 1990).
16. The commercial rouble/dollar exchange rate at the beginning of January 1991 (R1.66 per dollar) was roughly three times more beneficial for convertible currencies than the official rate. However, as of January 1992, the Russian Central Bank introduced a 'special commercial' rate of

exchange and devalued the rouble to R55 per dollar. At the 'official' market exchange rate the dollar cost R110.

17. A realistic assessment of the value of foreign investment also depends on the methods used in evaluating the foreign and local contributions to the statutory capital of joint ventures. A recent survey of several hundred joint ventures showed that convertible currency made up 20 per cent of foreign contributions; 59 per cent was in the form of capitalised machinery and equipment, and 12 per cent consisted of technology (*Business in the USSR*, June 1991, p. 19). The techniques used for allocating rouble values to foreign machinery and equipment, technology and know-how on the one hand, and land tenure rights on the other, have long been regarded as commercial secrets, and have therefore not been thoroughly documented in the literature.
18. According to the traditional concepts of Soviet statistics, 'productive' fixed assets belong to enterprises engaged in material production and material services (such as transport and communications). Enterprises in other services, including financial services, are regarded as 'non-productive' assets.
19. ECE database on Joint Ventures, and *Ekonomika i Zhizn'*, No. 40, 1990.
20. *Vneshneekonomicheskiye Sviazi SSSR, Ejekvartal'nyi statisticheskii byulleten'*, No. 3, p. 104; No. 4, p. 108; No. 6, p. 128; *Ekonomika Respublik v Yanvare–Noyabre 1991*, pp. 103–4.
21. *Ekonomika i Zhizn'*, No. 43, October 1990, p. 15; *Vestnik Statistiki* 1991, No. 6, p. 12; *Ekonomika Respublik v Yanvare–Noyabre 1991*, p. 103; *Ekonomika i Zhizn'*, No. 43, October 1991, p. 7.
22. Calculated from *Narodnoye Khozyaistvo SSSR v 1990*, p. 5.
23. Estimated from *Narodnoye Khozyaistvo SSSR v 1990*, p. 5, and *Ekonomika i Zhizn'*, No. 43, October 1991, p. 7.
24. The Soviet classification of joint venture activities depends on the industrial allocation of the local partners, and not on the nature of operations of the ventures themselves (See UN document *Trade/R.575*, p. 34). This principle has resulted in some inconsistencies: cooperative joint ventures (that is, those which have cooperative partners) are juxtaposed to those in industrial sectors. This also explains the implausibly high percentage of R & D-based output.
25. *Vestnik Statistiki*, 1991, No. 6, p. 10; *Osnovnye Pokazateli Balansa Narodnogo Khozyaistva SSSR i Soyuznykh Respublik, Statisticheskii Sbornik*, Moscow, 1990, p. 22.
26. See, for example, *Moscow Narodny Bank Press Bulletin*, 16 August 1989, p. 7; *Commersant* (English edition), 31 December 1990.
27. ECE *East–West Joint Venture News*, No. 7, 1991, and UN document *TRADE/R.575*, p. 36.
28. *Ekonomika Respublik v Yanvare–Noyabre 1991*, p. 104, and *Ekonomika i Zhizn'*, No. 43, October 1991, p. 10.
29. Already in 1990, joint ventures produced 8.9 million pairs of shoes, R13.6 million worth of garments, 138 400 telephone appliances and 75 000 tonnes of fish and sea products (*Vestnik Statistiki*, No. 6, 1991, p. 11).

30. This calculation was made on the basis of the industrial structure of foreign investment registrations according to the International Standard Industrial Classification (ISIC). Such a breakdown, however, cannot take full account of individual differences between enterprises, and should be viewed primarily as a working hypothesis.
31. *Press Release ECE/IND/3*, 18 February 1991.
32. *The Financial Times*, 18 June 1990.
33. *The Financial Times*, 7 June 1990.
34. *Business in the USSR*, March 1991, p. 28.
35. *Moniteur du Commerce International* (MOCI), 28 May 1990, p. 14.
36. *The Financial Times*, 20 June 1990.
37. *Commersant* (Russian edition), 9–26 December 1991.
38. *Business in the USSR*, March 1991, p. 26.
39. *The Financial Times*, 22 June 1990.
40. *Business in the USSR*, March 1991, p. 30.
41. *The Financial Times*, 13 June 1990; *Journal of Commerce*, 14 November 1991.
42. See, for example, *Business Eastern Europe*, 17 December 1990.
43. *Byulleten' Inostrannoi Kommercheskoi Informatsii*, No. 126, 21 October 1989.
44. *Pravda* , 11 October 1989; *The Financial Times*, 15 January 1990.
45. See *The Economist*, 3 February 1990.
46. *Journal of Commerce*, 28 June 1990.
47. See, for example, the experience of one of McDonald's subcontractors in *Izvestiya*, 11 April 1991.
48. See a detailed report of one of the Soviet supply cooperatives in *Link Barometer*, No. 1, 1990, pp. 22–30.
49. *Ekonomika i Zhizn'*, No. 31, 1990, p. 21.
50. *Link Barometer*, No. 5, 1990, pp. 3–4.
51. According to a Vneshekonombank representative, in mid-1990 the Bank planned to advance eighty convertible currency credits worth R15 billion (*Ekonomika i Zhizn'*, No. 31, 1990, p. 21).
52. See the Law on Currency Operations, and *Link Barometer*, No. 3, 1990, p. 13.
53. When the industrial ministry structure was still in place, in some cases the branch ministries guaranteed loans to joint ventures, in which they were partners (*Trade Finance*, May 1989, pp. 26–7). However, legal regulations stipulated that the State and domestic participants to a joint venture 'should not be liable for its obligations'. By implication, the industrial ministries were often unwilling to accept responsibility for joint venture commitments. In turn, Western banks were reluctant to accept guarantees from the ministries on the grounds that the latter enjoyed the special status of state authorities and did not constitute separate legal entities.
54. *The Financial Times*, 1 June 1990.
55. *Moscow Narodny Bank Press Bulletin*, 21 November 1990, pp. 1–2.
56. *Business Eastern Europe*, 9 December 1991.
57. *Nachrichten für Aussenhandel*, 2 January 1991.

58. *The Financial Times*, 18 October 1990; *Nachrichten für Aussenhandel*, 23 December 1991.
59. *Nachrichten für Aussenhandel*, 18 March 1991; *International Herald Tribune*, 14 June 1991.
60. One of the preconditions for the transition to a market economy and the inflow of foreign investment is the deregulation of the insurance market. The largest foreign groups in this sector, together with specialised Government agencies, are launching new insurance packages for joint ventures in Eastern Europe to insure against political risks (such as expropriation and nationalisation), as well as commercial risks (for example, the non-transfer of profits). For details, see the *Journal of Commerce*, 5 March 1990; *Izvestiya*, 23 May 1990; and *Business Eastern Europe*, 17 December 1990, and 2 December 1991.

    In 1989, the Council of Ministers issued a decree prohibiting foreign insurance companies from operating on Soviet territory. Recently, however, new insurance companies have been founded: for example, the Russian Insurance Joint-Stock Society, which has several joint ventures as its co-founders. Several other joint ventures are also being negotiated. In the Russian Federation, a new insurance law is being drafted, which will end the monopoly of the state and enable Western companies to take over a portion of the domestic insurance market (*Journal of Commerce*, 18 January 1990; *East European Markets*, 20 April 1990, p. 14; *Izvestiya*, 15 August 1990; *Pravda*, 4 March 1991; *The Journal of Commerce*, 9 December 1991; *Interflo*, 10/91).
61. *Ecotass*, 11 June 1990, p. 19; *Vneshnyaya Torgovlya*, 1991, No. 5, p. 22–6.
62. *Commersant* (Russian edition), 9–16 September 1991.
63. *Business in the USSR*, January 1991, pp. 42–3.
64. *Business Eastern Europe*, 13 January 1992.
65. These have been common obstacles to Western investors in the other Central and East European countries. See, for example, P. Artisien, *Joint Ventures in Yugoslav Industry*, Gower, Aldershot, 1985; and W. Jermakowicz and C. Drazek, 'Joint Venture Laws in Eastern Europe: A Comparative Assessment', Chapter 9 in this book.
66. D. Holtbrügge, *Managerial Problems of Joint Ventures in the Soviet Union*, Universität Dortmund, Arbeitsbericht, No. 8, November 1989, p. 18.
67. Calculated from the UN document *TRADE/R.575*, p. 35.
68. UN document *TRADE/R.575*, p. 35; and *Ekonomika Respublik v Yanvare–Noyabre 1991*, p. 104; *Ekonomika i Zhizn'*, No. 43, 1991.
69. For example, the Soviet–Swedish fish and sea products processing joint venture, Neptune, with an initial capital of R15 million started operations in January 1988. The estimated value of exports in 1989 was $50 million, and 95 per cent of the processed fish and sea products were sold for convertible currency in the USA and Japan. In the first nine months of 1990, the value of export sales amounted to about $38 million (at official exchange rates) (ECE Secretariat interview, and *Vneshnyaya Torgovlya*, No. 6, 1991, p. 34).

In a handful of cases, the Western partner targeted its local subsidiary to supply components and parts to other subsidiaries abroad. This was the case of the US camera producer Polaroid, which subcontracted the production of a built-in electronic circuit to its Svetozor joint venture. This guaranteed the enterprise an inflow of convertible currency (*Ecotass*, 11 June 1990, p. 20). However, under conditions of shrinking demand on the world market, the US parent has planned to assemble and sell cameras in Russia and the other Republics, rather than export components to the West (*International Herald Tribune*, 25 November 1991).

70. *Ekonomika i Zhizn'*, No. 48, November 1991.
71. *US Mission Daily Bulletin*, 31 March 1989.
72. *Vneshnyaya Torgovlya*, No. 6, 1991, p. 35.
73. *Narodnoye Khozyaistvo SSSR v 1990*, pp. 7, 159; *Ekonomika i Zhizn'*, No. 5, January 1991.
74. *Ekonomika i Zhizn'*, No. 43, October 1991; Information provided to the ECE Secretariat by the USSR State Committee on Statistics.
75. ECE *East–West Joint Venture News*, No. 7, 1991.
76. ECE database on Joint Ventures.
77. See weekly and monthly surveys of foreign investment in *Commersant*.
78. ECE database on Joint Ventures: *Osnovnye Pokazateli Balansa Narodnogo Khozyaistva*, pp. 34–40.
79. *MOCI*, 2 April 1990, p. 13.
80. *Business in the USSR*, February 1991, p. 51.
81. *Commersant* (Russian edition), No. 47, 2–9 December 1991.
82. *International Herald Tribune*, 6 February 1992.
83. *Commersant* (Russian edition), No. 47, 2–9 December 1991.
84. *Russia Express*, No. 71, 3 February 1992, p. 11.
85. *International Herald Tribune*, 7 February 1992.

6 Foreign Direct Investment in Hungary

David G. Young

INTRODUCTION

This chapter provides a general overview of foreign direct investment (FDI) in Hungary over the past few years. An attempt has been made to analyse the existing data, but many of the statistics are still too 'raw' and our experience too short to draw final conclusions about the move of foreign capital and know-how to Hungary. Taking this into consideration, this chapter proposes to outline foreign investment to date, using the available statistics and the author's own experience. The level of investment, its sectoral and geographical distribution and the profitability of joint ventures will be examined. At the same time, an attempt will be made to identify emerging investment trends, while the conclusion will discuss whether there is a limit to Hungary's ability to absorb FDI. The Appendix will present a concise summary of legislation pertinent to foreign investment.

The statistics used in this chapter have, on the whole, been derived from the publications and press releases of the Hungarian Central Statistical Office (KSH).[1] The KSH has collected an admirable amount of data through the use of quarterly questionnaires sent out to newly-formed companies. The data for the 1980s and 1990s, although not perfect, are felt to be relatively reliable. However, at the time of writing (February 1992), experts at the KSH stressed that preliminary data for 1991 probably represented an underestimate of the amount of foreign investment which entered the country that year. This has been taken into consideration when discussing FDI in 1991 and duly noted in the text and tables.

BACKGROUND: FOREIGN INVESTORS MOVE IN

When Western business interest in Central and Eastern Europe was stimulated by the collapse of communism in 1989 and the rise of

Table 6.1 Joint Ventures and 100% Foreign-owned Companies in Hungary

1987	*1988*	*1989*	*1990*	*1991*
130	227	1 350	5 693	11 000

Source: Hungarian Central Statistical Office.

democracy in 1990, Hungary was better prepared to attract FDI than its former socialist allies. By the end of 1989 much of Hungary's foreign investment legislation was already in place; tax incentives were available for foreign investors; company and transformation laws spelled out company forms and how a state-owned company could become a limited liability company (Kft) or public limited company (Rt); profit repatriation was guaranteed; and a foreign investor could have a 100 per cent owned subsidiary in Hungary (see the Appendix to this chapter). Moreover, years of economic reform and relative openness to the West had created a modest entrepreneurial atmosphere which foreign businessmen found familiar and conducive to their needs.

Joint venture numbers: In 1989 and 1990 (and probably in 1991 as well) Hungary attracted about half of the foreign investment directed at Central and Eastern Europe. In 1989 the number of companies with foreign participation was 1350, compared to 130 at the end of 1987 and 227 at the end of 1988 (joint ventures have been permitted in Hungary since 1972). By the end of 1990 that number had reached 5693. Preliminary results indicate that this rapid growth continued in 1991, with perhaps as many as 5000–5500 new companies being formed with foreign participation, bringing the total of joint ventures and 100 per cent foreign-owned companies operating in Hungary at the end of 1991 to approximately 11 000 (see Table 6.1).

Investment capital: The total amount of capital invested in companies with foreign participation in 1990 was Ft274.1 billion ($4.3 billion), of which Ft93.2 billion ($1.5 billion) was contributed by the foreign partner in cash or kind. By the end of 1991 the amount contributed by foreign investors was estimated to have more than doubled to $3.2 billion. Thus the rate of increase of foreign investment grew very rapidly during the period 1989–91, increasing four times between 1989 and 1990 (from $250 million to $1.0 billion) and almost doubled between 1990 and 1991 (to $1.7 billion). This may be modest when compared to investment levels in Southeast Asia or

Table 6.2 Share of Foreign Capital in Hungarian Companies, 1989–91

Foreign share %	No. of enterprises			Foreign contribution		
	Dec. 1989	Dec. 1990	Established between Jan. and June 1991	Dec. 1989	Dec. 1990	Established between Jan. and June 1991
20	195	793	502	0.9	3.8	0.9
21–30	176	798	352	2.4	8.2	3.5
31–50	817	3279	1287	21.5	49.0	12.3
51–80	118	433	306	4.5	23.2	5.1
81–99	17	146	115	0.2	3.1	0.4
100	27	244	515	0.4	5.9	3.8
Total	1350	5693	3077	30.0	93.2	26.0[a]

[a] Probably a significant underestimate.

Source: Hungarian Central Statistical Office.

Southern Europe, but is high when compared to Central and Eastern Europe's recent past.

Generally, the majority of companies with foreign participation in Hungary have been established with a small amount of initial capital. In fact, the average foundation capital has decreased over the period 1989–91. In 1989 the average capital investment was Ft22 million ($370 000), in 1990 Ft16 million ($250 000) and in the first six months of 1991, Ft8.5 million ($115 000). These numbers reflect the counter-balancing effect of thousands of small – often service and retail sector – investments weighed against major investments in manufacturing by multinational corporations (MNCs).

Nevertheless, the share of the foreign partner grew steadily over the same period. Thus the average share of the foreign contribution to the starting capital in 1989 was 24 per cent, in 1990, 34 per cent and in the first six months of 1991, 37 per cent. Table 6.2 reveals that while the majority of investors in 1991 still preferred taking shares in the region of 30–50 per cent, an increasing number were taking a controlling share (that is, above 50 per cent). In addition, the number of 100 per cent foreign-owned companies grew rapidly in 1991, with the number of such companies formed in the first six months of 1991 double those formed in the whole of 1990. This tendency reflects the increasing confidence of the Western businessman in investing in

Hungary. It also could reflect a growing frustration on the part of the foreign shareholder with a lack of control over his Hungarian investment.

Company form: Foreign investors clearly preferred the limited liability company (Kft) to the joint stock holding company (Rt), with the vast majority of investments in 1990–91 taking the form of Kfts. Kfts are the form generally more suitable to the needs of small business: they have a smaller initial capital requirement, Ft1 million ($13 000), compared to Ft1 billion ($13 million) for Rts.

Sectoral distribution: A review of FDI in 1990 by sector reveals a more even than expected distribution of investment across the economy. As Tables 6.3 and 6.4 show, about half of foreign capital invested in Hungary went into industry (Ft46 billion – $730 million). Within industry engineering (Ft14.9 billion – $235 million) and light industry (Ft9.8 billion – $155 million) led the way, followed by investments in the region of Ft6.0–6.5 billion ($100 million) in building materials, chemicals and food processing.

As has been well reported in the Western press, a significant part of FDI has been in the service sector. With tremendous demand for improved services and initial start-up costs relatively low, it is not surprising that this sector received Ft19.2 billion ($300 million), or 20.6 per cent of total investments in 1990.

Retail trade also received a significant share of foreign investment: Ft12.7 billion ($200 million) or 13.6 per cent of total investment in 1990. In 1990–91 large investments were made by Tengelmann (Germany), which took a controlling stake of the second largest chain of department stores (Skala); McDonald's, Burger King and Pizza Hut (USA); and Kleider Bauer (Austria). The largest number of joint ventures – 1661 – was formed in this sector.

Agriculture was one potentially attractive sector which was neglected by foreign investors. Given the sector's importance to the economy as a whole, at first glance it appears surprising that only seventy-eight joint ventures were formed with a foreign capital contribution of Ft494 million ($7.8 million). The reluctance of foreign investors to consider an investment in Hungarian agriculture can be attributed to the remaining questions concerning land ownership and the lack of legislation for the transformation of agricultural cooperatives (which was passed only in early 1992). Moreover, the collapse of domestic and former CMEA demand has led to a deterioration in the profitability (and hence attractiveness) of most Hungarian farms.

Origins of investment: Data on the source of FDI in Hungary are

Table 6.3 Joint Ventures Founded in Hungary in 1990

Sector	*Number*	*Founding capital (forint million)*	*Foreign capital investment (forint million)*
Mining	1	700.0	210.0
Electric energy	2	2.0	0.6
Metallurgy	29	5 905.1	2 017.2
Machine industry	691	41 968.0	14 875.2
Building materials	71	20 249.3	6 526.1
Chemical industry	187	30 005.3	6 209.9
Light industry	384	24 754.9	9 823.5
Other industries	31	802.6	372.9
Food industry	130	18 717.8	6 066.8
Total industry	1 526	143 105.2	46 102.3
Construction	518	13 020.2	6 058.6
Agriculture	78	5 896.7	494.0
Transportation	130	5 449.0	2 029.7
Domestic trade	1 661	42 318.8	12 715.7
Foreign trade	675	15 059.9	3 552.3
Water management	6	32.0	17.6
Other material sectors	199	3 571.5	1 532.0
Total industry and other	4 793	228 453.3	72 502.2
Personal and economic services	543	42 349.6	19 206.0
Health services	304	3 021.7	1 359.7
Communal services	53	323.9	150.8
Services	900	45 695.2	20 716.5
Total	5 693	274 148.5	93 218.6

Source: Hungarian Central Statistical Office.

difficult to obtain. The general consensus is that by far the greatest number of joint ventures have been formed by German and Austrian companies, which, with few exceptions, have entered the Hungarian market with small ventures targeted at weak spots in the domestic market. On the other hand, the largest amount of foreign capital (35 per cent) has been brought into the country by US firms, which have concentrated on strategic investments, often aimed at markets outside Hungary. For example, US companies such as Ford, General

Table 6.4 Joint Ventures Founded in Hungary in 1991 (January to September)

Sector	*Number*	*Founding capital (forint million)*	*Foreign capital investment (forint million)*
Mining	–	–	–
Electric energy	2	2.3	1.4
Metallurgy	10	3 329.7	1 226.0
Machine industry	343	12 047.9	6 208.3
Building materials	35	3 383.1	1 551.3
Chemical industry	77	5 815.6	3 259.5
Light industry	192	5 705.9	1 615.8
Other industries	16	163.7	87.3
Food industry	93	34 855.1	11 137.8
Total industry	768	65 303.3	25 087.4
Construction	325	11 518.9	2 809.1
Agriculture	54	294.6	130.3
Transportation	85	1 419.6	551.9
Domestic trade	1 459	9 579.3	3 528.8
Foreign trade	776	2 224.9	1 229.5
Water management	3	5.9	1.8
Other material sectors	71	1 695.2	1 115.6
Total industry and other	3 541	92 041.7	34 454.4
Personal and economic services	331	10 750.9	4 384.6
Health services	197	925.2	515.5
Communal services	29	150.8	73.7
Services	557	11 826.9	4 973.8
Total	4 098	103 868.6	39 428.2[a]

[a] Probably a significant underestimate.

Source: Hungarian Central Statistical Office.

Electric, General Motors, Guardian Glass and Sara Lee, are looking to markets in Western Europe (and someday perhaps in Eastern Europe) as well as in Hungary, to justify their investments (see Table 6.5).

Despite the dominance of small ventures within Austrian and German investment, companies from those countries still account for an important share of foreign capital invested in Hungary. Up to the

Table 6.5 Top Investments in Hungary

Investor	*Nationality*	*Share (%)*	*Deal ($ mn)*	*Sector*
Sanofi	French	40	75	Pharmaceuticals
General Electric	US	50	150	Lighting
Guardian Glass	US	80	115	Glass
Ford	US	100	83	Vehicles
Prinzhorn Group	Austrian	40	82	Paper
General Motors	US	67	66	Vehicles
Electrolux	Swedish	100	65	Refrigerators
Sara Lee	US	51	60	Food
Nestlé	Swiss	97	38	Food
Agrana	Austrian	49	35	Food
Suzuki	Japanese	40	30	Vehicles
Tengelmann	German	50+	200	Retail Trade

Source: *The Financial Times*, Hungarian press reports.

end of 1990 Austrian companies had contributed 23.5 per cent and German companies 22 per cent of foreign capital invested in Hungary. Other major investments have been made by companies originating from France, Korea, Switzerland, Italy and Sweden. Japanese companies, however, have been much more cautious in approaching the Hungarian market. With the exception of Suzuki and two other relatively large manufacturing ventures, Japanese investment in Hungary has been notable by its absence.

Geographical distribution of FDI: A significant proportion of foreign investment has been attracted by two regions: Budapest and the northwestern counties (see Table 6.6).

Budapest: Budapest is the dominant city in Hungary. It is the country's centre of government, business, culture and entertainment, and contains 20 per cent (2 016 000) of Hungary's population. It is also the centre of banking and finance. Skilled employees in this sector, and other service sectors, are much more difficult to find outside of the capital. Its infrastructure, while lagging behind Western levels, is ahead of the rest of the country. Public transport is good, Ferihegy International Airport is nearby and all but one of the nation's bridges across the Danube are located in the Budapest area.

The above are several of the reasons why Budapest and the surrounding counties of Pest and Fejér attracted over 50 per cent of FDI in 1990. Foreign companies invested in 3305 ventures in Budapest

Table 6.6 Territorial Breakdown of Enterprises with Foreign Capital per County

County	31 December 1990		1 January–30 June 1991	
	No. of enterprises	*Statutory capital in foreign currency*	*No. of enterprises*	*Statutory capital in foreign currency*
		forint million		*forint million*
Budapest	3 305	54 762.6	1 730	13 279.2
Baranya	153	2 115.1	68	683.1
Bács-Kiskun	201	1 839.5	107	460.8
Békés	63	728.7	41	43.8
Borsod-Abaúj-Zemplén	110	3 930.5	64	664.8
Csongrád	137	710.6	79	423.5
Fejér	130	5 419.8	65	177.1
Győr-Moson-Sopron	231	3 466.4	139	2 389.2
Hajdú-Bihar	113	893.3	42	1 530.8
Heves	43	109.7	33	170.3
Komárom-Esztergom	134	2 458.2	72	1 200.6
Nógrád	46	448.8	28	912.4
Pest	450	8 384.4	250	1 963.1
Somogy	100	1 279.9	59	49.3
Szabolcs-Szatmár-Bereg	68	2 708.4	40	71.1
Jász-Nagykun-Szolnok	56	1 073.3	41	133.9
Tolna	69	243.0	30	67.3
Vas	87	998.7	68	320.2
Veszprém	111	795.3	71	1 448.2
Zala	86	852.4	50	47.9
Total	5 693	93 218.6	3 077	26 036.6[a]

[a] Probably a significant underestimate.

Source: Hungarian Central Statistical Office.

alone and contributed foreign currency and in kind to the value of Ft54.8 billion ($865 million), or 58.8 per cent of FDI in that year. In 1991 a similar pattern developed, although statistics are not yet complete.

Northwest Hungary: Covering 9600 km^2, this region includes Vas, Györ–Sopron–Moson and Komárom–Esztergom counties, and is situated on the borders with Austria and Slovakia. The largest cities in the region are Györ, Sopron, Komárom, Szombathely and Esztergom. Traditionally, this part of Hungary has been more developed than the Eastern parts of the country. Austria has had and continues to have a strong influence in the region. The number of people living in this area is 1 016 000, about 10 per cent of Hungary's population. Living standards are relatively good – the average monthly wage exceeds the national average. Unemployment in the region is below, while the quality of infrastructure is above the national average. Although dwarfed by FDI in Budapest, the amount of foreign capital invested in northwest Hungary sets this region apart from the rest of the country. In 1990 Ft6.9 billion was invested there by foreign companies, the equivalent of 7.4 per cent of total FDI for that year. Major investments in this region have been made by Purina in Györ and Suzuki in Esztergom.

Overall, it is clear that Budapest and the northwest region of Hungary have attracted a large share of foreign direct investment in Hungary. On the one hand, they have done this by offering better business prospects and a higher level of infrastructural development. On the other hand, the northwest of Hungary has also benefited from its close proximity to Austria and the rest of Western Europe.

Profitability: One of the more surprising facts to arise out of this review of KSH statistics for 1990 is the relatively high level of profitability among joint ventures in Hungary. Given that most joint ventures are 'new' companies, with high initial start up costs, it would be expected that the majority would make losses in the first few years. This is not the case in Hungary, where, in 1990, 56 per cent of companies with foreign participation recorded a profit. In fact the total profits of joint ventures doubled between 1989 and 1990 – to Ft49.6 billion ($785 million) – although it should be noted that the number of joint ventures increased by about five times. Losses increased even more rapidly, but the net effect was a 68 per cent increase in overall profits to Ft37 billion ($585 million).

Joint ventures in some branches of the economy naturally fared much better than others. For example, joint ventures in engineering recorded significant losses in 1990 (see Table 6.7) as did the iron and steel industry. But all other sectors recorded profits, with retail trade leading the way with profit within the sector of Ft14.4 billion ($225 million).

Generally, joint ventures were more profitable than Hungarian companies without foreign participation. (However, tax incentives

Table 6.7 The Profitability of Joint Ventures by Sector, 1990 (forint million)

	Profit	*Losses*	*Profit minus losses*
Mining	–	2.6	(2.6)
Electricity supply	0.0	0.1	(0.1)
Manufacture of basic metals and casting	641.0	849.1	(208.1)
Manufacture of machinery and equipment	5 461.6	6 859.5	(1 397.9)
Manufacture of building materials	1 915.5	418.3	1 497.2
Manufacture of chemicals	3 186.0	261.9	2 924.1
Light industry	2 490.3	870.9	1 619.4
Manufacture of other products	79.8	14.2	65.5
Food industry	1 242.9	575.5	667.4
Mining and manufacturing	15 017.1	9 852.4	5 164.7
Construction	1 439.8	362.3	1 077.5
Agriculture and forestry	1 137.9	112.9	1 025.0
Transport, post and telecommunications	1 283.6	88.3	1 195.3
Trade	15 673.8	1 319.4	14 354.4
Water works and supply	3.2	1.3	1.9
Other material services	2 120.3	177.9	1 942.4
– Material branches together	36 675.7	11 914.4	24 761.3
– Non-material branches together	12 911.9	934.1	11 977.8
Total	49 587.6	12 848.6	36 739.0

Source: Hungarian Central Statistical Office.

granted to joint ventures and 100 per cent foreign-owned companies did give them an added advantage). In 1990 joint ventures paid Ft12.4 billion ($200 million) in dividends, or 44 per cent of all dividends granted by companies in Hungary. Of this amount Ft4.2 billion ($65 million) was eligible for repatriation by the foreign partners. According to the National Bank of Hungary, foreign investors chose to repatriate only Ft2.3 billion of this amount, with the remaining saved and/or re-invested in the company or other ventures in Hungary. Thus only 4.6 per cent of net profits were taken out of the country.

CONCLUSION: IS THERE AN INVESTMENT THRESHOLD?

There is little argument among Hungary's leaders about the need for foreign investment, and since the late 1980s the Hungarian government has made commendable efforts to encourage foreign investors to come to Hungary. It has done so because it realises the clear benefits to the economy of foreign participation. FDI brings in badly needed capital to a cash-poor economy; foreign businessmen bring with them modern technology and know-how; foreign partners can assist their Hungarian counterparts in marketing products abroad and in training the domestic labour force; and new companies from abroad can introduce competition to a market long held in the vice-like grip of state monopolies.

Already companies with foreign participation are having a significant impact on the Hungarian economy. As early as 1990 joint ventures accounted for 10.7 per cent of total sales in Hungary, and in 1991 that figure probably neared 20 per cent. This is a remarkable achievement in a two-year period. Moreover, while most Hungarian companies have been making workers redundant (unemployment stood at 8.3 per cent at the end of 1991), joint ventures doubled the number of employees to 4.5 per cent of the workforce at the end of 1990. Productivity was twice as high in joint ventures, while wages were 35 per cent higher for white-collar workers and 11 per cent higher for blue-collar workers.

Clearly FDI into Hungary has grown rapidly in recent years. In 1989 about $250 million was invested in cash and in kind by foreign companies; in the twelve months of 1990 $1.0 billion was put into the country by foreign investors; and in 1991 an estimated $1.7 billion was transferred into Hungary ($1.45 billion in cash and $250 million in kind). Thus total investment by foreign companies in Hungary was estimated at $3.2 billion at the end of 1991, with growth rates of 100 per cent recorded in 1989 and 1990, and of 50–70 per cent in 1991. However, the real question for Hungary is whether this rate of growth will continue, or whether there are limits to Western demand and Hungary's ability to absorb foreign capital.

Foreign demand to invest in Hungary is naturally difficult to measure. In 1991 Western MNCs, independent investment funds and international financial institutions were all actively searching for investment possibilities throughout the country. Although concrete data do not exist, anecdotal information gained from discussions with frustrated potential foreign investors indicates that demand to invest in Hungary exceeded the country's ability to absorb it. This is not surprising. Hungary's economic underdevelopment and practical (and policy) problems surrounding privatisation placed constraints on inbound investment. Hungary's obstacles to foreign investment have been discussed at length in many publications, but, in brief, include her poor infrastructure, the slow company registration process, the Hungarians' lack of experience in dealing with foreign investors and the inefficient banking system. Perhaps just as discouraging for the foreign investor was the relatively slow pace of privatisation, which in part was due to government policy, and in part to the practical difficulties of privatising state-owned companies under adverse conditions. That many Hungarian companies are deeply in debt, inefficient and uncompetitive on Western markets helps to explain the difficulties of privatisation and the reluctance of foreign investors to invest. Thus it can be argued that these factors, *inter alia*, place limits on the amount of FDI that can be absorbed by the country.

Nevertheless, the rapid growth in FDI in recent years lends credence to the thesis that Hungary's threshold for investment expanded significantly during the period 1989–91. The pace of privatisation, while slower than hoped for, was faster in 1991 than in 1990; several practical infrastructural problems were lessened (the availability of Western standard office space increased in 1991); and perhaps most importantly, Hungarians gained more experience in dealing with FDI, while Western investors developed a greater knowledge of the Hungarian market.

However, this does not mean that we should expect similar exceptional rates of growth in the coming years. The rapid increase in FDI took place against a background of negligible foreign investment in the period prior to 1989. Now that reasonable investment levels have been achieved, it will be much more difficult for Hungary to reach the annual growth rates of 100 per cent achieved during 1989–91. Yet modest growth should be possible, and the key will be the privatisation process and the improvement of the investment incentive framework. Thus the government will need to make companies undergoing privatisation more attractive by easing the negotiation process and finding creative solutions to the company debt situation. The authorities should also consider implementing additional investment incentives – from tax concessions to outright grants – in order to maintain the country's lead as the primary destination of FDI in the region and to compete successfully with other developing markets worldwide. If it can do this, Hungary should be able to maintain and even increase current investment levels.

Appendix

Legislative framework

The following is a brief survey of legislation relevant to investing in Hungary.

The Company Law defines the forms of business which companies may take, primarily public limited liability companies (Rts) and limited liability companies (Kfts) – other forms are also legislated.

The Transformation Act provides the framework for state-owned companies to transform into Plcs and Ltds.

The Foreign Investment Act reiterates and amplifies many of the provisions contained in the Companies Act and in the tax laws where they apply to foreigners. It also includes a number of additional provisions, mostly either granting further incentives to foreigners or guaranteeing their interests.

A new Accounting Act takes Hungary much closer to international accounting standards (from 1 January 1992).

Other important pieces of legislation cover the State Property Agency (Privatisation), banking, bankruptcy, compensation (for expropriation), and gambling.

Hungary also has a relatively well-developed tax framework, which includes:

- Corporate profits tax: 40 per cent;
- Three rates of VAT: 0, 15, 25 per cent;
- Personal income tax: top rate 40 per cent (from 1 January 1992).

It should be noted that the overall tax burden is increased by local taxes and various changes on wages.

Investment incentives

Tax legislation as of 1 January 1992 sets a deadline after which tax concessions on foreign investment will no longer be granted. The Law states that foreign investors will not be able to qualify for tax concessions after 31 December 1993. But concessions prior to this date will remain in effect for the specified period.

Thus a company registered before the end of 1993 can qualify for a 60 per cent reduction in the profits tax rate in the first five years and a 40 per cent reduction in the second five years if it meets the following conditions:

- the company is established with a foundation capital of more than Ft50 million ($650 000);
- foreign investors take at least a 30 per cent share of the issued capital;
- more than 50 per cent of the company's annual income is derived from manufacturing.

The possibility of obtaining a 100 per cent tax holiday for the first five years and a 60 per cent reduction in the second five years will also remain intact, if the investor meets the above three requirements and makes the investment in a priority sector.

Tax concessions are also available for companies in which the dividends of a foreign investor are invested.

Tax concessions are available for investments in designated 'underdeveloped' regions.

Government grants are available for the development of a company's infrastructure if a foreign investor is involved and if certain requirements are met.

Hungary has investment guarantee agreements (against expropriation) and double tax treaties with a number of countries.

Repatriation of profits is guaranteed.

Note

1. 'Foreign Joint Ventures in Hungary', Hungarian Central Statistical Office, 1991. The author wishes to thank Anna Mesko, who wrote the report, for her pioneering research and willingness to share information.

7 Foreign Direct Investment in Poland: 1986–90

Zbigniew Bochniarz and
Wladyslaw Jermakowicz

INTRODUCTION

The opening up of the Polish economy to Foreign Direct Investment in the post-war period began in earnest in 1976, when the First Joint Venture Decree was passed by the Council of Ministers. This Decree was intended for foreign companies established by citizens of Polish origin; these became known as 'Polonia' firms to emphasise that most participants shared a Polish and foreign background. The 1976 legislation was a cautious move towards allowing inward foreign investment, and contrasted markedly with the more liberal laws in existence at the time in Hungary and Romania. In 1986, after several revisions to the initial legislation, 693 companies were operating under the 'Polonia' Firms law.[1] The 'Polonia' companies were relatively small: 80.3 per cent had fewer than 200 employees, and the average investment amounted to $144 000. Their operations were restricted to domestic trade, restaurants, hotels and some other services (Decree 123, 1976 and Orders 10 and 100, 1976). These restrictions were lifted by the 1979 Law, but the basic industries remained closed to foreign capital.

The first joint venture law allowing full foreign participation was passed by the Polish Sejm on 23 April 1986, and serves as a starting point in this analysis. The data used in this study originate from the official register of the Foreign Investment Agency in Poland.

THREE LAWS, THREE PERIODS

The time period under consideration has been divided into three sub-periods (1987–8; 1988–9 and 1989–90) to mark the introduction of new laws on foreign investment in April 1986, December 1988 and December 1989, respectively.

The 1986 law on Joint Ventures widened the fields of activity for foreign investors to most sectors of the economy, with the exceptions of the defence industry, railways and air transport, communications, telecommunications, insurance, banking, publishing (but not printing), and foreign trade. This represented a significant departure from the 1979 legislation, which prohibited joint ventures in heavy engineering, basic chemicals, micro-electronics and metallurgy. Some restrictions, however, subsisted: the joint venture's Chief Executive or Chairman of the Board of Directors must be a Polish national; the foreign partner's equity participation was limited to 49 per cent; a proportion of hard currency earnings – between 15 and 25 per cent at the time of registration – had to be sold to a Polish foreign exchange bank; and 10 per cent of profits were automatically channelled to the reserve fund. The new law, however, allowed for the transfer abroad of foreign currency profits resulting from the excess of export earnings over import outlays in proportions commensurate with the partners' entitlement to company profits. The Ministry of Foreign Relations was the ultimate authority in charge of the activities of joint ventures.

The second law of 23 December 1988 established the Foreign Investment Agency whose main functions were to supervise the activities of joint ventures and issue registration documents. The approved period for applications was reduced from three to two months, whilst the spheres of activity were extended to yet more areas. The ceiling on the foreign partner's share of the joint venture's capital was raised to a possible 100 per cent (with a minimum participation of 20 per cent). The new law also permitted foreign nationals to be elected Chief Executives, reduced the compulsory sale of hard currency profits to a fixed 15 per cent, extended tax holidays from two to three years (up to six years for priority projects) and abolished the permits required for foreign trade operations.

The third law of 28 December 1989 liberalised further the conditions for foreign investment, primarily with regard to the repatriation of profits. This law allowed the unrestricted transfer abroad of all profits from sales, and permitted an additional 15 per cent repatriation of profits from goods and services sold on Polish markets.

A comparison of the three laws in Table 7.1 suggests that the most radical legislative changes came about in December 1988. This law

Table 7.1 Comparison of Foreign Investment Laws in Poland, 1987–90

Degrees of:	First period 1987–8	Second period 1988–9	Third period 1989–90
Economic openness (Areas excluded from investment)	Defence, rail, air transport, communications, insurance, publishing, foreign trade	Defence and areas requiring protection of State interests and environment	Defence and areas requiring protection of State interests and environment
Length of Decision Period	Three months	Two months	Two months
Repatriation of Profits	Repatriation of partial foreign currency earnings subject to reselling to the Polish foreign exchange Bank between 15% and 25% of earnings, and after transfer of 10% of profits to reserve fund	Repatriation of profits to the extent of hard currency earnings after reselling 15% of export proceeds to the State	Repatriation of all hard currency profits plus 15% of profits from domestic market sales
Foreign Partner's Share	Less than 49% share allowed	20–100% foreign share allowed	20–100% foreign share allowed
Corporate Income Taxes Paid	50% Tax rate decreases by 0.4% for each 1% of the share of export turnover in total turnover (but not less than 10%)	40% Tax rate decreases by 0.4% for each 1% of the share of export turnover in total turnover (but not less than 10%)	40%
Tax Deductions	For investment outlays	For investment outlays and charitable contributions	None
Length of Tax Holidays	Two years	Three to six years	Three to six years
Nationality Requirements	Only a domestic person can occupy top management	Both CEO and Chairman of the Board may be foreigners	Both CEO and Chairman of the Board may be foreigners

altered the principle of profit repatriation, established new supervisory authorities and liberalised the registration procedure by shortening the time period required for issuing permits.

The third law, probably because of time constraints, added merely cosmetic changes to its 1988 predecessor. They were prompted largely by nascent economic reforms, including the introduction of internal convertibility, the further liberalisation of international trade and anti-inflationary measures.

THE GROWTH OF JOINT VENTURES, 1986–90

Between April 1986 and December 1990, the authorities received 3330 applications from foreign investors wishing to start operating in Poland. Some 1886 registration permits were granted with a total initial capital value of $547 million; of these, 50 per cent did start operations.[2] The analysis of data in the three aforementioned periods shows a steady growth in the number of newly established firms. As Figure 7.1 illustrates, fifty-two firms were approved in the period 1987–8, 863 in 1988–9, and 1005 in 1989–90. The tendency, however, was for a decrease in the average size of firms, when measured against initial investments. The largest firms were those established in 1987–8, when the average initial capital amounted to $576 900; this fell by over 40 per cent to $237 339 in 1989–90. The same trend is observed in the value of joint ventures: Figure 7.2 shows that in period I, 58.1 per cent of joint ventures had an investment in excess of $200 000; this fell to 6.5 and 11.2 per cent respectively in the next two periods.

A positive development, however, was the increase in the average share of foreign capital participation in joint ventures. The removal of ceilings on the foreign partner's share under the 1988 Law resulted in a noticeable growth in foreign ownership. As Figure 7.2 further illustrates, the proportion of foreign firms holding a majority investment in joint ventures increased from 9.6 per cent in 1987–8, to 76.7 per cent in 1988–9, and 88.7 per cent in 1989–90. In this last period, the number of foreign firms with wholly-owned Polish subsidiaries increased to 25 per cent. The above data are confirmed by the share of foreign capital in the joint ventures' total investment measured as a ratio of foreign to total capital in Figure 7.2. This rose from 30 per cent in the first period, to 41 per cent in the second, to 74 per cent in the third.

During the same period a noticeable growth was recorded in the registration index, defined here as the ratio of issued registrations to the number of applications received (see Figure 7.3). The growing rate of registrations reflects the Polish government's readiness to encourage foreign firms in areas previously excluded from foreign

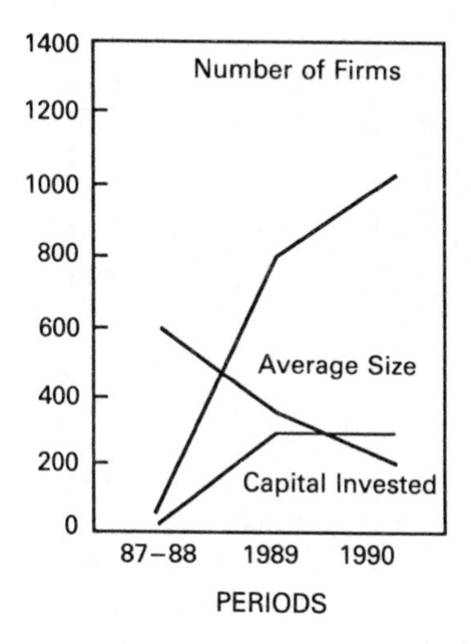

Figure 7.1 Number, Size and Initial Investment of Foreign Firms in Polish Joint Ventures, 1987–90

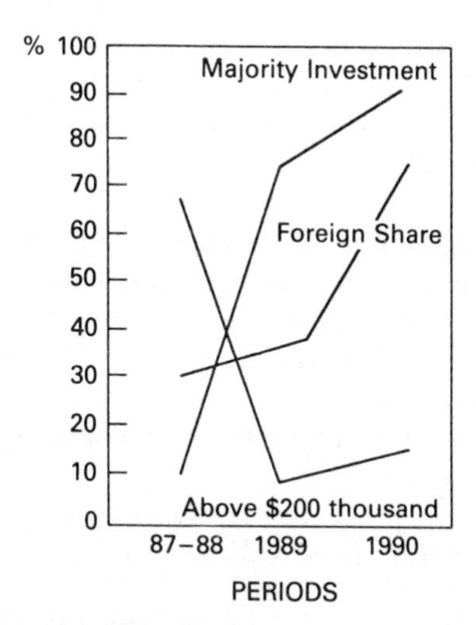

Figure 7.2 Extent of Foreign Participation in Polish Joint Ventures, 1987–90

penetration (such as banking and insurance), but also improvements in the thoroughness with which applications are filed for the establishment of new firms. Few applications were turned down (four in 1989, and twelve in 1990), in the main as the result of one of the partners' voluntary decision to withdraw from the registration process.

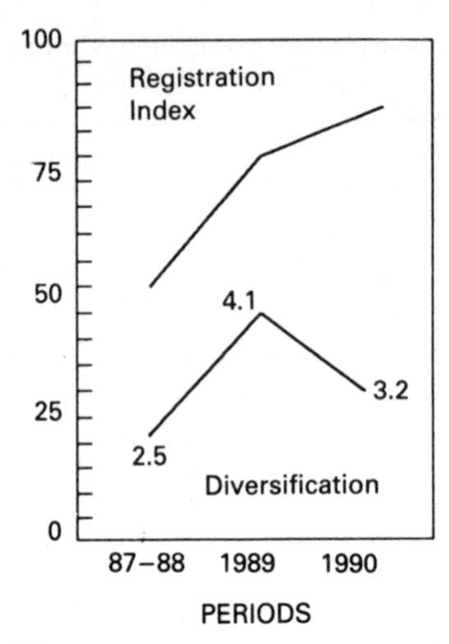

Figure 7.3 Joint Venture Registrations and Levels of Diversification in Poland, 1987–90.

The level of diversification in firms' activities is also measured in Figure 7.3: in 1987–8, firms declared their willingness to start operations in 2.5 areas; this nearly doubled in 1988–9, when the Polish joint venture law stipulated that any change in activities required official permission from the Foreign Investment Agency, a process which could take up to a month. Firms responded by registering under a variety of operational areas, thus avoiding delays and increasing flexibility. Somewhat surprisingly, in 1990, new firms abandoned this strategy: the diversification index fell back to 3.2, confirming a stabilisation of Poland's economic and legal conditions, as well as better knowledge on the part of foreign investors of potential investment areas.

FINANCIAL CHARACTERISTICS

An analysis of the development of joint ventures between Polish and Western firms would be incomplete without a survey of financial data, which cover 416 sample firms (or 50 per cent of the population) for the second half of 1989, and 564 firms (63.5 per cent) for the first six months of 1990.

Table 7.2 shows a significant increase in most average financial indicators for 1990, except for a decline in initial investment caused by a significant increase in credits that year.[3]

Table 7.2 Basic Financial Indicators of Joint Ventures in Poland, 1989–90 (millions of dollars)

	Aggregate indicators (for six month period)			*Average indicators (per firm) (for six month period)*		
	July–Dec. 1989	*January–June 1990*				
	*J-Vs**	*J-Vs**	*Total economy***	*1989*	*1990*	*Increase in %*
				(only joint ventures)		
Sales	191 826.9	782 624.1	35 639 473 000	461.1	1 387.6	301
Export	68 028.8	342 907.8	1 444 210 500	163.5	607.9	372
Income tax	1 057.7	1 843.9	3 489 578 900	2.5	3.3	129
Net profit	77 334.4	164 970.0	4 849 578 900	185.9	292.5	157
Credits (total)	55 528.8	391 666.7	–	133.5	694.4	520
Credits (in zl)	13 581.7	240 602.9	–	32.6	426.6	1308
Credits (in $)	41 947.1 (75.5%)	151 063.8 (38.7%)	–	100.8	267.8	266
Investment	–	–	–	336.2	245.0	(27)
Profit margin			.136	.401	.210	(52)
Return on investment			–	1.106	1.007	(9)
Return on assets			–	.792	.415	(52)
Export ratio			.041	.353	.444	(126)

Sources: * (Activity 1990); ** (Informacja 1990: 43).

A strong increase was recorded in the export index (372 per cent) over the six-month period, as well as in the export/sales ratio (0.44 per cent). This was most noticeable in the case of joint ventures, whose export/sales ratio was some ten times higher than that of the whole economy. An increase in exports in 1990, resulting in a $5 billion surplus, was caused by a fall in domestic demand due to the tight monetary policy of the Mazowiecki government.

The increase in the net profits of joint ventures in 1989–90 was 157 per cent, or half the increase in average sales. As a result, the net profit margin ratio (returns on sales) decreased by some 48 per cent.

In terms of employment, joint ventures with Western partners tend to be small, with an average labour force of seventy-three employees in 1989 and eighty-seven in 1990. The employees of joint ventures earned $496 in wages and salaries in 1989 ($42 monthly); their annual income increased to $988 in 1990 (or $82 a month). This represented a relative increase in total wages, but a sharp fall in real purchasing power in conditions of 280 per cent inflation.

Overall, joint ventures in Poland have been more profitable than domestic firms: the former's net profit margin (net income to sales), although falling from 40 per cent in 1980 to 21 per cent in 1990, remained two to three times higher than that of domestic firms. The rates of return on investment (110 per cent in 1989 and 100 per cent in 1990) and on assets (79 per cent and 41 per cent respectively) were very favourable, and indicated that joint ventures were employing their assets efficiently. The financial leverage was deemed positive as the returns on investment exceeded those on assets.

ORIGINS OF FOREIGN PARTNERS

For the purpose of this chapter, foreign investors in Poland have been divided into four categories. The first group consists of firms from the Federal Republic of Germany and West Berlin which, until October 1990, were treated separately; the second comprises joint ventures with US capital; the third is made up of joint ventures with capital from at least two foreign countries. The fourth and final group includes companies from all other countries. Groups one and two are the most homogeneous, as they consist of partners from a single country. Group three includes partners from two or more foreign countries (usually Germany, the USA and Sweden). The fourth group is the most heterogeneous, consisting of ten foreign countries in 1988, thirty-three in 1989, and forty-seven in 1990.

A comparison of the absolute numbers of foreign firms in 1986–90 shows a steady decrease in the presence of US firms and multinationals from at least two countries. Whilst, in 1986–8, they made up 24.9 per cent of all firms, in the last period (1989–90), their share declined to a modest 11.6 per cent. Over the same period, a fast growth was recorded in the numbers of German firms and 'others'. In 1989, 41 per cent of newly-registered foreign firms were of German origin.

In terms of the initial value of foreign investments, German and US firms recorded a modest growth over the period 1988–90, whilst 'others' saw a significant increase. An analysis of the average size of firms with foreign capital in the period 1988–90 reveals a relative growth for German firms, and a decline in the size of 'others'. US firms remained unchanged. The data also confirm that, in spite of some growth, firms with German capital remain the smallest in the total population.

CONCLUDING REMARKS

We observed that an increase in the absolute numbers of new joint ventures was accompanied by a lowering of the average foreign investment, which implied a rapid fall in the size of new firms. The reluctance of large multinationals to enter the Polish market was clearly visible, and surprisingly so in 1990, the transition year to a market economy. By comparison, both Hungary and Czechoslovakia were more successful in attracting large inflows of FDI. The absence of a mechanism for the full repatriation of profits abroad was an obvious drawback in Poland; by contrast, foreign investors repatriated $20 million from Hungary in 1990. Moreover, Poland does not offer either investment incentives or state support to large investors, unlike Czechoslovakia where the government is eager to extend tax holidays and state guarantees: the recent negotiations between Škoda, Volkswagen and Renault are cases in point. Large multinationals have also experienced difficulties at the negotiating stage, particularly in their search for suitable Polish partners. Former state-owned domestic enterprises appear to lack the necessary independence and financial confidence to take part in such negotiations. In this respect, the acceleration of the privatisation process might alleviate this problem.

In the medium term, FDI in Poland is likely to be a driving force behind a number of objectives, including privatisation, capital inflows, the introduction of modern technology and management techniques, and the supply of quality products to local markets. To date, however, none of those goals has been fulfilled, and the economic impact of operational inward investments has been marginal.

First, the privatisation of Poland's economy is still in its infancy. The total amount of subscribed initial capital – at $526 million – is equivalent to only 6 per cent of the book value of the economy's assets, 1.0 per cent of overall employment and 0.6 per cent of total income taxes. There is little doubt that the internationalisation of Polish firms to date has been a weak link in the plan for economic recovery.

The second objective of attracting foreign capital has remained largely unfulfilled. Of the total capital of $526 million subscribed to joint ventures, the foreign share amounts to only $282.9 million, or 53.9 per cent. Furthermore, only half of the firms which were granted registration licenses did start operations. Most foreign investors have restricted their financial commitments to the minimum amounts required by law.

Thirdly, according to the Foreign Investment Agency, the inflow of modern technology has been modest. The foreign partners to joint ventures are reported to be transferring dated equipment and keeping capital stocks artificially low.

Finally, FDI has failed to fulfil the expectation of supplying the local market with quality products. The majority of foreign firms are concentrating on unsophisticated activities in the food processing and textile industries. Exports remain a priority over the local market.

The present foreign investment legislation clearly requires urgent adaptation to the conditions of a market economy. The legislation dates back to December 1988, when it was targeted at a centrally planned economy.

Within the economic sphere the thrust of further liberalisation of the foreign investment law should be aimed at the following:

- to promote the full unrestricted transfer of profits abroad;
- to make the zloty externally convertible;
- to lift restrictions on taking credits with foreign banks;
- to introduce a maximum 30 per cent tax on the foreign partner's dividends;
- to eliminate the $50 000 minimum foreign investment requirement, which currently prevents members of the last generation of Polish émigrés from entering the Polish market.

Within the institutional sphere, the Foreign Investment Agency should be relieved of the task of licensing new companies. The Agency should become the government's principal instrument in attracting foreign capital to Poland.

Notes

1. See J. G. Scriven, 'Joint Ventures in Poland: a Socialist Approach to Foreign Investment Legislation', *Journal of World Trade Law*, No. 14, 1980.
2. The official data, issued by the Polish Investment Agency on 15 December 1990, show a sharp acceleration in the number of new registrations during the second half of 1990. Between 1 January and 1 December 1990, the Agency granted 1567 permits.
3. The growth in credits received in 1990 was in excess of 500 per cent.

8 Foreign Direct Investment in the Newly-Independent Republic of Slovenia: Experiences and Policy Options

Matija Rojec

INTRODUCTION

The future development of the newly-independent republic of Slovenia will depend crucially on her ability to establish long-term access to the West European markets, especially those of the European Communities. In the short and medium terms, it is anticipated that the former socialist countries will no longer face the high government-induced entry barriers on the West European markets, but instead that these barriers will be gradually reduced. However, they are likely to face increased *natural* entry barriers to those markets, particularly those originating from the determinants of national competitive advantage.[1] The former socialist countries will, in the medium term, remain subordinated to their Western counterparts, with regard to physical resources (which were abused and resulted in serious ecological problems); the lack of financial capital (particularly in the short term); infrastructural deficiencies; the lack of strong market segments and sophisticated buyers; weak supporting industries and inter-industry linkages; and deficiencies in the fields of management and labour relations.[2] According to Czinkota, Foreign Direct Investment (FDI) contains several of the aforementioned factors and determinants, particularly in the areas of management and resources, which explains why it is one of the main instruments for lowering natural entry barriers to Eastern Europe.[3]

THE RECENT EXPERIENCE OF FDI IN SLOVENIA

The new institutional set-up

The newly-independent republic of Slovenia has only recently begun to define her constitutional and legal structures. In the constitutional legislation covering the independence and sovereignty of the Republic (published in the Official Gazette of the Republic of Slovenia, January 1991), the Slovene Parliament decreed that the Foreign Investment Law passed by Yugoslavia in 1988 (Official Gazette of Yugoslavia, 77–88) would continue to apply in Slovenia.

Yugoslavia introduced legislation in 1967 allowing foreign firms to invest directly through joint ventures. In December 1988, a new Foreign Investment Law liberalised the investment environment with the objective of bringing it in line with international standards: foreign capital enjoyed full national treatment; most sectors of the economy were open to foreign firms operating through joint ventures;[4] foreign investors could engage in foreign trade activities, invest in banks, insurance companies and public sector enterprises, as well as purchase domestic enterprises either in whole or in part. Virtually all types of investments were open to foreign capital, including:

- equity joint ventures with local partners;
- wholly (100 per cent) foreign-owned companies;
- contractual joint ventures, involving investments in existing domestic companies based on a contract on capital investment;
- concessions: investments to exploit natural resources or public goods;
- 'build-operate-transfer' deals: these include financing, building and exploitation, for a set period of time, of industrial, infrastructural and other facilities.[5]

Four legal forms of equity joint venture and wholly foreign-owned company were made possible: a joint-stock company, a limited liability company, a limited partnership, and a general partnership or company with unlimited joint liability. In joint-stock and limited liability companies, the partners are liable up to the amount of their capital share in the company. In limited partnerships, some partners' liability includes their entire property (general partners), whilst others are liable up to the amount of capital invested. For general partnerships, all partners are liable with their property. Mixed banks can only be set up as joint-stock or limited liability companies.

The relations of the parties in a contractual joint venture are of a purely contractual nature. The foreign investment does not alter the character of the enterprise in which it was made: the enterprise does not become a joint venture company. The characteristic of this form of industrial cooperation is that the capital invested in a domestic enterprise does not entitle the foreign partner to ownership rights in that enterprise; instead, he acquires the right to participate in the enterprise's management and to share in its profits. The share of profits accruing to the foreign partner, and the terms of capital repatriation, are normally set out in the contract.

The gradual liberalisation of FDI legislation in Yugoslavia between 1967 and 1988[6] stayed, nonetheless, within the framework of specific, *sui generis* contractual joint ventures, the only permissible type of FDI at the time. The major change of attitude towards FDI, ushered in by the 1988 Law, reflected domestic developments (such as modest inflows of foreign capital, problems associated with foreign loans often used for financing 'white elephants', and heavy foreign indebtedness), rather than international trends (such as the ongoing liberalisation of FDI legislation in other countries). Essentially, the current FDI legislation of Slovenia is the outcome of the market-oriented economic reforms launched in 1989.

The increasing value and number of FDIs in the early 1990s

Notwithstanding the deep economic and political crises of the late 1980s, the liberalised FDI legislation, together with the market-oriented economic reforms, brought about a major increase in the value and numbers of annually-registered FDI projects.

Data from the Social Accounting Service show that, in 1985, twenty-six joint ventures were operational in Slovenia, of which the foreign investment share was estimated at $37 million. As Table 8.1 illustrates, over the next three years another eighteen joint venture contracts were signed (an average of 4.5 contracts per year) worth $34.4 million of foreign investment (or an average $8.6 million a year). In 1989, the inflow of new FDIs increased to 174, and their value reached $96.7 million. Figures for 1990 were still higher: 616 new FDIs worth $333.2 million of invested foreign capital.[7] Predictably, as the hostilities intensified in the first six months of 1991, the

Table 8.1 Foreign Direct Investment in Slovenia, 1985–91

Type of contract	*Number of registered contracts*	*Value of contracted foreign capital (millions of dollars)*
1985	5	3.7
1986	3	1.5
1987	6	11.4
1988(1)	4	17.8
1989(2) – Total	174	96.7
1. Equity Joint Ventures	135	30.1
2. Wholly foreign-owned	17	1.5
3. Contractual Joint Ventures	22	65.1
1990(3) – Total	616	333.2
1. Equity Joint Ventures	443	119.2
2. Wholly foreign-owned	85	8.9
3. Contractual Joint Ventures	88	205.0
1.1.–9.5. 1991(4) – Total	85	125.0
1. Equity Joint Ventures	51	17.0
2. Wholly foreign-owned	22	0.1
3. Contractual Joint Ventures	12	107.9

1. Only contractual joint ventures were allowed up to this date.
2. The original data were in DM; the exchange rate of 1$ = DM 1.68 was used.
3. The original data were in DM; the exchange rate of 1$ = DM 1.50 was used.
4. The original data were in DM; the exchange rate of 1$ = DM 1.70 was used.

Source: Centre for International Cooperation and Development, Ljubljana, data base.

number of new FDIs recorded a sharp downturn. However, since the end of the armed conflict in the late summer of 1991, some important new contracts have been concluded.[8]

By far, the greatest numbers of new FDI registrations in Slovenia between January 1989 and May 1991 consisted of equity joint ventures (71.9 per cent of all projects). They were almost exclusively in the form of limited liability companies; joint-stock companies were the exception.

As far as the value of invested foreign capital is concerned, contractual joint ventures dominate (with 68.1 per cent), while equity joint ventures are less important (30.0 per cent). Wholly foreign-owned subsidiaries are still of marginal importance, both in terms of numbers and capital invested.

A comparison of FDI in Slovenia and in the ex-Yugoslav Federation

Slovenia has always attracted the highest share of FDI in Yugoslavia; in 1985, of all *operational* joint ventures in Yugoslavia, nearly one-third were located in Slovenia. In the 1986–8 period (just before the adoption of the current Foreign Investment Law), foreign investment in Slovenia witnessed a temporary downturn, as Slovene companies (unlike their Yugoslav counterparts) favoured long-term industrial coproduction and leasing, in preference to joint ventures, as channels for the import of foreign equipment.

Since December 1988, Slovenia's share of Yugoslavia's total inward foreign investment has increased significantly, reaching a level on a par with her share in Yugoslavia's total foreign trade (see Table 8.2). This was due mostly to Slovenia's hosting of a much higher share of *contractual* joint ventures than the other republics of the ex-Yugoslav federation. In this context, *contractual* joint ventures amount to quasi credit arrangements (for duty-free imports of machinery and equipment), which enable foreign investors to minimise risk. Another characteristic of FDI in Slovenia is the high profile of equity joint ventures and wholly foreign-owned subsidiaries established with the legal minimum amount of initial capital.[9]

Slovenia, in terms of inward FDI, has fared on a par with some of the other ex-socialist countries of Eastern Europe. From January 1988 to July 1990, the number of equity joint ventures increased from twenty-three to 1830 in the Soviet Union; from 102 to 1600 in Hungary; from thirteen to 1550 in Poland; from seven to sixty in Czechoslovakia; and from nine to thirty in Bulgaria. In the Soviet Union, the foreign capital invested as of March 1990 was estimated at $1.9 billion, an amount equivalent to the stock of inward direct investment in Sweden, Denmark or South Korea (see Chapter 5 for details). In Hungary, it amounted to $263 million (about the same as the FDI stock in Sri Lanka, Paraguay or Tanzania,[10] and in Poland to $187 million.[11]

Origin and sectoral distribution of investments

The distribution of foreign investors by county of origin has remained more or less unchanged over the past two decades. By far the greatest

Table 8.2 Slovenia's Share of FDI in the Yugoslav Federation, 1968–91 (*percentage*)

Type of contract	*Number of registered contracts*	*Value of contracted foreign capital*
1968–85[1]	33.1	20.3
1985	19.2	16.4
1986	11.1	2.5
1987	15.8	5.3
1988	15.4	25.6
1989 – Total	30.1	28.5
1. Equity Joint Ventures	34.6	20.7
2. Wholly foreign-owned	17.7	7.9
3. Contractual Joint Ventures	23.9	37.3
1990 – Total	20.8	28.2
a) By type		
1. Equity Joint Ventures	21.9	23.9
2. Wholly foreign-owned	15.0	4.5
3. Contractual Joint Ventures	23.8	38.4
b) By quarter of year		
1st quarter	22.1	8.4
2nd quarter	23.0	36.7
3rd quarter	22.5	20.9
4th quarter	16.6	29.3
1.1.–9.5. 1991 – Total	19.3	60.3
1. Equity Joint Ventures	24.4	25.6
2. Wholly foreign-owned	13.7	0.7
3. Contractual Joint Ventures	17.1	86.8

[1] Data for the 1968–85 period relate to joint ventures operational in 1985. Other data relate to new FDIs for each year.

Sources:

a) Social Accountancy Service of Slovenia;
b) Federal Secretariat for Foreign Economic Relations;
c) Centre for International Cooperation and Development, Ljubljana, data base.

Table 8.3 Countries of Origin of Foreign Investors in Slovenia (1 January 1989–9 May 1991[1])

Countries of origin	*Number of registered contracts*	*Percentage share*	*Value of contracted foreign capital* (millions of dollars)	*Percentage share*
Germany	174	19.9	227.9	41.1
Austria	245	28.0	158.1	28.5
Italy	291	33.3	98.9	17.8
Australia	4	0.5	24.0	4.3
France	3	0.3	21.5	3.9
USA	18	2.1	4.6	0.8
Switzerland	39	4.5	3.7	0.7
Liechtenstein	8	0.9	3.5	0.6
Netherlands	19	2.2	1.2	0.2
Others	77	8.8	11.5	2.1
EC – Total	507	57.9	350.3	63.1
EFTA – Total	301	34.4	166.0	29.9
Total	875	100.0	554.9	100.0

[1] Only those investments in newly established FDIs are taken into account; additional capital injections in existing FDI projects are excluded.

Source: Centre for International Cooperation and Development, Ljubljana, data base.

number of investments originate from Germany (19.9 per cent of new FDI projects, and 41.1 per cent of the foreign capital invested between January 1989 and May 1991), Austria (28.0 per cent, and 28.5 per cent respectively), and Italy (33.3 per cent, and 17.8 per cent respectively). In fact, the European Communities and Austria are the dominant sources of FDI in Slovenia. US companies accounted for less than 1 per cent of FDI inflows in the aforementioned period (see Table 8.3). Three sets of factors explain this distribution.

a) The political crises, which engulfed Slovenia in the early 1990s, were a lesser impediment to companies from neighbouring countries, which had traditionally enjoyed strong trading links with the republic.

b) Strong economic ties with the European Communities made it easier for trading partners to upgrade their cooperation to direct investment.
c) The Slovene *gastarbeiter* in Germany and Austria, and the subsidiaries of Slovene companies in Germany, Austria and Italy, which make up an important section of foreign investors in Slovenia, are formally registered as foreign investors from those countries.

The largest FDI projects, in terms of invested foreign capital, are concentrated in manufacturing, but the majority of newly registered investments has been channelled to the business service and trade sectors. FDI in services is a new phenomenon in Slovenia, and should enrich the supply side in the process of economic restructuring. The importance of FDI in services, however, should not be overstated. First, investment in services and trade often acts as a supporting activity for the production requirements of equity joint ventures, subsidiaries or even parent companies. Secondly, many inward investments have yet to start operations, or are extremely modest in scope and scale. They were established, first and foremost, on a 'just in case' basis, to take advantage of one-off business opportunities.

New FDI projects tend to cover a greater range of activities. This reflects the foreign investor's lack of knowledge of the Slovene market, as well as the unpredictability of domestic conditions. A more diversified registration clearly gives the foreign investor greater flexibility[12] and the ability to switch, at short notice, to more profitable activities.[13]

The upsurge in new contracts has not been accompanied by a parallel increase in their value. As Table 8.4 illustrates, in 53.4 per cent of FDI projects registered between January 1989 and May 1991, the foreign stake was below DM5000, in only 4.3 per cent of cases was the foreign investment in excess of DM5 million. Notwithstanding the new legislation, *contractual* joint ventures[14] – for so long the object of criticism in foreign business circles – continue to absorb the largest inflows of FDI.

Several factors account for this trend: first, contractual joint ventures are used as quasi credit arrangements, allowing firms customs-free entry into Slovenia of capitalised assets (foreign machinery, equipment and know-how) in lieu of capital investments. Under this arrangement, the share of profits accruing to the foreign partner and his right to transfer back his capital are set out in the contract and

Table 8.4 Distribution of FDI Projects According to the Value of Contracted Foreign Capital (January 1989–May 1991)

Foreign Investment (DM 1000)	*Number of contracts*	*Percentage Share*
Up to 5	467	53.4
6 to 10	46	5.3
11 to 20	52	5.9
21 to 50	78	8.9
51 to 100	42	4.8
101 to 200	32	3.7
201 to 500	34	3.9
501 to 1000	27	3.1
1001 to 2000	26	3.0
2001 to 5000	25	2.9
in excess of 5001	38	4.3
Unknown	8	0.9
Total	875	100.0

Sources:
Centre for International Cooperation and Development, Ljubljana, data base.

normally backed by a Slovene bank guarantee, thus minimising risk. This type of FDI will remain relevant as long as the domestic economic and political climate continues to be unstable. Secondly, the capital in a *contractual* joint venture need not be invested in full in the year of registration, thus enabling the partners to spread the capital inflows over the life of the project. Conversely, in *equity* joint ventures and wholly foreign-owned subsidiaries, the foreign investment legislation stipulates that the entirety of the subscribed capital be paid in on registration. Given Slovenia's high rates of inflation, the start-up capital invested by foreign partners is often barely above the legal minimum.[15] This suggests that the data on FDI in equity joint ventures and foreign-owned subsidiaries at the time of registration underestimate the size of the projects. Thirdly, just under two-thirds of foreign investors in *equity* joint ventures, and three-fourths in wholly foreign-owned subsidiaries are natural persons. In contrast, over 80 per cent of *contractual* joint ventures have been entered into by legal entities (companies). This distinction is significant in that the investments of natural persons tend to be much smaller than those of companies. Finally, there is a preponderance of *equity* joint ventures and foreign-owned subsidiaries in the service sector, where the average size of the investment is of rule quite small.

The latest Foreign Investment Law (referred to above) clearly stimulated Slovenes residing abroad to invest in Slovenia, where they make up, as foreign investors, just under 20 per cent of FDI projects initiated since 1988. In addition, Slovene expatriates have transferred considerable amounts of private capital back into the republic and set up private businesses as 'domestic' investors.

A third category of foreign investors in Slovenia consists of foreign subsidiaries of Slovene companies. It is estimated that one third of FDI projects are, directly or indirectly, of 'Slovene origin'.

SLOVENIA AS A PROSPECTIVE LOCATION FOR FOREIGN INVESTMENT

In spite of the 'take off' of FDI in Slovenia at the turn of the decade, the paucity of large investments raises question marks over future developments. Foreign investors seem intent on penetrating the Slovene market in order to establish a presence, rather than actively exploit market opportunities. Large multinationals are still avoiding Slovenia, which by international risk assessment criteria, is a high-risk location.

According to Dunning in Chapter 2, three possible models of development are available to the ex-socialist countries of Central and Eastern Europe in the field of FDI, depending on the pattern and pace of restructuring in individual countries. These include the *developing country model*, the *reconstruction model*, and the *systemic model*. The reconstruction model points to the most widespread involvement of FDI, as the present situation in Eastern Europe is comparable to the post-war reconstruction period in Germany and Japan. In the words of Dunning, East Germany is in fact already following the course of the reconstruction model, with Hungary and Czechoslovakia one or two steps behind. Slovenia would probably fall within this category, whilst Albania, Bulgaria and Romania would be more likely to fit into the developing country model. The systemic model depends on the speed and extent to which each country introduces its programme of privatisation. This systemic change can be seen as a 'passport' for inward foreign direct investment, and in this context is relevant for all ex-socialist countries.

Thus, in spite of similarities in their systemic background, the potential for attracting FDI will vary between countries, and depend on a number of factors: the speed and extent of systemic changes, the location of specific advantages, infrastructural capacities, the development of human capital (managerial, marketing and organisational expertise), and levels of political and economic stability. In general, the role which foreign investors might play in future industrial restructuring will hinge on the specific competitive and innovative advantage of each host East European country.

The recognition by the European Communities of Slovene independence has removed a major obstacle to inward foreign investment. It is anticipated that Slovenia will no longer be perceived as a high-risk investment location. Assuming further that her economic situation stabilises in the medium term, Slovenia's potential for attracting foreign investment would in principle depend on the government's success, in the words of Dunning, in 'reshaping the attitudes to work and wealth creation; in redesigning the business and legal framework, especially with respect to property rights and contractual relationships; in setting up a market system; and in introducing macro-economic policies, which encourage domestic savings, but accept the discipline of currency convertibility and an open trading system'.[16] First and foremost, the *type* of inward foreign investment will be crucially important. Until now, FDI in Slovenia has been predominantly oriented to the local, that is the ex-Yugoslav, market. If Slovenia moves towards a common market or free trade area with some of the other ex-Yugoslav republics, it is likely that *local market-oriented* FDI will prevail. The continued political uncertainty in Croatia and war in Bosnia should persuade foreign investors that Slovenia is a minimum risk location, from where to supply the other republics of the ex-Yugoslav federation. In the words of *Business International*: 'Foreign investors will find out that Slovenia and Croatia are the most developed republics, while Serbia and the southern republics lag somewhat behind. . . . The acquisitions of companies are especially attractive in Slovenia and, to a lesser degree, in Croatia'.[17] As tariff and non-tariff barriers are by far the most compelling inducement for local market-oriented FDI, the other republics would be unlikely to reduce Slovenia's competitive advantage through special investment incentives.

In Slovenia, as in other ex-socialist countries, the pace of privatisation and of systemic changes will, to a large extent, determine the future growth of FDI,[18] particularly that of *export-oriented* FDI, for as long as the local market continues to be protected from foreign competition.

Slovenia, with a market of only two million, is unlikely to attract large inflows of *local market*-oriented FDI unless she gains preferential access to some of the other ex-Yugoslav republics, as few foreign investors could justify establishing production for such a limited market. The alternative is to compete predominantly for *export-oriented* FDI, as an export base for the ex-COMECON countries, or the OECD countries themselves, where competition from other investment locations would be extremely high.

The opening up of the East European market has prompted Western companies to seek new locations, from which to supply that market. Some of these firms have been quick to explore the new possibilities which the Central European countries of Czechoslovakia, Hungary, Poland and the republics of the ex-Yugoslav federation offer, particularly as locations from where to supply the large Russian market, without encountering the problems of setting up production in Russia itself. This was a major motivation behind the acquisitions of Škoda by Volkswagen, and of Galenika in Serbia by the US company ICN.[19]

Another motive of foreign investors is to set up export bases in Central Europe to service Western markets, with the joint objectives of reducing production costs and acquiring the market share of the enterprises taken over.

In Slovenia, the issue of lower production costs is dominated by labour costs, which although higher than elsewhere in ex-socialist Central Europe, are compensated for by higher productivity and more dynamic entrepreneurship. The proximity of Slovenia to the more demanding Austrian, Italian and German markets, as well as a history of intensive business relations with Western companies, have given Slovene companies a head-start over firms from the other ex-socialist countries.

The other objective – the takeover of East European companies with subsidiaries and representative offices in the West – serves the dual purpose of 'purchasing' a new market share, and of protecting existing Western market segments from East European competitors. According to *Business International*, the principal motive of the Austrian firm, Brigl & Bergmeister, in acquiring a majority stake in the Vevče Paper Mill, near Ljubljana, was the Slovene firm's market shares in Germany and Italy.[20]

This last motive raises the question of firm-specific inducements for inward foreign investment. In a number of large multinationals, a transformation is taking place from a conglomerate to a more specialised type of activities and corporate structure. This type of multinational invests abroad *only* if the investment fits into the development strategy (namely, if suitable partners can be found). On these grounds, we might conclude that foreign investors in Slovenia would be searching for companies with (a) technological advantages, (b) R & D capabilities, (c) an established market share, and (d) a will among staff to become market leaders. Some Slovene companies possess firm-specific advantages: for instance, products which have made significant inroads into foreign markets. Therefore we can expect Slovenia to attract a greater share of foreign investment from European rather than US-based multinationals, and from small and medium-sized rather than large firms.[21] The available data on FDI in Slovenia from early 1989 confirm this observation.

SOME POLICY OPTIONS: INWARD FDI AND PRIVATISATION

Although Slovenia is going through a transition period, in which both the economic and political situations are rather fluid, she needs to spell out a clear strategy towards FDI. Potential investors will need to know Slovenia's policy objectives *vis-à-vis* FDI, and the instrument to achieve them.

The major long-term objective behind inward FDI is the faster development and restructuring of the economy. Inflows of additional foreign capital are just one aspect of the potential development contribution of inward FDI. Others include the restructuring of the economy, access to modern technology, management and marketing skills, and integration into international production processes.

On gaining independence from Yugoslavia, Slovenia took over the existing Yugoslav Foreign Investment Law, and major changes are not expected in the immediate future. When Slovenia does draft her own FDI law, it is anticipated that it will be more accommodating to Slovene characteristics. The experience of other host countries suggests that Slovenia's legal framework for foreign investment should include the following elements: first, the Government should have the discretion to stimulate foreign investment in areas it considers crucial to national economic interests. This would require accompanying legislation on antitrust cases, environment protection and the role of the state in some sectors. Secondly, all FDI projects, bar those specifically referred to in the Foreign Investment Law, should be allowed to enter the country; thirdly, investment incentives should not, in principle, discriminate between legal entities with or without foreign equity participation. Other legislation pertinent to foreign investors (except for the Foreign Investment Law itself) should not contain specific references to entities with *foreign* equity.

The administrative and organisational framework will be another critical determinant for the future development of FDI in Slovenia, including approval and registration procedures for foreign investments, the qualifying procedure for investment incentives, and the setting up of government bodies with the task of coordinating with foreign investors. Selectivity should be paramount in approving inward FDI projects: the competent government bodies should not waste time with small or marginal projects, but concentrate instead on larger investments and private acquisitions of socially-owned companies.

From an organisational viewpoint, a coordinated and centralised approach seems most appropriate. This would imply a single governmental department or agency, whose task would be to coordinate with other interested departments. These contacts could either be on an *ad hoc* basis, or in the form of a permanent commission with representatives from all interested departments. Under this system, a coordinating body would enable the foreign investor to conduct most administrative procedures in one location.[22]

The Slovene Government will need to formulate a consistent long-term economic policy for inward FDI by combining investment incentives and performance requirements. If in future, as suggested above, Slovenia is to encourage *export-oriented* FDI, this will require an aggressive investment incentive policy to counter the growing competition from other countries as well as from the other ex-Yugoslav republics. In practice, this policy should put the accent on factor (especially capital/financial) incentives, and give priority to foreign investments (as discussed above). It should be based further on the equal treatment of foreign and domestic investors (particularly with regard to investment incentives), and aim at the integration of FDI incentives in the country's overall investment and development strategy.

These objectives argue strongly for an investment incentive policy based on the individualised treatment of each substantial FDI project; the provision of 'incentive packages' tailor-made for individual projects; and discretion in granting 'extraordinary' incentives to priority investments. This approach would reduce the volume and number of incentives and increase their efficiency; ensure that individual investors have access to the most relevant incentives; facilitate the monitoring of incentive schemes in case corrective measures are needed; and encourage the competent government bodies to tender internationally for investment projects, which they consider to be of particular interest.[23]

Whilst greenfield investments are principally governed by the Foreign Investment Legislation, for foreign takeovers and mergers, the antitrust legislation is equally important. Moreover, when socially-owned Slovene companies become the target of foreign acquisitions, the law on privatisation becomes paramount. Clearly, FDI cannot be separated from privatisation wherever the domestic partner is a socially-owned company. The types of FDI in question include: first, the partial or total acquisition of a socially-owned company; second, the recapitalisation of a socially-owned company; and third, a joint venture involving a socially-owned company. In value terms, it is anticipated that the bulk of future FDI in Slovenia will involve an element of privatisation, and that indirect acquisitions – the setting up of joint ventures with former socially-owned companies – will continue to prevail.

Finally, in their quest to stimulate the interest of foreign investors in domestic companies, the priorities of the Slovene authorities should be as follows:

- to stimulate the acquisitions of local companies which broadly pursue the desired restructuring of the economy;
- to impart on foreign investors the importance of modernising and restructuring the acquired companies, with a view to creating new jobs;
- and to speed up the role of FDI in the privatisation process through foreign debt-equity swaps.

Notes

1. A. M. Rugman and A. Verbeke, *Corporate Strategy after the Free Trade Agreement and Europe 1992*, Ontario Centre for International Business, Working Paper No. 27, March 1990, p. 11.
2. For details, see M. E. Porter, *The Competitive Advantage of Nations* (New York: The Free Press, 1990).
3. M. Czinkota, 'The EC, 1992 and Eastern Europe: Effects of Integration vs. Disintegration', *Columbia Journal of World Business*, Vol. 26, No. 1, 1991.
4. Wholly foreign-owned companies are not allowed in the manufacturing

and distribution of armaments and military equipment, rail and air transport, communications and telecommunications, insurance, publishing and the mass media.

5. For details of Slovenia's FDI legislation, see *Investing in Slovenia*, Centre for International Cooperation and Development, Ljubljana, 1990.
6. In 1985, the 49 per cent ceiling on the foreign share in joint ventures was abolished.
7. The original data are in Deutschemarks: 499.8 million.
8. For example, the acquisition of the Ljubljana Tobacco Factory by Reemtsma (Germany) and Seita (France) was estimated at DM 100 million.
9. The minimum initial capital to establish a new company is 8000 Slovene Tolars (SLT), or approximately DM200, for limited liability companies, and SLT 55 000 (approximately DM1400) for joint-stock companies.
10. More up to date data on joint ventures in Hungary are available in David Young's chapter in this book.
11. United Nations Economic Commission for Europe data, quoted in J. H. Dunning, 'The Prospects for Foreign Direct Investment in Eastern Europe', Chapter 2 in this book.
12. For example, a company not registered for the purpose of foreign trade, is not permitted to conduct foreign trade activities. An additional registration may be lengthy.
13. This concurs with the findings of Maecki on FDI in Poland. See M. Maecki, *The Development of Foreign Enterprises' Activities in Poland* (1976–85), World Economy Research Institute, Working Paper No. 10, Warsaw, 1987.
14. The average foreign investment of *contractual* joint ventures established in the period January 1989 – May 1991 was DM4 921 312. The respective foreign share in *equity* joint ventures was DM410 652, and that in wholly foreign-owned entities DM129 839.
15. Prior to March 1992 the legal minimum was set at SLT8000 (approximately DM160). On 27 March 1992 it was raised to SLT100 000 (DM2000) for newly-established limited liability companies, and SLT1 million (DM20 000) for joint-stock companies.
16. See Dunning, Chapter 2 of this book.
17. Business International, *Joint Ventures, Acquisitions and Privatization in Eastern Europe and the USSR: A Practical Guide to Investment*, Report No. 2105, London, 1991.
18. See for example David Young's chapter in this book on Hungary.
19. *Business International*, op. cit., p. 7.
20. Ibid., p. 9.
21. Quoted from K. M. Zapp addressing a Seminar on Methods and Techniques of Privatisation at the Centre for International Cooperation and Development, Ljubljana, on 22 June 1990.
22. For details, see S. E. Guisinger *et al.*, *Investment Incentives and Performance Requirements* (New York: Praeger, 1985).
23. For details, see OECD, *International Investment and Multinational Enterprises – Investment Incentives and Disincentives: The Effects on International Direct Investment* (Paris, 1989).

9 Joint Venture Laws in Eastern Europe: A Comparative Assessment

Wladyslaw Jermakowicz and
Cecelia Drazek

INTRODUCTION

The velocity of business activity in Central and Eastern Europe has greatly increased since the political changes of 1989–90. Countries which previously subscribed to centrally planned economies have enacted new legislation designed to open their economies to market forces. They have 'liberalised' their policy towards private economic activity for a number of reasons. First, the ideological obstacles against private and Western-owned property in socialist economies have been gradually removed. Second, these heavily indebted countries have developed a growing awareness of the potential benefits of foreign direct investment. The emerging business class of Central Europe is increasingly willing to enter into joint ventures with Western partners in order to gain access to the much-needed capital and expertise.

The number of joint ventures has increased significantly since 1989. The most recent data point to three significant periods: April 1990, December 1990 and July 1991, and are summarised in Table 9.1.

In absolute numbers, Hungary, the ex-Soviet Union and Poland occupy the leading positions; in relative terms (according to the number of joint ventures per million of population), the order is different, with Hungary ranked first, Poland second and Czechoslovakia third.

We consider, next, whether these numbers alone reflect the real level of attractiveness of a country's legal and economic conditions. On their own, the aforementioned figures do not seem to account for the advancement of market principles in these economies. For instance, Albania enacted its first joint venture law on 31 July 1990, but does not have any record of joint venture activity. Bulgaria ranks well

Table 9.1 Number of Joint Ventures Registered in Central and Eastern Europe, as of 15 April 1990, 4 December 1990 and 1 July 1991

Country	*Total Number of Joint Ventures*			*Joint Ventures with US Partners*			*Population (in millions)*	*Number of Joint Ventures per million of population*		
	April 1990	*Dec. 1990*	*July 1991*	*April 1990*	*Dec. 1990*	*July 1991*		*April 1990*	*Dec. 1990*	*July 1991*
Soviet Union	1400	2900	3700	140	230	–	289.0	4.8	10.3	12.8
Poland	866	1903	2500	60	149	177	38.2	22.7	49.8	65.4
Hungary	600	2800	4500	14	200	200	10.6	56.6	264.1	424.5
Bulgaria	60	60	75	10	10	13	9.0	6.6	6.6	8.3
Czechoslovakia	32	600	1000	1	35	40	15.6	2.0	38.5	64.1
Romania	5	587	1000	1	53	55	23.2	0.2	25.3	43.1

Source: United States Department of Commerce.

behind other East European countries in joint venture activity, due partly to the late introduction of joint venture legislation, and its previous government's negative attitude towards foreign investors. Surprisingly, the pace of joint venture activity in Romania accelerated in the second half of 1990.

A comparison of 'verbal declarations' to assess the receptiveness of a host country to foreign investment has proved to be of little assistance. Each country points to different aspects of its joint venture law to emphasise that its treatment of FDI is more liberal than that of its neighbours. The Hungarians stress the availability of real estate to foreign workers and the unrestricted transfer of profits. Until recently, Poland emphasised its six-year tax holidays and investment guarantees. Czechoslovakia, Bulgaria and the Czech and Slovak Republics, Bulgaria and the Commonwealth of Independent States stress the attraction of their low tax regimes. Thus, an objective criterion of measurement of the attractiveness of different countries' joint venture laws is still lacking. In this chapter, we present a comparative analysis of the investment opportunities in six East European countries. The analysis rests solely on a comparison of the newly adopted joint venture laws; it is of a purely formal character, as it does not take into account the informal conditions which prevail in each country. This approach, which we believe represents an important first step in measuring the attractiveness of opportunities in the emerging economies of Eastern Europe, rests on the correlation of two sets of measures: Makarov's classification,[1] which describes the evolutionary process of liberalisation in business legislation, and the authors' own criteria, referred to as 'descriptors', which exhibit specific aspects of legal conditions.

LEVELS OF FORMAL LIBERALISATION

The *first level* of liberalisation consists of granting limited autonomy to joint ventures, which are permitted mostly in the manufacturing sector, with severe restrictions on the foreign partner's participation in management. Chairmanship positions on supervisory and executive boards are restricted to nationals from the host countries. Profit-sharing is under strict state control, and the repatriation of profit is usually limited to a percentage of foreign currency earnings. The host country does not provide any protection against expropriation or nationalisation.

The *second level* is characterised by the adoption of more liberal legislation, which increases the autonomy of joint ventures and adds incentives for their development, whilst preserving specific conditions for their functioning. At this level, the foreign partner, whose share cannot exceed 49 per cent, is allowed to occupy one of the top management positions. Investment is allowed outside the manufacturing sector, whilst special incentives and tax relief are available for joint ventures operating in priority sectors. Additional concessions are granted for export activities, and registration procedures are simplified. Some countries introduce limited guarantees against the expropriation of foreign investments.

The *third level* liberalises the legislation further, by permitting the formation of joint ventures with foreign participation in excess of 50 per cent but still short of full ownership. The repatriation of profits arising from international trade is guaranteed by law. Additionally, firms have the right to transfer abroad part of the surplus from their trade in domestic currencies. Joint ventures can operate in all spheres of the economy, with some limitations in the military sector. Firms enjoy freedom in international trade, but export and import licences are still required. *Domestic* laws guarantee protection against expropriation and nationalisation.

The *fourth level* is that of the most liberal legislation, which permits 100 per cent foreign participation, thus 'transforming' joint ventures into wholly foreign-owned subsidiaries. Equal rights are granted to both local and joint legal entities, and full repatriation of profits is guaranteed by law. Joint ventures operate in all spheres of the economy without any restrictions, and enjoy full freedom in international trade: export or import permits are no longer required. International laws guarantee protection against nationalisation and expropriation. At this level of liberalisation, joint venture firms in Eastern Europe enjoy the same rights as those in the developed Western economies.

METHODOLOGY

To enhance the understanding of the specific characteristics which can make or break newly-established businesses, the authors developed a system of indicators, which measure the direction and attractiveness of legal changes in Eastern Europe. Each of the

Table 9.2 Descriptors used in the Measurement of Legal Liberalisation

	Number of Responses	*Weight Assigned*
Possibilities of Profit Repatriation	51	4.3
Maximum Share of Foreign Partner's Ownership	46	3.1
Possibility of Owning Real Property	35	4.2
Level of Income Taxes	31	3.6
Length of Tax Holidays	27	3.7
Income Tax on Foreign Partner's Dividends	26	2.2
Length of Repatriation Procedure	19	3.1
Nationality Requirements for Managerial Positions	17	2.8
Economic Choice Measured by the Opportunities to Invest in Different Spheres of the Economy	17	2.3
State Guarantee of Compensation for Expropriation	10	2.7
Import Duty Exemptions	3	1.3
Total	282	33.3

aforementioned levels of formal legislative liberalisation is identified through the application of eleven parallel descriptors.

The descriptors were selected on the basis of responses to a questionnaire, which was sent to 823 members of the Polish–American Economic Forum, an organisation consisting of people of Polish extraction living in America. The respondents were asked to identify five areas of joint venture legislation which influenced their consideration of Eastern Europe as an investment area: 172 respondents (or 20.7 per cent of the sample) identified more than thirty different areas. For the purpose of this research, the eleven most frequently mentioned responses were selected as descriptors.

In the second stage of the research, conducted between July and December 1990, members of the Forum were asked to assign a relative weight to each of the descriptors on a 0 (irrelevant) to 5 (very important) point scale: 156 responses (18.9 per cent of the sample) were received. The findings are summarised in Table 9.2.

A comparison of numbers of responses and weightings allocated to each of the descriptors shows slight differences. The single highest group of respondents (fifty-one) thought that profit repatriation (with a weighting of 4.3 points) was most important; forty-six respondents listed the majority share of the equity (although this only carried a weight of 3.1). The possibility of owning real property was most important to thirty-five respondents and given a weight of 4.2.

Each descriptor pertaining to the first level of liberalisation was assigned one point. At the other end of the spectrum, fourth level descriptors were allocated four points. Additionally, for each descriptor, a different weight varying from 1.3 to 4.3 was assigned. The degree of formal legislative liberalisation (DFLL) is made up of the sum of specific descriptors for each country. Thus, if a host country's law is fully liberalised, the total number of points will be 133.3 (eleven descriptors times four points, and times the weight of each descriptor, totalling 133.3 points). As the legislation moves from a lower to a higher level, the point value of each descriptor increases, as does the indicator of DFLL.

The DFLL is the sum of the points for each descriptor. The descriptors, point values and weightings are discussed in Table 9.3.

A COMPARISON OF JOINT VENTURE LAWS

What follows is a comparison of the most pertinent legal acts regulating foreign investment activities in Eastern Europe: the Law on Foreign Investment of 23 December 1988 (amended on 28 December 1989) in Poland;[2] the Law on Corporations with Foreign Capital Participation of 14 June 1991, and Act XXIV of 1988 on Investments of Foreigners in Hungary;[3] Decree 56 on Economic Activity in Bulgaria;[4] Joint Venture Code No. 173 in Czechoslovakia;[5] the Act on Enterprises with Foreign Property Participation (Amendment, 19 April 1990) in Czechoslovakia;[6] Decree No. 1074[7] and Decree No. 1405 of the USSR Council of Ministers;[8] in Russia, Osnovy Zakonodatiel' stava ob investicionnoj diejatiel' nosti v CCCR, of 11 December 1990;[9] and Laws 26/1990 and 31/1990, governing Commercial Companies in Romania.

Each country's legislation is discussed in each descriptor area. Each analysis starts with a description of the most liberal legal provisions and ends with the most restrictive ones. The criterion for identification of the laws' liberality is measured in accordance with the scale developed in Table 9.4. In each case, points for the levels of each law's liberalisation are determined.

The *repatriation of profits* is considered to be the most important aspect of a host government's legislation. Profit repatriation is guaranteed in Hungary. A joint venture company can sell its output for Hungarian forints; the foreign partner's share of profits may be converted into hard currency and repatriated without any special permits. The company's only obligation is to obtain a bank certificate, confirming that it has sufficient funds to cover the amount to be repatriated in hard currency. It is assumed, however, that profit repatriation by a joint venture takes place only at year end, when the company declares its annual profits and/or dividends, although the law is vague on this point (four points).

Poland stipulated that the amounts of foreign currency transferred abroad in a given year by a foreign investor could exceed by 15 per cent the surplus of exports over imports in convertible currencies in the preceding accounting year. According to the Law of 14 June 1991, foreign investors have the right to transfer abroad 100 per cent of the company's post-tax profits as of 1 January 1992 (three points for 1990 and four points for 1991).

In Czechoslovakia, the law on joint ventures implicitly states that joint ventures earn their hard currency through exports, and no legal provisions exist for repatriating local currency earnings. In other words, Czechoslovak law permits the repatriation of profits only to the extent of hard currency earnings (two points). Because repatriation of local currency profits is not addressed in the amendments of the Law of 19 April 1990, the repatriation of local currency profits is possible only if there is 'sufficient availability of foreign exchange' (two points).

In Romania, according to the 1990 Law (confirmed in the legislation of 29 March 1991), foreign investors are entitled to transfer abroad between 8 and 15 per cent of domestic profits, in addition to export profits. Domestic profits can be converted into Western currencies at exchange rates set by the Romanian Bank for Foreign Trade, or other authorised banks (1990a – one point; 1990b – three points).

According to Bulgarian law, a foreign entity may remit abroad the profits earned in foreign exchange and the original foreign currency investment. A permit from the National Bank is required for each transfer of domestic or export profits (two points).

The *foreign partner's maximum share of ownership* varies between countries. In Hungary and Poland, a foreign firm may establish a fully-owned subsidiary (four points). That right was granted to Romanian joint ventures in the second half of 1990 (1990a – two points; 1990b – four points).

Bulgarian regulations allow the foreign investor to hold an ownership interest up to a maximum of 99 per cent (three points). Similarly, in Czechoslovakia, the joint venture Code (173/1988)

Table 9.3 Degrees of Legal Liberalisation and Descriptors

Degrees of Liberalisation	*First Degree (1 point)*	*Second Degree (2 points)*	*Third Degree (3 points)*	*Fourth Degree (4 points)*
Descriptors				
Repatriation of Profits (4.3 points)	Law permits repatriation of partial foreign currency earnings	Law permits repatriation of profits to the extent of hard currency earnings	Law permits repatriation of profits above the hard currency earnings	Law permits full repatriation of profits
Foreign Partner's Share (3.1 points)	Less than 30% foreign share allowed	31–49% foreign share allowed	50–99% foreign share allowed	100% foreign share allowed
Real Property Ownership (4.2 points)	J-V cannot own any real property	J-V needs permit for real estate acquisition	Only J-V with majority of foreign ownership needs government permit	J-V can acquire any real property
Lowest Income Taxes Paid (3.6 points)	Between 41% and 50%	Between 31% and 40%	Between 21% and 30%	20% and less
Maximum length of Tax Holidays (3.7 points)	No Tax Holidays	Between one and two years	Between three and five years	More than five years
Income Tax on Dividends (2.2 points)	21% and more	Between 11% and 20%	Between 1% and 10%	No taxes on dividends

Registration Procedure (3.1 points)	Multi-stage process requiring consent of more than one government institution	All J-V registrations require consent of a government institution	Only majority foreign owned firms require government permit	Free registration
Nationality Requirements (2.8 points)	Only domestic persons can occupy top management positions	Foreigners can either be CEO or Chairman of the Supervisory Board	Both positions of CEO and Chairman of Supervisory Board can be occupied by foreigners	Full freedom to appoint foreigners to top positions
Investment Opportunities (Choice) (2.3 points)	Investment only in manufacturing sector	Investment in manufacturing and service sectors. Export-import licences required.	Investment in all sectors is possible with the exclusion of defence. No separate export-import permits required.	Investment in all sectors without restrictions
Compensation Guarantees for Expropriation (2.7 points)	No guarantees. No legal statement regarding guarantees.	Limited guarantees. Expropriation only within rules of Act, with compensation.	Full guarantees under the host country law.	Full guarantees under international law.
Import Duty Exemptions (1.3 points)	No import duty exemptions.	Exemption only for goods intended for export.	Import duty exemptions granted for limited period of time	Import duty exemptions for all initial capital.

Table 9.4 Degrees of Formal Liberalisation in Bulgaria, Czechoslovakia, Hungary, Poland and the Former Soviet Union, 1990–91
(a = first half of 1990; b = second half of 1990; c = first half of 1991)

Country	*Bulgaria*			*Czechoslovakia*			*Hungary*			*Poland*			*Romania*			*Former Soviet Union*		
Descriptor	a	b	c	a	b	c	a	b	c	a	b	c	a	b	c	a	b	c
Repatriation	2	2	2	2	2	2	4	4	4	3	3	4	1	3	3	2	2	2
of profits	8.6	8.6	8.6	8.6	8.6	8.6	12.4	12.4	12.4	12.9	12.9	17.2	4.3	12.9	12.9	8.6	8.6	8.6
(4.3 points)																		
Foreign	3	3	3	3	4	4	4	4	4	4	4	4	2	4	4	2	2	4
Partner's	9.3	9.3	9.3	9.3	12.4	12.4	12.4	12.4	12.4	12.4	12.4	12.4	6.2	12.4	12.4	6.2	6.2	12.4
Share																		
(3.1 points)																		
Real Property	1	1	1	1	1	1	4	4	4	3	3	3	1	1	1	1	1	1
Ownership	4.2	4.2	4.2	4.2	4.2	4.2	16.8	16.8	16.8	12.6	12.6	12.6	4.2	4.2	4.2	4.2	4.2	4.2
(4.2 points)																		
Income Taxes	3	3	3	4	3	3	3	3	3	2	2	2	2	3	3	3	3	3
(3.6 points)	10.8	10.8	10.8	14.4	10.8	10.8	10.8	10.8	10.8	7.2	7.2	7.2	7.2	10.8	10.8	10.8	10.8	10.8
Tax Holidays	3	3	3	2	2	2	3	3	3	4	4	2.5	2	2	3	1	1	1
(3.7 points)	11.1	11.1	11.1	7.4	7.4	7.4	11.1	11.1	11.1	14.8	14.8	9.2	7.4	7.4	11.1	3.7	3.7	3.7

Tax on	3	3	3	1	1	1	4	4	4	1	1	2	1	1	1	2	2	2
Dividends	6.6	6.6	6.6	2.2	2.2	2.2	8.8	8.8	8.8	2.2	2.2	4.4	2.2	2.2	2.2	4.4	4.4	4.4
(2.2 points)																		
Registration	3	3	4	2	2	2	3	3	4	3	3	4	2	2	2	1	1	2
Procedure	9.3	9.3	9.3	6.2	6.2	6.2	9.3	9.3	9.3	9.3	9.3	12.4	6.2	6.2	6.2	2.1	2.1	2.1
(3.1 points)																		
Nationality	3	3	3	1	4	4	4	4	4	4	4	4	2	4	4	1	1	1
Requirements	8.4	8.4	8.4	2.8	11.2	11.2	11.2	11.2	11.2	11.2	11.2	11.2	5.6	11.2	11.2	2.8	2.8	2.8
(2.8 points)																		
Economic	2	2	2	2	2	2	3	3	3	3	3	3	2	2	2	2	2	2
Choice	4.6	4.6	4.6	4.6	4.6	4.6	6.9	6.9	6.9	6.9	6.9	6.9	4.6	4.6	4.6	4.6	4.6	4.6
(2.3 points)																		
State	3	3	3	2	2	2	3	3	3	4	4	4	3	3	3	1	1	2
Guarantees	8.1	8.1	8.1	5.4	5.4	5.4	8.1	8.1	8.1	10.8	10.8	10.8	8.1	8.1	8.1	2.7	2.7	5.5
(2.7 points)																		
Import Duty	2	2	2	3	3	3	4	4	4	4	4	4	2	2	4	1	1	1
Exemptions	2.6	2.6	2.6	3.9	3.9	3.9	5.2	5.2	5.2	5.2	5.2	5.2	2.6	2.6	5.2	1.3	1.3	1.3
(1.3 points)																		
Total	84	84	87	69	77	77	112	112	115	105	105	109	59	83	87	51	51	60

which became operative on 1 January 1989, allows up to 99 per cent foreign ownership, but is implemented on a case-by-case basis. Amendments introduced on 19 April 1990 allowed foreign firms and private persons to own 100 per cent of the equity (1990a – three points; 1990b – four points). In the Commonwealth of Independent States, a presidential Decree enacted in October 1990 gave foreigners, as of 1991, the right to establish wholly foreign-owned subsidiaries and to purchase shares in joint stock companies formed from large state enterprises (1990 – two points; 1991 – four points).

The *ownership of real property* is a very important factor in encouraging investment and providing a feeling of security and stability. In Hungary, a joint venture company may acquire real property necessary for the conduct of its business (for example land and buildings). Real estate companies, however, are not allowed (four points).

In Poland, a joint venture with less than 50 per cent foreign ownership can acquire real property. In cases where the foreign ownership exceeds 50 per cent, the consent of the Ministry of Internal Affairs is required (three points).

In Bulgaria, Romania and Czechoslovakia, companies with foreign participation cannot own land, sub-soil resources, forests or water on their territory (one point). Whether foreign firms can own land in the Commonwealth of Independent States is not addressed in the Decrees on foreign investment. These only state that 'foreign investors will receive land-use rights, including long-term leasing rights' (one point).

Income tax systems vary from one country to another, depending on economic policy. For the purposes of this study, the lowest taxes after all possible exemptions are considered the most desirable.

In Czechoslovakia, the income tax rate for foreign companies amounts to 40 per cent. If the taxable income of a joint corporation is below Kčs 100 000, the rate of corporate income tax is 20 per cent. In addition to income tax, however, joint ventures are required to make contributions to various wage and social funds, including 50 per cent of the wage bill to the social security fund, and 5 to 10 per cent of earnings to the 'reserve, cultural and remuneration funds'. The Federal Ministry of Finance is entitled to grant a reduction in the rate of corporate income tax for social welfare contributions. Amendments in April 1990 kept tax rates at the same level of 40 per cent on profits and 25 per cent on dividends. The number of obligatory funds was reduced from three to one 'reserve fund', which must include both convertible and local currencies. In this respect, the new law seems to be more restrictive than its predecessors (1990a – four points; 1990b – three points).

In Hungary, the income tax rate is 40 per cent on profits up to Ft3 million, and 50 per cent above this amount; however, a number of exemptions are available. For joint ventures in which the foreign partner's share equals 20 per cent or exceeds Ft5 million, 20 per cent of the tax bill is deductable. These joint ventures may be eligible for an allowance of up to 100 per cent of the tax bill in the first five years of operations, and up to 60 per cent from the sixth year. In the latter case, the taxes paid will amount to only 30 per cent (three points).

In the former Soviet Union, the income tax rate of 30 per cent applies to joint ventures in which the foreign share exceeds 30 per cent; other joint ventures are taxed at 35 per cent. Tax reductions must be applied for (three points).

In Bulgaria, the profits of joint stock companies with more than 20 per cent of foreign ownership, and of subsidiaries of foreign entities are taxed at 30 per cent (as compared with 50 per cent for domestic companies). Companies with less than 20 per cent foreign ownership are taxed at 40 per cent. An additional 20 per cent reduction may be granted to foreign companies; to date, few applications have been successful. Foreign companies may apply for tax reductions for up to three years after the start of production. Such decisions rest with the Ministry for Foreign Trade (three points).

The Polish Law on Foreign Investment sets a 40 per cent income tax rate, with tax deductions granted for investments in social projects (two points).

In Romania, the tax rate is set at 40 per cent of annual profits, defined as the difference between total income and expenses incurred. The law provides 50 per cent exemptions for re-invested profits, and 25 per cent exemptions for large exports, imports and R & D activities, as well as for the creation of at least fifty new jobs (1990a – two points; 1990b – three points).

The main purpose of *tax holidays* is to provide additional incentives for foreign investors to enter new markets. In other words, they secure a 100 per cent tax exemption for a limited number of years, which vary between each East European country. Up until June 1991, the Polish law granted companies with foreign ownership three years of tax holidays. For companies operating in 'priority sectors', tax holidays could be extended for another three years. The new Law of 14 June 1991 is more restrictive: the Ministry of Finance may grant a company corporate tax exemptions in cases where the foreign partner's contribution to the company's initial capital exceeds ECU2 million. In addition, if a company introduces new technologies, exports a minimum of 20 per cent of sales, or locates its operations in a region of high unemployment, tax cuts are available (1990 – 4 points; 1991 – 2.5 points).

Hungarian tax holidays are used rather modestly and apply only to large joint ventures in certain priority sectors. These joint ventures are entitled to a 100 per cent allowance with regard to taxes in the first five years (three points).

According to Romanian law, full exemptions from tax on profits are granted for five years to investments in manufacturing, agriculture and construction; for three years in the natural resources, communications and transportation; and for two years, in services, trade and banking (1990 – two points; 1991 – three points).

The Federal Ministry of Finance in Czechoslovakia is empowered to grant tax holidays for a maximum period of two years (two points).

In Bulgaria, limited liability companies with foreign participation in excess of 49 per cent or with investments of more than $60 000, joint stock companies with foreign ownership exceeding 20 per cent, and the subsidiaries of foreign firms, can all be exempted from taxation for the first five years if their activities are in high-technology sectors specified by the Council of Ministers (three points).

Until 1991, there were no tax holidays in the Soviet Union. Under the new legislation, foreign capital companies are granted a two-year tax holiday (1990 – one point; 1991 – two points). In most of these countries, tax holidays begin on the date of establishment of the joint venture. The exception is in the CIS, where they are granted when the joint venture declares its first profits.

Income tax on the dividends of foreign partners is paid in almost all East European countries, except Hungary (four points). The tax rules are 10 per cent in Bulgaria (three points), 20 per cent in the ex-Soviet Union (two points), 20 per cent in Romania and Czechoslovakia (one point each).

The old law on foreign capital companies in Poland provided for a 30 per cent tax rate on the dividends of foreign partners. The 1991 law reduced the tax to 20 per cent (1990 – one point; 1991 – two points). As Poland is a signatory to double taxation agreements with many countries, including the United States, the actual tax rate varies from 10 to 15 per cent.

Bureaucratic delays encountered with the registration process are considered below. In Poland, under the 1989 Law, foreign investors followed the registration procedure of the Foreign Investment Agency. According to the 1991 Law, companies need only register with a regional court, and no longer require a permit from the Agency[10] (1990 – three points; 1991 – four points).

In Hungary, foreign investors with a minority ownership need to be registered with the Central Court of Registration prior to their establishment. Joint ventures, which are majority foreign-owned, must receive a licence from the Ministry of Finance. If the Ministry of Finance fails to respond to a joint venture application within sixty days, the application is considered accepted (1990 – three points). The law introduced in 1991 no longer requires any registration (1991 – four points).

In Bulgaria, the introduction of Decree 56 on Economic Activity simplified the procedure for setting up joint ventures, and decreased the duration of the registration period. If foreign participation exceeds 45 per cent in a limited liability company, or 20 per cent in a joint stock company, a permit for registration from the relevant state body is required (1990 – three points; 1991 – four points).

In Czechoslovakia, the 1990 amendments reduced the authorisation procedure from 90 to a maximum of 60 days (two points).

In Romania, the registration procedure remains complex. Foreign investors apply for registration at the Romanian Development Agency, which requests information from the respective ministries to ascertain the 'reliability of the investor, the field and the legal form of the investment and the amount of capital to be invested' (Article 20, 1991) (two points).

In the Commonwealth of Independent States, the registration process contains three phases: phase one requires a letter of intent; in phase two, a joint venture contract is concluded; finally, the joint venture is registered. At each stage, the consent of the Council of Ministers and of the appropriate Ministry is required (one point).

Nationality requirements for the selection of executives often determine the success of a company. Limiting the choice can hamper a firm's development and create barriers to effective cooperation. With an understanding of this interdependence, Polish law no longer restricts the Presidency or Directorship of the Board to Polish citizens. Currently, appointments within the company are decided by the owners (four points). In Hungary, foreign companies enjoy similar freedom in appointing chairmen and management teams (four points). The same provisions were introduced in Romania in the second half of 1990 (1990a – two points; 1990b – four points).

In Bulgaria, Decree 56 empowers foreign citizens to sit on or be elected Chairman of the Board of Directors of joint stock companies. This represents a significant improvement on previous laws, which restricted foreigners to the position of Vice-Chairman. When a foreign national occupies the position of Chairman, the Vice-Chairmanship is reserved for Bulgarian nationals (three points).

Whilst under former regulations, presiding members of executive bodies in Czechoslovakia had to be nationals, the new law opened up these positions to foreigners (1990a – one point; 1990b – four points).

The *degree of economic choice* is an important factor in determining an investment sector. The Polish Law of 1989, unlike its predecessors, allows foreign investors to conduct business in any branch of the national economy, including foreign trade. A few limitations remain in national defence and environmental protection (three points). Similar requirements apply to Hungary (three points), and were introduced in Romania in 1991 (1990 – two points; 1991 – three points).

In other post-socialist countries, the degree of choice is somewhat similar. However, joint ventures operating in foreign trade must obtain separate export/import licences, which increase the degree of governmental control. In Czechoslovakia, for example, under the 1989 law, joint ventures did not automatically receive the right to conduct foreign trade operations. Each joint venture company had to apply to the Federal Ministry of Foreign Trade for a trade licence. The 1990 Amendments partially removed this restriction by allowing Czechoslovak legal persons or firms to apply for foreign trade rights. However, a lengthy authorisation procedure remains in existence (two points). In the CIS, joint ventures can engage in export/import activities; these however, can be suspended in 'the event of unfair competition, or if the activity is detrimental to the interests of the state'[11] (two points).

Polish laws provide state guarantees of compensation – in the currency of the original investments – in the event of confiscation, nationalisation or expropriation. The new law of 1991 gives an automatic guarantee of 'prompt, adequate and effective' compensation for all losses resulting from expropriation. Compensation would be equivalent to a fair market value and be paid without delay (four points).

The Hungarian law is very similar, although it is more vague as to how the investment would be valued. At any rate, joint ventures with US participation are now eligible for political risk insurance from the US Overseas Private Investment Corporation (OPIC) (three points).

Decree 56 in Bulgaria provides guarantees that 'investment made by foreign entities shall not be subject to confiscation or expropriation in an administrative manner' (three points). In Romania, the law states that 'foreign investment shall not be nationalized, expropriated, requisitioned or subjected to similar measures' (Article 5, 1991) (three points).

In Czechoslovakia, the multinational's property may be expropriated or its rights restricted only in accordance with Act XXIV. If such measures are taken, the foreign shareholders receive compensation to cover the value of their property (two points). New legislation in the CIS compensates for the absence of guarantees in previous Soviet laws and devotes an entire Chapter to 'Guarantees of Rights and Investment Protection'. Chapter IV, Article 23 stipulates that 'the state guarantees the protection of investment, independently of the form of ownership or of foreign investment' (1990 – one point; 1991 – two points).

Import duty exemptions are a significant allowance, although they are not connected to income tax. In Poland, they cover capitalised assets such as machinery, equipment, materials and intermediate products, during the first three years of operations. The companies may also take advantage of import duty refunds in accordance with the same principles which apply to state-run enterprises (four points).

In Hungary, as in Poland, capital goods, technology and patents brought into joint ventures as capitalised assets, as well as those purchased with hard currency from an original cash investment, enjoy duty-free entry (four points).

In Romania, imported machinery, equipment, and means of transport are exempt from customs duties. Raw materials, supplies and components imported for production purposes are exempt from import duties for two years from the date the project was commissioned (1990 – two points; 1991 – four points).

Customs duty exemptions in other East European countries are of a more limited scope. Under Czechoslovak regulations, duty exemptions may be granted on request by the Federal Ministry of Foreign Trade (three points).

In Bulgaria a company may be exempted from import duties if imported materials, intermediate products, or equipment are intended for export production. Such exemptions are also available for imports of equipment necessary for the realisation of an industrial cooperation agreement (two points). Legal provisions in the CIS do not include customs duty exemptions (one point).

The observations discussed in this chapter offer a perspective on investment opportunities in Eastern Europe which is based on the strengths and weaknesses of each country's legislation. We outlined the individual aspects of laws, and their effect on foreign participation in business ventures. Next, we consider the impact of legislation on FDI at two levels: a) the impact of legal openness on the number of joint ventures; b) the impact of legal changes on the growth in the numbers of firms with foreign participation.

(a) The level of legal liberalisation and the number of joint ventures

This study shows that Hungary and Poland have the most liberal joint venture legislation, with 115 points and 109 points respectively. The CIS has the most conservative legal environment, with sixty points. Romania, Bulgaria and Czechoslovakia are located between those two extremes. By virtue of the laws passed to date, Hungary and Poland can be classified as liberal market economies. They allow for currency convertibility, 100 per cent foreign ownership, duty exemptions, and the import of capitalised assets; moreover, they do not impose restrictions on the employment of foreign nationals in top management positions.

The Romanian, Bulgarian and Czechoslovak joint venture laws are going through a transitional stage: they contain liberal provisions which permit foreign ownership interests to a maximum of 99 per cent and set an income tax rate of 30 per cent for new ventures. However, they do not allow real property ownership, or the repatriation of profits.

The most conservative legal environment is found in the CIS' joint venture law. Decrees 1405 and 1074 restrict foreign ownership to a maximum of 49 per cent, reserve senior management positions to host nationals, use a complicated and bureaucratic registration procedure, and do not offer tax incentives. The emerging republics of the CIS need to be monitored closely for nascent business opportunities.

As Table 9.4 suggests, the level of openness expressed in a country's joint venture law has a positive correlation with the number of joint ventures per million inhabitants (see also Table 9.1). In the first half of 1990, the correlation coefficient was 0.9441; 0.6918 in the second half of 1990; and 0.6626 in the first six months of 1991. The falling correlation coefficients in each successive period would suggest that factors other than the law itself did influence the foreign investors' choice of host countries.

Hungary and Poland, with the most liberal laws, also recorded the most joint ventures per million inhabitants. It is interesting to note the relatively high position of Czechoslovakia, and the lowly position of Bulgaria in 1991. 'Over-investments' in the former might be explained by its historical ties with Austria and Germany, and their high levels of technical and managerial cultures. Conversely, Bulgaria has retained the image of a centrally managed economy.

The place of different countries on the scale expresses different degrees of formal liberalisation and the progress of their economic reforms. The opposite is also true. Different levels of marketisation have impacted on the attractiveness of different descriptor areas. The less developed host countries (including the CIS, Bulgaria and Romania) are attempting to attract foreign capital through lower income taxes. Given the current regulations against profit repatriation, these exemptions are unlikely to have the desired effects. At best, they are an indirect incentive for the re-investment of profits in the host country, not for fresh capital inflows.

(b) The dynamism of legal liberalisation

This study of legislative developments has shown that the countries of Central and Eastern Europe are moving towards a more liberal model. Arguably, the slowest pace of change has been in Hungary and Poland; the fastest in the countries which were closest ideologically to a command economy. Of particular significance is the foreign investment legislation in Romania, which has witnessed the most dramatic liberalisation, resulting in an impressive increase in joint venture registrations.

An analysis of the laws' dynamism in the three periods under consideration shows a high positive relationship between legal changes and the number of registered joint ventures. The correlation coefficient for all countries was 1.000; for Bulgaria, it was 1.000; for Romania 0.9726; for Czechoslovakia 0.9148; for Hungary 0.8352; for Poland, 0.7772; and for the CIS 0.7414. The highest correlation was in Bulgaria, where the domestic situation was the most stable. The DFLL increased by only three points, and the number of joint ventures by fifteen. Conversely, the lowest correlation was found in the CIS, reflecting the unstable political situation and ambiguity of the joint venture legislation.

Finally, it appears that no country has a law which combined all elements on a single level of openness. Each host country displays a combination of solutions exhibiting different degrees of liberalisation. The most consistent countries are probably Hungary, which combines elements of the third and fourth degrees, and Bulgaria, which displays the largest number of elements from the third degree. The least consistent legislation is that of Czechoslovakia which combines elements from all four DFLLs. This may result from the speed with which the laws were prepared. This situation is changing: at the time of writing (January 1992), a new, more liberalised joint venture law was in preparation. We can expect the number of joint ventures in Czechoslovakia to grow rapidly, and to exceed that in Poland and Hungary by the mid-1990s.[12] The dynamic aspect of this evolution warrants closer attention and can be recommended as a field for further study.

Notes

1. I. Makarov and I. Puzin, *Ekonomicheskoe Sotrudnichestvo v Evrope. Itogi i Perspectivi*, Moscow, 1987.
2. Ustawa z 23 grudnia 1988 o dzialanosci gospodarczej z udzialem podmiotow zagranicznych, as amended on 23 December 1989 (Poland).
3. Act XXIV 1988 on Investments of Foreigners in Hungary, Budapest, 1988.
4. Decree 56, Economic Activity, Sofia Press, Bulgaria, 1989.
5. Joint Venture Code (173/1988), Prague, Czechoslovakia, 1989.
6. Act on Enterprises with Foreign Property Participation, and on Business Activity and Joint Ventures, Prague, Czechoslovakia, 19 April 1990.
7. Decree 1074 of the CPSU Central Committee and the USSR Council of Ministers of 17 September 1987: 'Additional Measures to Streamline Foreign Economic Activity in the New Conditions of Economic Management', Moscow.
8. Decree of 2 December 1988, No. 1045, of the USSR Council of Ministers: 'The Further Development of Foreign Economic Activity of State, Cooperative and other Public Enterprises, Associations and Organizations', Moscow 1988.
9. *Izvestiya*, 16 December 1990, No. 349.
10. It is widely accepted that the role of the Foreign Investment Agency will shortly be changed to that of a 'promotional' agency.
11. Decree of 2 December 1988, No. 1045, see above.
12. S. Anderson, 'The Eastern Block Investment Report Card', *The Soviet Union and Eastern Europe Business Journal*, Vol. 2, No. 2, pp. 1–13, 1990.

Part III
Current and Future Trends

No attempt will be made in this section to undertake a comprehensive summary of, or to present definitive conclusions on the varied selection of papers (both theoretical and empirical) contained in this volume. Instead, we asked Professor Pinder to reflect on the recent course of East–West relations, and to consider the potential for closer economic and political integration in Europe to the turn of the century.

10 The European Community and Investment in Central and Eastern Europe

John Pinder

An explicit aim of the European Community's policy towards the countries of Central and Eastern Europe is to help them establish market economies and constitutional democracies.[1] Foreign Direct Investment can make an essential contribution to economic strength and hence to the consolidation of stable democracy. Conversely, the investment will flow sufficiently abundantly only if the investors are confident enough that the host countries are going to have prosperous market economies and stable, reasonable politics: in other words, that the Community's aim will be broadly fulfilled.

More precisely, the conditions that favour investment in these countries and can be influenced by Community policies include a market economy with a satisfactory performance, a stable government with policies that are friendly to foreign investment and, externally, adequate security and good access to export markets, especially, in this case, the Community itself. The Community has a number of policy instruments that can exert such influence: trade and cooperation agreements; the generalised system of preferences; quota liberalisation; aid, with the PHARE programme and the European Bank for Reconstruction and Development, in which the Community holds the majority of shares; association agreements; admission to membership; and, increasingly, instruments of security policy.[2]

How the Community uses these instruments, and how effectively and energetically it does so, depends on the nature of its interests in the relationship with its Eastern neighbours. Until 1985, the Community's defensive and unyielding diplomacy demonstrated the depth of its distaste for Soviet hegemony in Central Europe and the Balkans. Caution at first coloured the Community's reaction to Perestroika after 1985. Then, when the radical reforms began in 1989, the

Community responded rapidly and enthusiastically. The more recent experience provides the best basis for judging future prospects. But the earlier periods also have some relevance. So first, 'un peu d'histoire', as the Michelin green guides put it, about the years up to 1985.

TO 1985: THE COMMUNITY'S RESISTANCE TO SOVIET HEGEMONY IN CENTRAL AND EASTERN EUROPE

Soviet hegemony cut across the Community's interests in a number of ways: security was threatened by the Red Army and the Warsaw Pact; trade was impeded by the centralised state-trading system; the regimes were perceived to be unfriendly; and the Community disliked the Communist dictatorships for their disrespect of human rights. All this was felt particularly acutely in the Federal Republic of Germany, with the Soviet oppression of the Germans to the East.

Soviet policy had been hostile to the Community since its foundation. But after 1968 a new element emerged. The integration of Comecon was seen as a more convenient way of securing quiescence in Central Europe and the Balkans than the military intervention that was employed to prop up the regime in Prague; and Soviet leaders believed that a joint Comecon approach to relations with the Community would be an element in this. Talks between Comecon and the Community began in 1973, and they continued to no avail for over five years. The Community rejected the idea of negotiating with Comecon as a group about trade, where the East European countries had enjoyed a certain autonomy hitherto. The Community saw no benefit in accepting a tighter Soviet hegemony. Its policy was to seek negotiations with Comecon's member states, which, unlike the member states of the Community, had retained their competence for foreign trade. Negotiations dragged on in a desultory way until 1979, when they were shelved in the aftermath of the intervention in Afghanistan and the martial law in Poland. The members of Comecon remained almost the only countries in the world that refused to have formal relations with the Community.

Not that formal relations would have made a big difference to trade. As its exports, mainly oil, gas, timber, diamonds and other raw materials, encountered little protection on entering the Community, the Soviet Union had scant need to negotiate about trade barriers. Although the countries of Central Europe and the Balkans would have dearly liked to negotiate about the Community's heavy protection against their exports of agricultural products and low-technology manufactures, the Soviet Union kept them in line with the policy of seeking trade negotiations through Comecon. The real barrier, for the Community, was the Comecon countries' system, which was not negotiable; and until that system was changed, trade negotiations would have no more than a marginal effect.

TO TRADE AND COOPERATION AGREEMENTS: GORBACHEV AND THE TRANSITION

Soon after gaining power in 1985, Gorbachev evidently decided that he would accept the Community's requirement that it negotiate on trade directly with Comecon's member states. Comecon was to be satisfied with a joint declaration of interest that the two sides would meet regularly to discuss cooperation. Even this took nearly two years to negotiate. The reason was the cautious attitude of the Community, which wanted to be sure that it would indeed be able to complete bilateral trade negotiations with Comecon's members. So agreement on the declaration was reached only in June 1988, when it was already clear that the first bilateral agreement, with Hungary, would enter into force later that year; and this was followed by agreements with the other European Comecon countries.

These countries had changed their policy about negotiating with the Community, reflecting the new, more tolerant Soviet attitude towards them that was a notable feature of Perestroika. But as they had yet to change their economic systems, the agreements had only a modest significance for trade. The Community differentiated between those countries that still retained hard-line governments, which were accorded only trade agreements, and those that were embarking on substantial reforms – Poland and Hungary being the first – which were favoured with trade and cooperation agreements. The trade agreements signified that the two parties were at least on speaking terms at a formal level; for its part, the Community was certainly prepared to grant some liberalisation of import quotas. The trade and cooperation agreements added to this procedure for discussing cooperation in a number of listed fields. But the experience of such agreements which had been concluded in the past between the East European countries and the member states of the Community indicated that cooperation did not amount to much, unless it was accompanied by the provision of finance by the Western partner.

Export credits had been the main substance of these agreements – on a very large scale, as witnessed by the size of the debts of countries such as Poland to public authorities in the West. The member governments did not, however, allow the Community to include credits among the provisions of its trade and cooperation agreements.[3] This had been accepted in the Community's agreements with Mediterranean countries; but the governments saw credits as a political instrument in their relations with Eastern Europe, and were not yet ready to join their efforts in a common Community policy in this respect. So although the Community had signed trade and cooperation agreements with all the European members of Comecon, including the Soviet Union, by 1990 (with the exception of East Germany, which had joined the Federal Republic and hence the Community before its agreement reached that stage), these represented no more than a move towards the best that could be expected in relations with centralised state-trading countries. They were soon to be put in the shade by the Community's response to the process of radical reform in Eastern Europe that began in 1989.

THE COMMUNITY'S RESPONSE TO RADICAL REFORMS IN CENTRAL AND EASTERN EUROPE

The Community's response to the radical reforms was rapid and enthusiastic. Having constantly resisted Soviet hegemony and given no encouragement to the repressive Communist regimes, the Community had no words to eat before changing its policy towards Central and Eastern Europe; nor did it have much difficulty in defining its interests, which were the obverse of those it had defended in the past.

The Community was clear that its interest lay in the creation of market economies and constitutional democracies in its neighbours to the East. (The term it tended to use was 'pluralist democracies', underlining the contrast with the monolithic Communist regimes). The economic interest was certainly significant. The Community's trade with Sweden was about as great as its trade with the whole of Comecon. Sweden, with its market economy, was a much richer partner for the Community and, above all, much more open to trade. The Czechs, before the Second World War, had been at least as rich as the Swedes and postwar Czechoslovakia should alone, with an effective and open economic system, have continued to be as good a trading partner. The scope for prosperous relations with market economies in Central and Eastern Europe as a whole seemed vast, particularly when the opportunities for investment as well as trade were taken into account. But economics was overshadowed by the security interest. For over forty years, Soviet military power had occupied the heart of Europe and hung heavy over the West. Now, if the changes could be consolidated, this menace would be removed; and if Communism could be removed from the Soviet Union, its mission to spread its power across the world would come to an end. History had shown that democracies were safer neighbours than dictatorships. The success of democracy in Central and Eastern Europe would transform the security of the Community and of Europe as a whole. On top of that, the Community's member states felt a natural affinity with the new democracies. The idea of helping them went with the grain.

Appropriate policy instruments had already been fashioned in the course of the Community's development of its relations with other countries. They could be taken off the shelf and used again, with some adaptations; and given the difficulty of devising new instruments for such a complex Community, still heavily dependent on securing agreement among twelve member governments, this was of no small significance when urgent action was required. From its relations with less developed countries, the Community could take the Generalised System of Preferences (GSP) and its aid programmes; from its relations with European Mediterranean countries, agreements of association. There was also the experience of three rounds of accession of new members – although the accession of East Germany came through a novel route, by its union with an existing member state, the Federal Republic. For other Central and East Europeans, accession is a question for the future: possible in principle for all of them; difficult in practice for some; and not possible for Russia, which is so big that it would upset the Community's all-important political equilibrium. For Russia with a market economy and a democratic polity, partnership is a more suitable concept than membership, drawing on the pattern of the Community's relationship with the United States. But apart from East Germany, accession was not a suitable instrument for the early 1990s. It was the other instruments that the Community had to employ.

GSP AND QUOTA LIBERALISATION

The Generalised System of Preferences and quota liberalisation were big steps towards an open Community market for Central

Europe and the Balkans. The GSP allows tariff-free entry into the Community market for exporters from the countries that benefit from it, with certain important exceptions.[4] One exception is, as usual, agriculture: here there is no general removal of tariffs, let alone of the more restrictive import levies, although there are reduced tariffs on some agricultural products. For industry, there is a tariff-free entry except where it really hurts producers in the Community; when it does, the products can be classed as 'sensitive', and the tariff is applied again after a tariff-free quota has been filled. Since coal and steel are notoriously 'sensitive', the Community neatly excluded them by giving Central and East Europeans GSP for products covered by the EC Treaty; that is, almost everything except coal and steel, which come under the Treaty of the European Coal and Steel Community. As a long-stop, the Community also reserves the right to apply 'safeguards', which are protective devices, usually quotas, imposed when a product is imported 'so as to cause or threaten serious injury' to domestic producers. Despite these limitations, the GSP has been an important measure of liberalisation. It was accorded by the Community to Hungary and Poland from 1 January 1990; both increased their exports to the Community very rapidly in that year, with Hungary maintaining the expansion through 1991, although the appreciation of the zloty was by then hampering Polish exporters. In 1990 the GSP was also extended to Bulgaria and the Czech and Slovak Federal Republic, as they began to introduce serious reforms; and Romania, which had been granted GSP as far back as 1974 as a reward for its independent stance in foreign policy, unique among members of the Soviet bloc, received an improved scheme in 1991, after Ceausescu had been removed and there was a prospect of reforms. Yugoslavia, non-aligned since before the GSP was invented, received it at its inception in 1971, and Yugoslav exports to the Community responded vigorously in the 1970s, as those of Hungary and Poland were to do in 1990.

In addition to the GSP, the Community removed at the same time an important measure of trade protection, in the form of almost all its import quotas on industrial products coming from Central Europe and the Balkans. These had included numerous quotas directed specifically against the state-trading countries, which member states had applied during the Cold War period and had, with Community agreement, retained though accepting a gradual liberalisation year by year. The specific quotas were eliminated. 'Global' quotas, which were directed not specifically against state-trading countries but against low-cost imports more generally, were suspended, with the important exceptions of coal, steel, textiles and most of the agricultural products to which they apply; and the suspension has been renewed on an annual basis.

The GSP and the quota liberalisation have been important for the export trade of Central European and Balkan countries. They are no less significant for investment. For so long as the Community maintains these measures, they offer access to its market and thus enable investors to take advantage of exporting to it on the basis of the cheap and educated labour in its Eastern neighbours. There is the risk that the Community, where it is not bound by association agreements, could remove these favours which it has unilaterally granted. But it is not likely to put the policy into reverse. The risk for investors is, rather, that it will add new products to the GSP 'sensitive' list, or apply safeguards if competition bites too hard. Where there is such a danger, those who have invested will have to apply their lobbying skills to ensure that their enterprise is not penalised. For the East European partners, there is also the down side of the existing limitations, for agriculture, textiles, steel and the sensitive products; and for the republics of the former Soviet Union the question remains, early in 1992, of how far they will be accorded the advantages which countries of Central Europe and the Balkans have already received. The latter, and those who invest in them, would moreover benefit considerably if the GSP and the suspension of global quotas were to be entrenched in their trade and cooperation agreements for at least some years ahead. Here the countries with the association, or Europe Agreements, have a considerable advantage, because the prospect of free trade is written into their treaties.

AID: PHARE, EBRD, AID TO THE FORMER SOVIET UNION

An open EC market is not enough to give a reasonable prospect of economic success in the reforming countries. An economy just being released from the shackles of state control may not respond by supplying the goods which comparative advantage would potentially justify; and converting the domestic economy into a working market system is itself an enormous task. Economic aid can help the East European countries to effect this hard transition. The Community and its Western partners have been providing fairly satisfactory amounts of technical assistance, to contribute to the establishment of the market economy and its institutions. Apart from balance of payments support to pave the way for currency convertibility, less has been done to supply financial assistance to ease the transition. Already in 1989 the Community decided to launch its aid programme, under the title PHARE (the French acronym for Poland and Hungary aid for economic reconstruction). The seven leading industrial countries, at their G7 summit in July of that year, agreed to recommend a comprehensive programme to the G24 group of the OECD's advanced industrial states, which include the EC's twelve. The EC itself contributed collectively through its budget and the European Investment Bank; the International Monetary Fund and the World Bank were also brought in, as well as the European Bank for Reconstruction and Development (EBRD), when it was established in 1990.

The Community's budget for 1990 included ECU300 million (1 ECU = £0.7 or $1.3 early in 1992) for Hungary and Poland; this was increased to ECU500 million when reforms in the Czech and Slovak Federal Republic and the Balkan countries justified their inclusion in the programme, whose explicit objective was to assist the development of market economies and pluralist democracies. The allocation was renewed on an increasing scale for 1991 and 1992, rising to ECU1 billion in the latter year. If the contributions of the member states and the EC itself are taken together, their grants of up to ECU1.5 billion a year by 1992 amount to some three-quarters of the total of grants from all the G24 countries; and the loans from Community sources are running at ECU3–4 billion a year, about equivalent to the loans from other G24 countries together with, more importantly, the IMF and the World Bank. But about half of the total of loans from Community sources consisted of allocations for export credits on the part of the member states which, unless repayment is not expected, are scarcely to be classified as aid.

The aid for the Commonwealth of Independent States comes, not under the PHARE programme, but under a separate heading. In the summer of 1990, when there seemed for the first time to be a real prospect of serious economic reform in the Soviet Union, the G7 summit in July considered the possibility of aid on a large scale. In December, the European Council of the heads of state or government of EC member states allocated ECU1.15 billion in aid to the Soviet Union: ECU250 million of food aid, the guaranteeing of ECU500 million of credits to buy food, and ECU400 million of technical assistance. At once, political difficulties got in the way, when the Community suspended the programme because of repression in the Baltic republics; then there were administrative problems connected with, at first, the Soviet bureaucracy, then the confusion that followed its disintegration. But by the end of 1991, when the European Council, wanting to help Russia and the other republics after the failed coup and the change of regime, made a new decision to provide ECU200 million of food aid and ECU1.25 billion of loan guarantees, the way seemed to be clear for the aid to start to flow. Meanwhile, the member states too had initiated their own aid programmes, with that of Germany on a particularly large scale.

Soon after the radical reforms began in Central Europe in 1989, and a prospect of economic reform in the Soviet Union also emerged, the Community took another important initiative. The French government proposed the creation of an investment bank to help the transition; EBRD was established in 1990, with a capital of ECU10 billion, 51 per cent owned by the EC and its member states and the rest by a wide range of other countries, including the designated recipients in Central and Eastern Europe, but with the more significant contributions coming from the Community's partners among the G24. The statute of the Bank emphasises the aim of promoting private investment: 'to foster the transition towards open-market oriented economies and to promote private and entrepreneurial initiative in the Central and East European countries committed to and applying the principles of multi-party democracy, pluralism and market economies'. Not less than 60 per cent of its loans each year are to go to private borrowers. Up to 30 per cent of the Bank's paid-up capital can be put into equity investments. Since, when the Bank was established, the Americans in particular were highly suspicious of the Soviet Union's intentions, no more than the Soviet contribution to the Bank's capital, which was 6 per cent of it, was to be placed there in the first three years. If the Commonwealth of Independent States maintains the process of reform, it may be expected that this restriction will be lifted, should the amount of viable projects reach that limit.

At the beginning of 1992, the EBRD had already started to put money into projects bringing together Western and local firms, thus reducing risks for Western investors. The justification of the Bank, from an economic viewpoint, is of course that such investment, paving the way to a dynamic and prosperous economy, is a public good which justifies a public contribution to the bearing of risk. While significant investments have already been made without such support, the political and economic risks are still substantial enough to deter much of the investment which is required for economic success, and which would itself do more than anything else to bring such success about.

Not since the great depression of the 1930s has production in a Western country fallen by as much as 20 per cent in a year, if the Second World War and its aftermath are excluded. The political repercussions of that depression were catastrophic. Without expecting that history to repeat itself, one may be concerned that GDP in several Central and East European countries has fallen by 5, 10, or even 20 per cent or more from one year to another, following the launching of the reforms. Unemployment has risen in some of them to double figures and continues to rise. This has been the price of breaking the rigidities of the old system and of bringing down inflation. But the sound money policy may have to be sustained for some time if a macro-economic framework is to be established for successful reforms; and the consequent pain may be more than some of the new democracies can bear. There is the danger either of a relapse into authoritarian and perhaps nationalist governments, which would be uncomfortable neighbours, or of abandonment of the policies required for economic stability. Either way, foreign investors could suffer. Investors will form their own judgement of the risks, which will vary from country to country. But the more public authorities can share the risk, whether through EBRD or through investment guarantee schemes, the more likely the investors are to incur them; and the more the Community aids the transition, the less the risk is likely to be.

One risk is that governments can be blown off course by social discontent, particularly from the unemployed. It has been suggested that Western aid could include support for the budgetary costs of unemployment assistance, which would contribute to economic as well as social stability, because countries without a developed capital market can finance budget deficits only by printing money unless they can secure funds from abroad. So far there has not been much sign of such help from the Western side. If it does materialise, investors could feel that the risk is being reduced.

Another risk is that there may be macro-economic stability without growth, and hence disillusion with a market system that appears to bring no reward. The technical assistance and balance of payments support that the West has supplied so far may be enough to enable dynamic forces within these economies to be released, sufficiently to stimulate healthy growth. But the investment resources required for such growth are very large. It is estimated that half-a-dozen countries alone – Bulgaria, the Czech and Slovak Republics, Hungary, Poland and Romania – will together require physical investment of at least $100 billion a year for several years ahead, little of which will at first come from their own savings.[5] When private foreign investment flows confidently, much of this may be supplied. But until this happens, lack of capital and of the managerial and technological skills that come with foreign investment may be a critical constraint on development. A substantial part of the basic investment needs are, or at least can legitimately be, in the public domain: transport, communications and the cleaning of the environment. Financial assistance from the West for such purposes could do much to help the economies through the transition and into a phase of self-sustaining growth. Aid programmes on the scale envisaged up to the start of 1992 provide important things, but they contribute little to such investment. Substantial aid to promote it could, if forthcoming, offer some assurance to investors that the prospects for a successful transition were being improved.[6] But it must be recognised that help of this sort may not be provided; and investors will then place their money and effort in countries that can best do without it.

The problems of the Commonwealth of Independent States are worse than those in Central Europe or even the Balkans. The lack of experience of democracy and of the workings and structures of a market economy is more extreme. The disruption caused by disintegration of a hitherto intensely integrated Soviet economy is very great. The cost and pain of transition to a market economy are consequently accentuated; and the difficulty of carrying it through without financial as well as technical assistance is more pronounced. Professor Jeffrey Sachs, adviser to the Russian as well as the Polish government, estimated late in 1991 that Russia alone would need aid of $17 billion in 1992: $6 billion of food and medical aid; $6 billion of credits for critically needed goods; and $5 billion as a stabilisation fund towards a convertible rouble.[7] The Russian government asked for aid along these lines, but the American response was negative. The US Administration preferred to leave it to the IMF when Russia had been admitted to membership. But while the IMF can provide the stabilisation fund, it cannot deal with other elements of such an aid programme. The European Community, which, in the absence of Japanese willingness, is the other potential major supporter, may be confronted by the question of whether it is prepared to take a large initiative without the assurance of equivalent support from elsewhere.

The Community's interest in a successful transition on the part of Russia and other former Soviet Republics is the greatest. The security risks of wars between the republics or of authoritarian nationalist governments come nearer to the Community than to the other great industrial powers. The effect of economic collapse on oil and gas supplies and on migration flows could be highly inconvenient. On the up side, moreover, the benefits to the Community of a dynamic market economy and a pacific liberal democracy in Russia would be enormous. Most potential investors will wait and see what happens in the Commonwealth of Independent States before committing substantial resources there. A generous aid initiative by the Community could help to improve the prospects of success and shorten the time for those that wait for it.

ASSOCIATION: EUROPE AGREEMENTS

The Community has signed association agreements with four European Mediterranean countries that have been seen as possible eventual members: Greece, Turkey, Cyprus and Malta. Greece became a member in 1981; the other three have applied but are still waiting. Meanwhile, association is intended to provide, short of membership, a comprehensive framework for the relationship, and it carries with it an implication that membership is a potential outcome.

In using this instrument as part of its East European policy, the Community has been promoting its aims of pluralist democracy and market economy. But because of the closeness of the relationship envisaged, and beyond that, the prospect of future membership, the Community has also required 'practical evidence' of the East European partners' commitment to these aims before opening negotiations for association.[8] This it judged in 1990 to exist in the Czech and Slovak Republics, Hungary and Poland; and after almost a year of negotiations, it signed agreements, called Europe Agreements, with them in December 1991.

Each agreement is to establish an industrial free-trade area between the Community and the East European partner over a transitional period of ten years. The Community is to remove almost all remaining quotas on industrial products immediately, and the tariffs on them progressively in the first five years. The only exceptions are coal, steel and textiles, for which the quotas are to be progressively liberalised at the same time as the tariffs are reduced, with the period stretched to six years for textiles. The recourse to safeguards in the case of 'serious injury' to Community producers does, however, remain. For agricultural products, the Community concedes some tariff cuts and quotas for the import of particular products, with in addition the allocation of part of the aid for food supplies to the Commonwealth of Independent States to the purchase of food from these countries.

Because the GSP and the quota liberalisation that accompanied it gave so much free access already, the Europe Agreements have less immediate effect than would otherwise be the case. But, despite the few exceptions, they do offer a further early instalment of liberalisation; and they open up the prospect of free entry into the Community market in a time scale that should be a considerable encouragement to foreign investors who need the assurance of a wide market for the products of their investments.

The Central European partners, for their part, are to remove their import barriers over the ten-year transitional period. This, again, should on balance be of interest to investors because, even if they lose the protection of the Central European market, they will enjoy a more assured prospect of a healthy and outward-looking economy there. More directly relevant, the Europe Agreements provide for 'national treatment' for the establishment of companies; that is, no discrimination against Community investors. For most sectors this applies from when the agreement enters into force, although for some sensitive sectors there is a delay until the end of the ten-year transitional period; similar exceptions can be introduced (but not retrospectively) when a sector encounters particular difficulties; and some sectors are excluded altogether. Any discrimination against the operation of established Community firms is to cease from the start, as are restrictions on the repatriation of profits and on movement in either direction of capital related to direct investments. The Community's competition rules are to apply, which could bring some protection against cartels or other unfair practices on the part of local competitors. The supply of services is likewise to be freed 'progressively'. As for the other freedom that applies within the Community, the agreements are much more modest about the free movement of workers. The Community confined itself to a commitment to improve the situation for those already legally employed in the EC.

The Europe Agreements also provide, as the trade and cooperation agreements have done, for various kinds of 'cooperation', giving a comprehensive list of fields in which this is envisaged. Of particular importance is the cooperation to help the Central Europeans put in place the legislation that will enable them in due time to participate fully in the single market. Here, as in most other forms of cooperation, the effect depends on funds to finance it; and despite pressure from the Central Europeans to have such finance allocated separately to each one in a financial protocol to the agreements, the Community insisted on keeping aid and assistance as a matter for the PHARE programme, leaving the Community free to decide how much aid will go to which country in each year. The PHARE programme is, however, substantial enough to make a lively reality of cooperation, which relates mainly to industrial, economic and financial affairs but is also to have scientific and cultural aspects. A 'political dialogue' is also envisaged, meaning discussion with a view to cooperation in both internal and foreign policy matters.

The operation of each agreement is to be overseen by institutions set up for the purpose: a Council of Association, in which Ministers and Commissioners will meet at least once a year; a Committee of Association, comprising senior officials who will prepare the meetings of the Council and carry on business between times; and a Parliamentary Association Committee, bringing together Members of the European Parliament and parliamentarians from the associate. The role of the European Parliament is particularly significant, because it has the right of assent – which means also the right to refuse – with respect to acts of association, any amendments to such acts, and, eventually, accession. In addition to their interest in keeping the European Parliament happy, the associated countries may see advantage in working with parliamentarians from well-established democracies, as well as in learning about the European Parliament, in which they will participate after joining the Community.

The offer of Europe Agreements is open to Balkan countries too when the Community judges that they show enough 'practical evidence' of commitment to pluralist democracy and market economy. Bulgaria, having made fair progress in 1991, is already in line for negotiations; and Romania despite its difficulties, is also mentioned in this connection. Slovenia, now independent and close in many ways to the Central Europeans, should be able to qualify without too much delay, as should others among the remaining republics that have constituted Yugoslavia, whether independent from the former Yugoslavia or not, provided that they are securely at peace, are establishing pluralist democracies, and carrying through the remaining economic reforms to become genuine market economies. Albania, at some distance, could follow.

Among the republics of the former Soviet Union, the Baltic states have a special status as their incorporation by Stalin during the war was never recognised as legitimate by Western states. They are, moreover, small and thought to have fair prospects for economic viability and political stability. Perhaps Europe Agreements may in time be offered to them as well. But the other former Soviet republics have been classified differently by the Community. The Community's Commission and Council decided in January 1992 that while these new states should have something more substantial than the trade and cooperation agreements in order to encourage their movement towards markets and democracy, they would not qualify for full-scale Europe Agreements. Something in between would be appropriate, providing for 'the widest possible opening of markets' and 'support for institution-building and the strengthening of civil society'.[9] Russia, the Ukraine and Belarus would be the first in line for such intermediate agreements.

'Any European state may', according to Article 237 of the EC Treaty, 'apply to become a member of the Community'. The Europe Agreements with the Czech and Slovak Republics, Hungary and Poland affirm, in their preambles, that this is an ultimate objective. While these agreements themselves offer investors a good deal of reassurance, membership would anchor such countries more solidly in the single market and the Community's rule of law and political system. In this context, the prospects for future membership are relevant to the prospects for investment.

MEMBERSHIP

The East German way into the Community, through union with an existing member state, is not for others – unless, some time in the future, Romania should be a member and Moldova should decide to unite with it. For the others, the road is the stony one of application, negotiation, and acceptance through ratification by all the member states and assent by the European Parliament.

The Central Europeans have shown themselves eager to join when there is a realistic prospect of their being able to do so. They wanted an article envisaging this in the body of the Europe Agreements; but the Community's Council of Foreign Ministers, doubtless bearing in mind some embarrassment resulting from the inclusion of such an article in the association agreement with Turkey, whose accession the Community has so far declined to countenance, resisted this, and only reluctantly accepted the mention in the preamble. An expected time scale was indicated by President Havel when he visited Paris in 1991 and suggested that the Czechs and Slovaks might be able to join in about ten years' time; and this evidently reflected a strain of thought in the Community, because President Delors later cited him approvingly.[10] Hungarians have indicated that they might make a much earlier application. In order to evaluate the prospects, it is useful to consider the conditions that may have to be satisfied before accession becomes possible.

A number of these conditions concern the Community itself. At least some of those that have the power to say no (that is, member states and the European Parliament), will want to be sure that the Community is firmly enough integrated to accommodate these new members without diminishing its effectiveness. Some of these gatekeepers will want to be sure that the economic and monetary union is well enough under way not to lose its momentum as a result of the accessions.[11] There will also be insistence that the institutions of the Community should not be weakened. With more, and more diverse, member states, a search for unanimity among the ministers in the Council would be yet more time-consuming and unproductive. There will be a stand on the principle of majority voting as the general rule. The close supervision of the Commission's execution of Community laws and policies by committees of officials from the member states would likewise become unduly burdensome, and there will be demands for the Commission to become more like a government. With these changes, along with the increase in the Community's powers agreed at Maastricht, will come a requirement that the European Parliament's powers be enhanced so as to place it more on a footing with the Council; and this will be supported by some member states and, of course, the European Parliament. The list could be extended. But these examples have been given in order to show that 'widening' the Community will be a complex process, requiring 'deepening' that may take some time to accomplish.

The conditions that the Central or East Europeans must fulfil comprise mainly the fair assurance that they will be solid market economies and pluralist democracies. The Community system, as the single market programme demonstrates, could not contain a country with an incompatible economic system. It would moreover be difficult to accommodate a country without a reasonably well-functioning economy, because where democracy is not yet deeply rooted, economic failure is liable to place it at risk. Nor could the Community's institutions allow for the inclusion of undemocratic member states. Ministers who come from representative governments could hardly accept that decisions be determined by votes of people without such legitimacy. The European Parliament could not include members who had not been elected in free and fair elections. The Court of Justice requires complete independence for its judges; and the judgements made under Community law are for the most part made by the courts of member states, whose juridical systems must therefore conform to the principles of impartiality and the rule of law. The members of the Commission, too, must be allowed complete independence, which dictatorial regimes would find hard to tolerate. Giving the Eastern neighbours the benefit of the doubt, the Community might judge that their democracies were well enough established after a second round of fully free and fair elections. Beyond the compatibility of its internal politics, moreover, the Community may wish to be satisfied that the external policy and security stance of an applicant for membership would not be likely to disrupt the common foreign and security policy.

In case it should be thought useful for the writer to hazard a guess as to when these conditions will be deemed sufficiently fulfilled, it may be supposed that the Central Europeans and the Community itself can be ready some time in the later 1990s, although Poland has more difficulties to overcome than the Czech and Slovak Republics and Hungary. The Balkans and the Baltics might join in the following decade. As suggested, Moldova could perhaps join through merger with Romania, if Romania itself is ready. At some stage in this progression, however, members of the Community and the European Parliament might well consider that in order to maintain the coherence of the Community, or Union as it is to be called following Maastricht, further enlargement should be accompanied or preceded by integration of the member states' armed forces, thus creating a federal state rather than a union with federal institutions but mainly economic powers. Unless the member states are by then willing to go so far, at least one of the gatekeepers could conclude that new additions to the number and diversity of the members would risk introducing dissension and conflicts that the institutions could not contain; and further accessions would have to wait until the Community, with all its existing members, had become integrated and solid enough to cope with more.

Would Belarus, the Ukraine, Armenia and Georgia, which apart from Russia are the other parts of the former Soviet Union that can claim to be in Europe, always be republics too far? The same argument applies, with greater force. The Community or Union would probably need to have the self-confidence of a solid and mature federal state in order to take them in. Russia, as already suggested, being so big, would qualify for partnership rather than for membership.

To think of membership for Central or East Europeans is to think of the longer term. In no way is it a solution for present crises. But to those who make investment plans in a longer-term perspective, the prospects for membership must be an element in the assessment, even if successful Europe Agreements might go towards providing many of the benefits of full membership.

THE EC AND THE FUTURE FOR PRIVATE FOREIGN INVESTMENT IN CENTRAL AND EASTERN EUROPE

The Community has contributed to democracy in Central and Eastern Europe in two main ways: as a political example and through its economic assistance. The democracy of the member states and its evident link with their prosperity has attracted the Central and East Europeans and influenced their political choices. The knowledge that it is a condition of eventual accession may be a significant incentive to maintain the democratic system. Against this, the Community and its member states do not seem to have done much to support the institutions of democracy and civil society directly. It is possible to conceive of ways in which technical assistance could impart skills needed to run such institutions and provide resources for their establishment; but Western help does not seem to have been creative about this on any large scale. It is towards the market economy that technical assistance has been directed; and this, if it succeeds, will provide an essential underpinning for pluralist democracy.

The GSP and the quota liberalisation have given an immediate boost to the export sectors of those countries that can supply a range of industrial goods, even if the continuing restrictions on coal, steel, textiles and agricultural products are a serious limitation. The Europe Agreements offer a fairly firm prospect for the future, both in protection of foreign investors' interests and in access to the Community market, leading to integration in the European and international economies. The Czech and Slovak Republics, Hungary and Poland should be followed in the next few years by Balkan and perhaps Baltic countries; and the intermediate agreements being developed for states of the new Commonwealth should provide some similar benefits, though probably without any explicit reference to future accession. For the Central Europeans in particular, however, accession is a prospect in a time scale relevant to many investments.

The Community's emergency aid has, in certain cases, guarded against the destabilising influences of hunger and disease. The technical assistance is contributing much towards the human and institutional infrastructure for the market economy: enough, perhaps, when the PHARE aid from other Western countries is added to it, to do what is needed in that respect for Central Europe and the Balkans. But whether enough is to be provided for Russia and the other states of the Commonwealth is another question. Support for the balance of payments in view of convertibility is a routine in which the Western performance is usually adequate. But the big question remains whether financial assistance to support investment and perhaps social security is enough, given the consequences of failure with the reforms, to do what should be done to reduce the risks to reasonable proportions.

Considering what went before it, the Community has a magnificent record of peace and security among its member states. But the war in former Yugoslavia has demonstrated its lack of experience and of instruments for keeping the peace among its neighbours; and such conflicts may recur, particularly in the Balkans and the Commonwealth of Independent States. The Community has been able to bring to bear some of its economic weight and capacity for political conciliation. But it is evidently not yet equipped to guarantee security to investors in areas where there is the potential for such conflicts. Maastricht was a start in giving the Community, or rather the Union, access to some defence instruments. The Western European Union, which is to be closely associated with the Community, is to have a 'planning cell', meetings of Chiefs of Defence Staff, military units 'answerable' to it, and cooperation in logistics, transport, training and strategic surveillance; and the Union's common foreign and security policy is to include the 'eventual framing of a defence policy, which might in time lead to a common defence'. If the Community remains dynamic, it will in time acquire a substantial defence competence. But dangers in the Balkans and farther to the East remain and investors will not, for years ahead, be able to look to the

Community for any guarantee of protection against them. But the Community and its member states are making efforts to forestall potential problems, through consultations that the Western European Union, as well as NATO is offering to Central European and Balkan countries, and by making the process of the Conference on Security and Cooperation in Europe (CSCE) and the policy of disarmament and arms control in Europe, two of the first priorities for its common foreign and security policy.

The area in which the Community can give a fair guarantee of security will, however, be widened as the Community is enlarged to include Central European countries. As and when enlargement extends farther, its ability to guarantee security within its frontiers will depend increasingly on the extent to which it has integrated the armed forces of the member states. If Russia were to become authoritarian and nationalist, moreover, the security of Europe as a whole could depend on the counterweight provided collectively by the European and the North American pillars of NATO. But more hopefully, a democratic and pacific Russia could cooperate in a European and wider security system, whose other pillars could include a federal European Community or Union, the United States, Japan, and perhaps emerging Third World powers such as India and Brazil – and, stretching hopes somewhat farther – a suitably reforming China.

But that is to look far enough into the future: too far, doubtless, for the taste of many readers. Meanwhile the Community is, with its trade and aid measures and the Europe Agreements, helping to give Central European countries a status of good investment prospects and to give East Europeans a chance of becoming such. The more the Community can bring itself to be liberal in reducing protection and more generous about aid, the more those prospects are likely to improve. Russia in particular, if it can be brought through its extremely difficult transition to the point where it can become an efficient exporter of oil, gas and other primary products, will become externally viable and hence a good risk as a borrower and, it might be hoped, a good place for investment. There are many ifs. But the Community can help to reduce their number. A study of the development of its relationship with Central and Eastern Europe is a must for those who consider investing there.

Notes

1. See Commission of the EC, *Association agreements with the countries of Central and Eastern Europe: a general outline*, Communication from the Commission to the Council and Parliament, COM/90/398 final (Brussels, 27 August 1990); and Commission of the EC, *Action Plan: Coordinated Assistance from the Group of 24 to Bulgaria, Czechoslovakia, the German Democratic Republic, Romania and Yugoslavia*, SEC (90)843 final (Brussels, 2 May 1990).
2. For greater detail on these subjects than can be given in this chapter, see John Pinder, *The European Community and Eastern Europe* (London: Pinter for RIIA, 1991).
3. See Christian Lequesne, 'Les accords de commerce et de coopération Communauté Européenne–Pays d'Europe de l'Est', in Jean-Claude Gautron (ed.), *Les relations Communauté Européenne–Europe de l'Est* (Paris: Economica, 1991).
4. For an explanation of the Generalised System of Preferences, see R. C. Hine, *The Political Economy of European Trade: An Introduction to the Trade Policies of the EEC* (Brighton: Wheatsheaf Books, 1985), Chapter 12.
5. Centre for Economic Policy Research, *Monitoring European Integration: The Impact of Eastern Europe* (London: CEPR, 1990), pp. 38–9.
6. The leading article in the *Financial Times* of 28 December 1989 suggested as a 'benchmark' over ECU50 billion a year, as the current equivalent for the Community of the annual contribution of the US to Western Europe in Marshall Aid.
7. *Financial Times*, 25 September 1991.
8. *Association agreements, op. cit.* (n. 1, supra).
9. *Financial Times*, 12 January 1992.
10. *Der Spiegel*, 14 October 1991, pp. 23–4.
11. This was argued by, for example, Helmut Schmidt, in 'Deutschlands Rolle im neuen Europa', *Europa-Archiv*, 21/1991, p. 621.

Appendix: The Practicalities of Establishing a Joint Venture in the Commonwealth of Independent States

William Crisp

Business International, a private company in the field of management information services and a member of the Economist Newspaper Group, registered a joint venture in Moscow in October 1990. Its partner in the 50–50 joint venture was the Institute of World Economy and International Relations of the Academy of Sciences of the former Soviet Union.

Numerous lessons were learned during the negotiations, which could be helpful to prospective investors. Among the key points, it was deemed desirable to:

- establish a clear purpose for the joint venture;
- remember that the local partner has bona fide objectives of its own;
- ensure that the multinational's headquarters understands the joint venture's objectives;
- allow enough time for negotiations and intra-corporate coordination;
- be prepared for budget puzzles.

If a foreign company enters joint venture discussions in the Commonwealth of Independent States (CIS) without a clear idea of its objectives, the likelihood is that the negotiations will collapse. Business International, a publisher of business information, required bona fide business information on local commercial conditions, which it would market in its regular business publications. It was prepared to pay reasonable market rates to any ex-Soviet organisation, which was in a legal position to supply such information.

Business International believed that a joint venture established in Moscow could secure bona fide business information, and export such information to its editorial office in Vienna for publication. For this export service, a fair rate would be paid by Business International to the joint venture.

This pattern fitted a very simple purchase–export orientation. There was no requirement for complicated local sales or conversion of roubles into hard currency. While some rouble activities were not entirely ruled out, from the beginning the clear purpose of the joint venture was conceived as an export operation.

Negotiations began in Moscow in January 1989, and the contract was signed in Vienna in September 1990. Throughout this period, the basic clarity of purpose of the joint venture, along with the goodwill of both partners, ensured that negotiations did not break down.

Russian partners logically have their own objectives in negotiating a joint venture investment project. Given the non-convertibility of the rouble, the foreign partner should understand that access to hard currency earnings is usually a foremost objective. Such earnings under current circumstances may be obtained from local sales under limited conditions, special forms of trading and through exports. Additionally, the Russian partner is usually keenly interested in obtaining hard currency-denominated equipment and technology. Any proposal will be severely hampered if it ignores the partner's objectives, particularly as they usually relate to hard currency.

The foreign managers who initiate investment proposals usually have a clear understanding of joint venture regulations, the market situation, legal issues and currency questions in the CIS. However, their corporate superior executives at a distant regional or world headquarters may have no knowledge whatsoever of such details. Successful managers must, first of all, ensure that their headquarters officials understand the clear purpose of the joint venture, and how it can benefit the company. They must also ensure that, over time, key officials, particularly those in the finance department, familiarise themselves with the rewards and difficulties of operating in the CIS market. Special effort must be made to explain difficult legal and financial issues to corporate executives. Time spent on such 'education' is never wasted.

Most companies assume that great amounts of time will be required to negotiate each clause of the contract with their CIS counterparts. This is not always the case: if the joint venture concept is a clear one, and if the CIS objectives are met, then negotiations can be faster than anticipated.

Many companies find, however, that enormous amounts of time are required to secure final corporate approval of the contract. Usually, the company lawyer will review the contract. Details of CIS law and practice may be completely unknown to this person, who may seek a 'second opinion' from another lawyer.

This may take as much time as the original negotiations. Thus, it is a good rule to reserve an amount of time for headquarters consultation at least equal to the time required for negotiations in the CIS.

Surprises will always be encountered. A feasibility study must be written prior to registration, but data may be lacking to establish any firm business protection. Company headquarters will also want to see a business plan, budget, or cash flow projection. Such demands are difficult to meet even for the simplest of joint ventures. They pose extreme problems for larger ventures, especially those in the natural resources which are subject to world price fluctuations.

Companies should thus anticipate that the budgetary issue, and money projections, can form one of the greatest obstacles. Many projects have been killed by company headquarters, simply because no one could devise an acceptable budget. Numerous other guidelines may be added to the above key issues. Based on its own experience, Business International believes that one overriding requirement must be realised before negotiations begin: to ensure that the purpose of the joint venture is clear, and that its basic objective is plain for all to see. If this principle is established, then many subsequent difficulties in negotiations can be overcome in a constructive fashion.

Bibliography

S. Anderson (1990) 'The Eastern Block Investment Report Card', *The Soviet Union and Eastern Europe Business Journal*, 2, 2.

W. Andreff (ed.) (1990) *Réforme et échanges extérieurs dans les pays de l'Est* (Paris: L'Harmattan).

W. Andreff (1987) *Les Multinationales* (Paris: La Découverte).

P. Artisien and S. Holt (1980) 'Yugoslavia and the EEC in the 1970's', *Journal of Common Market Studies*, XVIII, 4, June.

P. Artisien (1981) 'Belgrade's Closer Links with Brussels', *The World Today*, 37, 1, January.

P. Artisien (1985) *Joint Ventures in Yugoslav Industry* (Aldershot: Gower).

P. Artisien (1989) *Yugoslavia to 1993: Back from the Brink?* (London: Economist Publications).

P. Artisien (1990) 'The Making of the East European Market', *Issues*, 10.

P. Artisien, C. H. McMillan and M. Rojec (1992) *Yugoslav Multinationals Abroad* (London: Macmillan).

A. Åslund (1985) *Private Enterprise in Eastern Europe* (London: Macmillan).

A. Besançon (1976) *Court Traité de soviétologie à l'usage des autorités civiles, militaires et religieuses* (Paris: Hachette).

J. Blaha (1988) 'Les sociétés mixtes Tchécoslovaquie – Ouest', *Le Courrier des Pays de l'Est*, 239, May.

M. Bornstein (1985) *The transfer of Western technology to the USSR* (Paris: OECD).

Business Eastern Europe, 2 January 1989; 11–13 March 1989; 12–20 March 1989; 17 December 1990; 26 August 1991; 2 December 1991; 9 December 1991; 13 January 1992.

Business International (1991) 'Joint Ventures, Acquisitions and Privatization in Eastern Europe and the USSR: A Practical Guide to Investment', 2105 (London: Business International).

Business in the USSR, January 1991; February 1991; March 1991; June 1991.

J. Cantwell (1990) 'East–West Business Links and the Economic Development of Poland and Eastern Europe' (Reading: University of Reading).

Centre for Economic Policy Research (1990) *Monitoring European Integration: The Impact of Eastern Europe* (London: CEPR).

Centre for International Cooperation and Development (1990) *Investing in Slovenia* (Ljubljana).

Cerem–Larea (1986) *Les stratégies d'accord des groupes de la C.E.E., intégration ou éclatement de l'espace industriel européen* (Nanterre: University of Paris-X).

Commersant (English Edition), 31 December 1990.

Commersant (Russian Edition), 9–16 September 1991; 2–9 December 1991; 19–26 December 1991.

Commission of the European Communities (1990a) *Industrial Cooperation*, *with Central and Eastern Europe: Ways to Strengthen Cooperation*, July (Brussels: European Communities).

Commission of the European Communities (1990b) *Association Agreements with the Countries of Central and Eastern Europe: A General Outline*, 27 August (Brussels: European Communities).

Commission of the European Communities (1990c) *Action Plan: Coordinated Assistance from the Group of 24 to Bulgaria, Czechoslovakia, the German Democratic Republic, Romania and Yugoslavia*, 2 May (Brussels: European Communities).

M. Czinkota (1991) 'The EC, 1992 and Eastern Europe: Effects of Integration vs. Disintegration', *Columbia Journal of World Business*, 26, 1.

J. H. Dunning (ed.) (1985) *Multinational Enterprises, Economic Structure and International Competitiveness* (Chichester: John Wiley).

J. H. Dunning (1988) *Explaining International Production* (London: Unwin Hyman).

East European Markets, 20 April 1990.

Economist, 3 February 1990.

Economist (1991) 'A Survey of Business in Eastern Europe', 21 September.

Ekonomika i Zhizn', 4, 1990; 31, 1990; 40, 1990; 5, 1991; 34, 1991; 43, 1991; 48, 1991.

Financial Times, 28 December 1989; 15 January 1990; 1 June 1990; 7 June 1990; 13 June 1990; 18 June 1990; 20 June 1990; 22 June 1990; 18 October 1990; 18 July 1991; 25 September 1991; 12 January 1992.

R. Girault (1973) *Emprunts Russes et Investissements Français en Russie*, 1887–1914 (Paris: Armand Colin/Sorbonne University Press).

R. Girault and M. Ferro (1989) *De la Russie à l'U.R.S.S. – L'Histoire de la Russie de 1850 à nos jours* (Paris: Nathan).

P. Grou (1989) *Les multinationales socialistes* (Paris: L'Harmattan).

S. E. Guisinger et al. (1985) *Investment Incentives and Performance Requirements* (New York: Praeger).

P. Gutman (1988a) Review of C. H. McMillan (1987) *Multinationals from the Second World – Growth of Foreign Investment by Soviet and East European State Enterprises, Revue d'Etudes Comparatives Est–Ouest*, 19, 1 March.

P. Gutman (1988b) 'Le couple exportation d'ensembles complets/compensation dans les relations Est-Sud, substitut à l'investissement direct? Une hypothèse de travail' *Revue Tiers-Monde*, XXIX, 113, January–March. (An English version appeared as Chapter 9 in B. H. Schulz and W. H. Hansen (1989) *The Soviet Bloc and the Third World – The Political Economy of East–South Relations* (Boulder: Westview Press).

P. Gutman (1980) 'Coopération Industrielle Est-Ouest dans l'automobile et modalités d'insertion des pays de l'Est dans la Division Internationale du Travail occidentale' *Revue d'Etudes Comparatives Est–Ouest*, 11, 2, June and 11, 3, September. (An English version appeared in *The ACES Bulletin*, 22, 3–4, Fall–Winter).

G. Hamilton (ed.) (1986) *Red multinationals or red herrings? The activities of enterprises from Socialist countries in the West* (London: Pinter).

P. Hanson (1981) *Trade and Technology in Soviet-Western Relations* (London: Macmillan).
P. Hanson and M. R. Hill (1979) 'Soviet assimilation of Western technology: a survey of U.K. exporters' experience' in *Soviet Economy in A Time of Change*, Volume 2, Joint Economic Committee, Congress of the United States (Washington, DC: USGPO).
R. C. Hine (1985) *The Political Economy of European Trade: An Introduction to the Trade Policies of the EEC* (Brighton: Wheatsheaf).
D. Holtbrügge (1989) *Managerial Problems of Joint Ventures in the Soviet Union*, 8, November (Dortmund: Universität).
Hungarian Chamber of Commerce (1988) *Joint Ventures in Hungary with foreign participation – Register*, second edition, February.
International Economic Insights (1991) 2, March/April.
International Herald Tribune, 25 November 1991; 6 February 1992; 7 February 1992.
Izvestiya, 23 May 1990; 15 August 1990; 16 December 1990; 15 March 1991.
P. Joffre and G. Koenig (1985) *Stratégie d'entreprise – Antimanuel* (Paris: Economica).
Journal of Commerce, 18 January 1990; 5 March 1990; 28 June 1990; 14 November 1991; 9 December 1991.
J. Kwiatowski and M. Sowa (1989) 'Nouveaux phénomènes dans la Coopération économique avec l'étranger en 1988', *Rynki Zagraniczne*, No. 32, 16 March.
M. Lavigne (1989) 'Joint Ventures within the Socialist Economic System', revised version of a working paper presented at the European University Institute, Florence, January.
M. Lebkowski and J. Monkiewicz (1986) 'Western Direct Investment in Centrally Planned Economies', *Journal of World Trade Law*, 20, 6, November–December.
C. Lequesne (1991) 'Les Accords de Commerce et de Coopération Communauté Européenne – Pays d'Europe de l'Est', in Gautron, J. (ed.), *Les Relations Communauté Européenne – Europe de l'Est* (Paris: Economica).
Link Barometer, 1, 1990; 3, 1990; 5, 1990.
F. Louvard (1985) 'Joint Ventures, sociétés mixtes et coopération industrielle dans le cadre des échanges Est-Ouest' in IFRI (ed.), *Les conditions préalables à la création d'entreprises mixtes entre l'Est et l'Ouest: expériences et perspectives* (Paris: IFRI).
M. Maecki (1987) The Development of Foreign Enterprises' Activities in Poland (1976–85), 10 (Warsaw: World Economy Research Institute).
I. Makarov and I. Puzin (1987) *Ekonomicheskoe Sotrudnichestvo v Europe* (Moscow: Itogi i Perspectivi).
P. Marer (1986) *East–West Technology Transfer-Study of Hungary 1968–1984* (Paris: OECD).
C. H. McMillan and D. P. St Charles (1974) *Joint Ventures in Eastern Europe: A Three Country Comparison* (Montreal: C. D. Howe Research Institute).
C. H. McMillan (1977) 'Industrial Cooperation', *East European Economies Post-Helsinki* (Washington: Joint Economic Committee, US Congress).

C. H. McMillan (1981) 'Trends in East–West Industrial Cooperation', *Journal of International Business Studies*, Fall.
C. H. McMillan (1986a) 'The International Organisation of Inter-Firm Cooperation', Chapter 11 in Watts, N. (ed.), *Economic Relations Between East and West* (New York: St Martin's Press).
C. H. McMillan (1986b) 'Trends in Direct Investment and the Transfer of Technology' in Csikos-Nagy, B. and Young, D. (eds), *East–West Economic Relations in the Changing Global Environment* (London: Macmillan).
C. H. McMillan (1987) *Multinationals from the Second World – Growth of Foreign Investment by Soviet and East European State Enterprises* (London: Macmillan).
C. H. McMillan (ed.) (1990), (1989), (1988), (1986), (1983) *The East-West Business Directory – A Listing of Contact Points in the O.E.C.D. Countries for the Conduct of Business with Eastern Europe and the Soviet Union* (Kettering: Duncan Publishing/Carleton University).
C. H. McMillan (1991) 'Foreign Direct Investment Flows to the Soviet Union and Eastern Europe: Nature, Magnitude and International Implications', *Journal of Development Planning*, No. 20.
C. A. Michalet (1976) *Le Capitalisme mondial* (Paris: PUF).
C. A. Michalet (1988) 'Les accords inter-firmes internationaux: un cadre pour l'analyse' in Arena, R., De Bandt, J., Benzoni, L. and Romani, P. M. (eds), *Traité d'Economie Industrielle* (Paris: Economica).
A. D. Mikhail, K. N. Nandola and S. B. Prasad (1990) 'Perceptions of US Executives on Doing Business in Eastern Europe and the USSR: Testing the International Exchange Framework' (Madrid: EIBA).
Moniteur du Commerce International (MOCI) 28 May 1990; 2 April 1990.
O. Morgatchev (1988) 'Un partenaire pour l'Occident', *Politique Internationale*, 13, Autumn.
R. Morawetz (1991) *Recent Foreign Direct Investment in Eastern Europe: Towards a Possible Role for the Tripartite Declaration of Principles Concerning Multinational Enterprises and Social Policy*, 71 (Geneva: ILO).
Moscow Narodny Bank Press Bulletin, 16 August 1989; 21 November 1990.
J. L. Mucchielli (1985) *Les firmes multinationales: mutations et nouvelles perspectives* (Paris: Economica).
Nachrichten für Aussenhandel, 2 January 1991; 18 March 1991; 23 December 1991.
E. Nadjer (1986) 'L'évolution récente du contrôle des changes en Pologne', *Revue d'Etudes Comparatives Est–Ouest*, 17, 4, December.
A. Nove (1969) *An Economic History of the U.S.S.R.* (Allen Lane: The Penguin Press).
K. Ohmae (1985) *La Triade* (Paris: Flammarion).
C. Oman (1984) *New Forms of International Investment in Developing Countries* (Paris: OECD).
Organization for Economic Cooperation and Development (1989) 'International Investment and Multinational Enterprises – Investment Incentives and Disincentives: the Effects on International Direct Investment' (Paris: OECD).
T. Ozawa (1991) 'Europe 1992 and Japanese Multinationals', in Bergen-

meier, B. and Mucchielli, J. L. (eds), *Multinationals and Europe 1992* (London: Routledge).
H. V. Perlmutter (1969) 'Emerging East–West Venture: The Transideological Enterprise', *Columbia Journal of World Business*, IV, 5, September–October.
F. Persanyi (1989) 'New Possibilities to Foreign Investors in Hungary', *Hungarian Business Herald*, 2.
J. Pinder (1991) *The European Community and Eastern Europe* (London: Pinter).
K. Plesinski (1986) 'Sur les sociétés à capital étranger', *Zycie Gospodarcze*, 18, 4 May.
M. E. Porter (1990) *The Competitive Advantage of Nations* (New York: The Free Press).
Pravda, 11 October 1989; 4 March 1991.
S. Rasloveff (1989) 'U.R.S.S.: entreprises conjointes avec les firmes occidentales' in NATO, *Soviet Economic Reforms: Implementation under way* (Leuven: Ceuterick).
A. Rowley (1982) *Evolution économique de la Russie du milieu du XIXème siècle à 1914* (Paris: SEDES).
A. M. Rugman and A. Verbeke (1990) *Corporate Strategy after the Free Trade Agreement and Europe 1992*, 27, March (Toronto: Ontario Centre for International Business).
J. P. Saltiel (1987) 'La victoire du capital', *Politique Internationale*, No. 36, Summer.
H. Schmidt (1991) 'Deutschlands Rolle im neuen Europa', *Europa-Archiv*, 21.
J. G. Scriven (1980) 'Joint Ventures in Poland – A Socialist Approach to Foreign Investment Legislation', *Journal of World Trade Law*, 14.
T. Sowell (1991) 'What Capital Shortage?', *Forbes*, 19 August.
M. Svetličič (1990) 'Providing FDI in Vietnam: A Lesson from the Yugoslav Experience', *Asia-Pacific TNC Review*, 7.
A. Tiraspolsky (1988) 'L'U.R.S.S. de Gorbachev et la politique d'intégration du CAEM' in NATO, *The Economies of Eastern Europe under Gorbachev's influence* (Leuven: Ceuterick).
I. Toldy–Ösz (1989) 'Joint ventures – More incentives needed', *Hungarian Trade Journal*, 39, 2, February.
UNCTC (1978) *Transnational Corporations in World Development – A Re-examination* (New York: United Nations).
UNCTC (1988a) *Joint Ventures as a Form of International Economic Co-operation* (New York: United Nations).
UNCTC (1988b) *Transnational Corporations in World Development – Trends and Prospects* (New York: United Nations).
United Nations Economic Commission for Europe (1979) 'East–West Industrial Cooperation' (New York: United Nations).
United Nations Economic Commission for Europe (1988) *East–West Joint Ventures – Economic, Business, Financial and Legal Aspects* (New York: United Nations).
United Nations Economic Commission for Europe (1989a) 'East–West Joint

Ventures – New Joint Ventures and Foreign Investment Regulations and Listing of Joint Ventures Domiciled in the European C.M.E.A. Member Countries at the beginning of 1989', ECE/TRADE 162, Rev. 1, 21 February, Geneva, United Nations.

United Nations Economic Commission for Europe (1989b) 'Statistical profile of joint ventures in the U.S.S.R.: first results', TRADE/A.C.2/C.R.P.5. 24 February, Geneva, United Nations.

United Nations Economic Commission for Europe (1989c) 'Recent trends in the formation of East–West joint ventures in the C.M.E.A. countries: main features of financing and marketing arrangements', TRADE/A.C.23/C.R.P.4. 26 February, Geneva, United Nations.

United Nations Economic Commission for Europe, *East–West Joint Venture News*, 1, 1989; 5, 1990; 6, 1990; 7, 1991.

Index